ISLAN

Sir Frank Fraser Darl[...] educated in Edinburgh. He has worked with a number of agricultural, ecological and conservation institutes and he has contributed greatly to preservation work especially in Scotland; between 1944 and 1950, he directed the West Highland Survey and he has also been Chief Officer for the Imperial Bureau of Animal Genetics and Rockefeller Special Research Fellow. For five years until 1958, he was senior lecturer in ecology and conservation at the University of Edinburgh. He is the author of a great many books on animals and conservation, including *A Naturalist on Rona*, *The Story of Scotland* and *The Unity of Ecology*. He now lives in Scotland.

ISLAND YEARS

FRANK FRASER DARLING
DSC, FRSE

With a new Preface by the author

UNABRIDGED

PAN BOOKS LTD : LONDON

First published 1940 by G. Bell and Sons Ltd.
This edition published 1973 by
Pan Books Ltd, 33 Tothill Street, London, SW1.

ISBN 0 330 23467 6

Printed in Great Britain by
Cox & Wyman Ltd, London, Reading and Fakenham

To Bobbie

CONTENTS

LIST OF ILLUSTRATIONS
(*between pages 78–79 and 158–159*)

PREFACE

Here is a chapter of experience, three years of three people's lives.

When I have given an account of research work done in these island years, naturally keeping to my argument in the lecture-theatre and telling of the lives of the animals I have watched, there has come a flood of questions afterwards – 'But what *we* want to know is how *you* lived, please.'

It is devastating. I have been trying for an hour to show the interest of the social life of animals, but once more it seems the chief interest of man is man. 'Here are real Crusoes,' those people have been saying to themselves instead of listening to my wordiness, 'and we are all Crusoes at heart as well; and dash it all, we may do it yet if only we can get out of this spider web of civilized life. We'll ask him a few questions at tea-time.' And I have been nervously wondering if my scientific discourse over which I have sweated for hours has been acceptable. Who knows?

It is imperative, this demand from society for an account of island life, and I can escape it no longer. I wrote a book of literary and scientific essays while I was on North Rona, and called it *A Naturalist on Rona* because that seemed to me a good title. One reviewer, himself a naturalist, gave me a dressing-down, not for what was in the book, but for what he expected to find in it and did not, namely, just what we were doing with ourselves.

Here, then, are joys and little sorrows, ease and hardship, mistakes and irritations, and some of the good things of life the islands have taught us. And still we are among the islands, making a little farm from land that was derelict, seeing new things and seeing old things again in a new beauty.

FRANK FRASER DARLING

Isle of Tanera,
Ross and Cromarty, Scotland
January, 1940

PREFACE TO THE PAN EDITION

Some lives are a steady progression as if on an appointed course; others appear odd and incidental without any guiding principle. My own might seem to have been of the latter kind, but to assume that might be too facile a conclusion. One thing is certain: attention to the matter of a career has been sadly lacking. But I have known from early life what most interested me and what I wanted to do, namely, natural history and living the life of a naturalist. When I was a child natural history was benignly looked upon by parents and schoolmasters as a good Saturday occupation which was healthy for the child and would keep him out of a lot of mischief. To follow it into late adolescence was not so good: you were a drifter, a loafer and lacking ambition or any notion of what was what.

Several happy coincidences got this fellow eventually through a scientific education in biology, but when he did get a proper going-on sort of a job which gave him plenty of that scarce commodity, reading time, he read where his heart lay, in animal behaviour and ecology. The award of a good fellowship was the end of a career in animal genetics, and our drifter studied the deer on a Highland hill and thereafter headed for the uninhabited islands where his inclinations also lay.

This book was written in the course of the island years, the great lesson of which was self-reliance. Now it was to be tested, for I had slipped on a slope of wet peat and broken a leg. My wife set it for me while I read out how from the little St John Ambulance book. And the war was a few weeks old. There was now no war for me and I decided to work our little farm with the design of making as few demands on sailors' lives as possible. We were down on the hard for nearly five years and because farming is not all studying natural history, I found myself almost fighting sea and weather instead of accepting it as part of the pattern of ecology. Farming was not new to me, but I understood that I didn't wholly like it in our day.

My first published writing using the phrase 'wildlife conservation' had been in 1934, when conservation as a philosophy of life had long replaced any youthful dependence on orthodox religion. By the later forties I found myself on Government committees having this subject as their *raison d'être*. The course had set itself, though still in ways far from islands – Arctic Alaska, Central Africa and elsewhere. The lessons were the same. Animals behaved differently and yet so similarly, and one gained a special kind of awareness of living rhythm and of interdependence.

Out of it all came another kind of awareness, that man and his habitat could also be an extension of natural history. Indeed, unless you studied man and his ecology in that way, you were missing a great deal. Once in this stratum of life, one can delve deep and not always in pleasant fashion. The pastoral nomad has no sewage problems, but civilization is beset by them, as we now know so well. So the drifter has reached his seventieth year and soon hopes to make his way back to the north of Scotland and some quiet natural history. But you cannot order life or turn your back on it.

It has surprised me to find how many friends of past years are now working in the fields of human ecology and anti-pollution. Gazing at the revolving screens at a sewage disposal plant is not an aesthetic pleasure, but then I think again: these engineers have adapted biological processes of natural purification to our repulsive needs. These worms and bacteria are doing a beautiful job of work and those of us who were thought to be escapist naturalists are not really so far away after all.

FRANK FRASER DARLING

Shefford-Woodlands House,
July 1972

Sula Sgeir   North Rona

Orkney
Islands

Atlantic Ocean

Caithness

Sutherland

Lewis

SUILVEN

The Minch

Summer
Isles

North
Sea

Harris

Shiant Is.

Scoraig

North Uist

AN TEALLACH
Ross and Cromarty

Little Minch

Inverness

Skye

South
Uist

Inverness

Rhum

The
West Coast
of
Scotland

Eigg

Coll

Tiree

Mull   Oban

Treshnish Isles

Iona

N

Colonsay   Jura

Islay

Edinburgh
Glasgow

0   Miles   50

Arran

North Rona

N

Lisgeir Mhor
Leac Mhor Fianuis
Fianuis
Nonet Cave
Sgeildige
Geodha Blatha Mhor
Huis
Langa Beirie
Marcasgeo
Ruins
Well
Tor 355
Sceapull
Poll
Heallair
Leac na Sgrob
Sron na Chadrach
Loba Sgeir
Gealldruig Mhor

Mile 0 — 1

The Treshnish Isles

Cairn a' Burg Beg
Cairn a Burg Mhor

N

Sgeir na h'Iolaire
Sgeir nan Erionnach
Creag a' Chaisteal
Dirty Inlet
Dun Cruit Harp Rock
Lunga
CRUACHAN
The Dorlinn
Fladda
Sgeir na Giugach
Cam
Sgeir an Mhor

Bac Mhor or Dutchman's Cap

Bac Beg or Little Dutchman

Mile 0 —

Eilean a' Chleirich

Tuill an Chleirich
Hidden Loch
East Cove
Long Geo
Cauldron
Acairseid (East Bay)
North Loch
Exchange
Lochan na h'Airidhe
Hut
ARD GHLAS
Rudder
West Landing
Lochan Iar
Lochan na Gleann 252
Ard Bheag
South Cave

Ross and Cromarty

Eilean Mullagrach
Isle Ristol (Ristole)
Ghlas Leac Mhor
Eilean a' Char
Isle of Tanera
Achiltibuie
Tanera Beg

Ghlas Leac Bheag
Eilean Dhuib
Horse Island

Eilean a' Chleirich
Carn an Iar
Carn Dheas
Bottle Island
Clerach Island

The Summer Isles

N

TO SCORAIG—8 MILES

Miles 0 — 1 — 2

Cailleach Head

CHAPTER ONE

PREPARATIONS

THE BRAE HOUSE OF DUNDONNELL in the north-west
corner of Ross and Cromarty is one of the finest houses in the
land – from a man's point of view – and that, perhaps, is an
important qualification. But for the moment accept a des-
cription flavoured by the masculine bias which is more concerned with the outside of a house than its inside.

The house nestles white and snug into the southern face of
a precipitous and wooded hillside, and this is the first and
only dwelling seen by the traveller new to the glen, who has
come over the long, dreary pass of the Dirie Mor and the
narrow, winding and atrociously surfaced road of the Feighan. Twenty miles from Garve railway station land you at
Braemore with the Dirie behind. Woods and rhododendrons
are before you, and the seductive view of Strath Mor, Loch
Broom and Ben More Coigeach in the far distance gives the
newcomer the false idea that the wilder part of his journey
is over. But the signpost says fourteen miles to Dundonnell
and this road is not going into the big strath at all. The
traveller is on the Destitution Road, so called because it was
constructed in the famine years of 1847–8 as a means of pro-
viding work and food for the stricken crofting population of
the West Coast. There are twelve miles to go before the next
smoke rises from a chimney.

Some people call it the Desolation Road, doubtless because
they have let their impressions colour their memory. I suppose it is desolate to one who sees scenery as a picture without
the detail of things which make up scenery. The high hills
are in front and to the left hand – the Forest of Fannich,

the double spear points of Slioch, looking very near beyond Loch a' Bhraoin, and then, as you turn away somewhat surprisingly from that glen, the spiry ridges and pinnacles of An Teallach. You have left the trees and are on a high moorland scarred with black gullies showing the grim, whitening skeletons of the trees which were once part of the ancient Forest of Caledon. It is not always raining up there, but it is very often, and the road seems never-ending. Feighan House, just past the summit, is like an empty skull showing black holes where once were windows and door. Tramps find it a useful port of call for a night's rest, and they are gradually burning up the mantelpieces and any other removable woodwork. The bogwood would burn longer and better, but that would mean work to get it.

Feighan means bog, and this bog and this house have an unpleasant history if all you hear is true. Feighan House was once an inn placed on the old drove road. I was going to say the drove roads were the arteries of the Highlands, but that would be bad physiology; arteries carry newly charged red blood from the heart to the extremities of the body, but Scotland's heart has been pulsating weakly since a long while, and what has come north and westwards along the drove roads these two hundred years has been poor anaemic stuff. Let us rather call them the veins and drainage channels of the Highlands. Great herds of cattle, slowly driven by a wild crowd of men, left the country west and north of the mountain backbone and disappeared into the hungry maw of the south. Year after year the cattle walked away and later the sheep, and now the men have gone as well.

The inn of Feighan was a halt for the drovers going and coming. They drank strong spirit in a place which the law did not reach, and if some of them disappeared and were not heard of again in their own time, they may turn up yet in those black gullies where the peat is disintegrating. Such then is Feighan, and now, the house well past, the road runs alongside a flat where the deer graze in the evenings and from where a walker may see a golden eagle soaring nine days out of ten.

I love this road myself, not for its own sake but because it is the road to home and the wild country it pierces is the bulwark against what is to me the less pleasant world of the east and south. Many, many are the times I have come tired over this stretch and in the half-light of evening, not grudging the badness of the road, yet with relief and joy crossing Feighan Bridge from where the road drops steeply under the great rampart of the Black Rock and enters the glen.

Here are the birch woods again, and after a few precipitous twists of the road the glen opens before the traveller now hungering for something kind. An Teallach appears in full grandeur above the foreground of trees, then the wooden sweep of the strath, and when the hills rise again on the northern side in slopes of great beauty, there is the little white house less than a mile away, a cheerful man-made thing in a big landscape – just a little West Highland house and nothing more. When I first came into the glen and saw the house where we should live, I remember saying to myself it would be a bad day when I should drive out of the glen to leave it. And now it seems that day will never be, because we have left the glen seawards to settle on the island of Tanera Mor.

As you leave the road which goes on a mile or two to the head of Little Loch Broom, and climb towards the Brae House, you will see that it is set in no garden but is almost part of the hillside. There is one door and five windows which are all too small when you are inside for long. A Highland house which is not a mansion does not usually have more than one door, for though two doors may have social advantages when you leave the level of simple folk and begin to climb in the world, they create conditions for a fine draught of wind to go through the place so that it is never warm. And you never yet met Highland folk who liked a cold house. It does not matter what the weather is outside, but when they come in and shed their shoes they like something more than what the thermometer calls temperate.

The beasts of the hill come about us; the roe deer very often, summer and winter; red deer in the very bad weather of winter, though more usually in spring when the grass

is shooting well but the nights yet cold; wild cats in autumn
and winter, and especially if we leave open the henhouse
door at night; rabbits always; the woodmice or long-tailed
fieldmice come inside in waves, and charming as I find them,
they have a wretched habit of emptying jars of jam and
marmalade in the store press; house mice are rare and not
encouraged; weasels are never far away, and we have had
the pleasure of one living under the house. Our red
squirrels are delightfully tame and are to be seen at all times
of the year.

Bird life is varied and pleasant; the eagle and the buzzard
are often overhead, and peregrine falcon and sparrow-hawk
are not uncommon. Chaffinches take the place of sparrows
about the door and are much to be preferred. Goosanders
and mergansers come up the glen on their way to the freshwater lochs where they breed. There are both tawny and
barn owls in the glen, and in wintertime you may find a tree
gay with a flock of four kinds of tits, tree-creepers and gold-
crests.

The rock behind us gets all the sun and no north wind.
There is hardly a month in the year when a primrose cannot
be found somewhere in the sheltered neuks, and once in the
midst of a hard winter, when all else seemed frozen, I found
a plant of the delicate and feathery herb-robert in flower.

So much for the man's view of the place. Marian Fraser
Darling, usually known as Bobbie and who as my wife is the
mistress of the Brae House, would tell you another side of
the picture. The burn is forty yards away and dries out sometimes in summer. Not only must water be carried into the
house but it has to be thrown out as well! And once inside,
you will see that the walls are so permeated with damp that
wallpaper will not retain its original colour for more than a
week or two and only with periodic help will it stick to the
wall at all. The floorboards are warped and lie open, and
when we first went there it took us nearly two years to get
top-side of the fleas. The boarded ceiling flakes whitewash
into your soup if someone should tread incautiously overhead. Our fireplace is a natural gem, just an open hearth with

two stone hobs, so impossible to keep clean that we never try – so why grumble, says the masculine element.

Despite these interior shortcomings, it is a house where people are happy. It is Alasdair's background, and the child dearly loves the place to come back to after a spell among the islands or at school. This house has seen our hopes grow, watched our work being done and our island ploys hatched. Here have come new faces, for it is known we keep open house when at home, and some of these acquaintances have ripened into friendship after hours of good talk which have stretched into the early mornings.

The one fault of the Brae House is that you cannot see the sea from its windows. It is necessary to climb a hundred feet through the bracken and up the cliff by the waterfall, and then a long view stretches away north-westwards. Flat parks and woods of the strath, and then the wrinkled saltings at the head of the Loch; green strips here and there by the sea's edge, and little white dots which are the houses of the crofts; and behind these on either side of the long sea loch the hills rise steeply, getting browner and more bare until the summits seem to be just naked faces of the red Torridonian sandstone.

The steep hills make Little Loch Broom a dangerous place for a boat when the winds blow, but from this perch behind the Brae House the sea looks calm enough until you put a telescope on it. If the day is clear you can see the Outer Hebrides and pick out the shape of the hills in the Forest of Harris. And from farther up the hill, where the view is unhindered, the crofts near Stornoway, over forty miles distant, are visible through the glass. There is an island between there and Little Loch Broom, and its long shape cuts off part of the Hebridean view. It is about eighteen miles from this rock behind our house, and now, after our years of island life, I do not care to look at it through my glass, for if I see the surf beating up in white puffs, distorted by mirage, I am reminded of anxious days of wishing to get there and knowing the swell would not allow; and if the sea is flat calm and the sun shining, I wish I was going anyway.

The island is Eilean a' Chleirich, a rugged little half-square mile of varied country, lying remote and uninhabited by man. It seemed heaven on earth to us when we first landed there, and each year when we went for odd days we would say – if only we could live there. The quietness, the number of birds and the beauty of the little freshwater lochans hidden away from the wild ocean, all pulled at our heart-strings. Was it the job of work or our own desires which drew us there to live in 1936? Call it fifty-fifty and let us not give way to introspection. The scheme of work on the social behaviour of birds and the inter-relations of the several kinds living there looked quite good on paper, and as we had at that moment no income from research fellowships we had only ourselves to satisfy.

We were satisfied and we began to plan.

Bobbie is an excellent quartermaster; I conceive the ideas and rough out the ways and means, and she fills them in to the minutest detail. Then we go through the lists together and think of the thousand and one things which might happen but which we hope never will. When we embark on these ploys we certainly do not seek adventure, for to our minds adventure often means incompetence somewhere or carelessness at some earlier time. Living on uninhabited islands is no lark but a responsible task, especially so when you add to the possibilities of trouble by taking a child. Alasdair spent his eighth and ninth birthdays on Eilean a' Chleirich, and since then has been on two other island expeditions. If I describe this first move to isolation in some detail it is because our growing-pains may have a value for someone else, and there is always a certain interest in seeing how things get done on an empty purse.

A man should never wait until he sees money running along in front of him so that he may follow. It is man that leads and money follows. I would say to Bobbie, if the work is worthwhile it will gather its own support, and if it isn't we shall go down to the nick, and good riddance. But before the summer was out we had a fellowship to live on and research funds to supply us with the instruments necessary for measuring weather in relation to the behaviour of the birds.

First of all, what were we going to live in? As we were going to Eilean a' Chleirich early in April, which is still wintertime in the West Highlands, it would be good to have a rigid structure. The idea was dropped because we had not money enough for a hut, and what was equally important, it was unlikely that a hut could be got over and landed so early in the year. We decided on a waterproofed bell tent with a collection of small tents, which had been used as bases for my work in the deer forest, for stores. It did not take us many weeks to grow wiser to this extent – if you are going to spend several months on an island where there is no covered shelter, it is necessary to have as good a tent for stores as for your own living. Two or three small tents are not enough, for canvas flaps and tends to loosen in a wind unless it is raining as well, and then it seems to find the corner of a packing-case to chafe against. The canvas wears thin and admits the rain, and you find yourself in all kinds of trouble.

A bell tent is a very well-designed piece of work. The whole strain is in a downward direction on the pole, and in windy weather there is no flat surface to check the wind, which is carried round and upwards to where it can do no harm. The sag which does develop on the windward side during a gale draws the apex of the tent towards it, and the pole slightly out of the perpendicular into the wind. The tent has, therefore, a compensating, self-strengthening action in a high wind. At least this is the theory. It works in practice until you get winds of force ten on the Beaufort scale, and then you can look out for something happening. We modified our bell tents on the next expedition by fitting intermediate guys all round and four long guy ropes of heavier type to the apex. These had a fine steadying effect, and for future trips they will always be fitted. The door-flaps of a bell tent can be wrapped either way and laced so that an uninterrupted cone faces the weather. When a bell tent is for two people only, beds can be placed on the outer edge at the lowest part of the roof and there is ample headroom for several feet round the pole. A circle of thirteen feet six inches

diameter is a good working space. Its faults are those common to any shelter made of canvas and rope, and in long
stretches of rainy weather the wish for a window becomes
acute.

Then sleeping arrangements: lying on the ground is fine for
a week or two when you are moving on each day, and when
I was with the deer in the forest I would have grinned at the
idea of taking a bed with me. But for a more or less permanent camp in all weathers, warmth and comfort at night go a
long way towards successful work during the day. Sometimes the weather causes you to lie up for a day or two, and
then the psychological factor cannot be ignored. Discomfort
added to the closeness of living and the makeshift character
of many camp arrangements tend to shortness of temper.
Bobbie and I realize this quite well and can modify our conduct to fit the circumstances, but children are complete ego-
tists and it is amazing what trivial things can rank as being
of primary significance in the mind of a child. So we bought
ourselves Hounsfield beds made of light tubular steel and
strong canvas. They bend and give to the stresses of the body
and are not as flimsy as they look. We put thin kapok mat-
tresses on these beds and each of us had an eiderdown
sleeping-bag. We have no cause to regret our choice, for this
equipment is still standard for our island expeditions, and so
far as the time spent in bed is concerned, we have never had a
cold or physically uncomfortable night.

Bobbie made lists of rugs, deck-chairs, books to take, pens
and paper, cutlery, crockery, cloths and cooking utensils;
everything to be packed in boxes which would be useful as
seats and cupboards on the island. We also wrote on all the
boxes with a blue pencil a complete list of what was inside
them. Even with all this care it was a fortnight before we
could find the Primus prickers! A large order was sent to
one of the Glasgow stores for groceries to be dropped by the
Clydesdale at Scoraig. These were sent in tea-chests, and we
felt at fault for not having asked for the groceries to be packed
in smaller boxes. As it was, we had difficulty in landing the
heavy tea-chests on Eilean a' Chleirich.

Cooking can make or mar camp life. Fires are all right for boiling or frying, but we had to think of good sound meals and baking bread over a long period. We took a Hestia oven, two Primus stoves and a Valor blue-flame heating stove. Yeast came from the Postal Yeast Company of Hull with the launch which was supposed to visit us fortnightly. We have read and been told of yeast being maintained as a culture in lonely places where fresh yeast cannot be got, but we have met no one yet who can tell us how they themselves have maintained a clean and satisfactory culture in the West Highlands. Our own efforts have not been successful, and the probable reason is that we have no means of keeping the yeast culture at a constant temperature. The yeast from Hull keeps for a fortnight without deterioration. Dried yeast tablets have never worked with us, and the bread made with them has been like lead. It was something of a problem, then, in 1938, to think how we could make bread on North Rona during six months of complete isolation. The Postal Yeast Company kindly helped us out by supplying tinned flaked yeast made by the Distillers' Company. This handy stuff is packed in half-pound airtight tins and keeps for at least eight months, as we know.

We could have carried a wish for simplicity to the point of building a stone oven to be heated by driftwood and peat. But the peat should have been cut the previous year and the oven would need to be built. I have seen attempts at these things from time to time, and think them as well left in the realm of story-books. A good outdoor oven which will be economical of fuel and will not burn food on one side and chill it on the other needs careful engineering and a good time to build.

The problem of fresh food is linked with that of cooking, especially when you have to think of a child. We decided to take our goats and hens and let them take pot-luck of the place. Islands are usually better grazing grounds for animals than the adjacent mainland. The reason for this, off the West Coast of Scotland, is that the small islands have less rainfall than the mainland and the ground is well manured by the birds which draw their food, rich in lime and phosphorus, from the sea. Also, being well out in the sea, temperature is more even than on the mainland and the grass comes earlier.

Green stuff was impossible to get. We could not make a garden in a few months, there are not enough nettles on the island for boiling, and Bobbie will not face up to very much in the way of seaweed. Alasdair and I used to chew dulse and enjoy it, and there was something pleasant about going down the rocks to the world uncovered by the low spring tides where the dulse grows, iridescent as the wings of a tropical butterfly. We did sow lettuce and mustard and cress in a box, but the hens found it before it was ready, unfortunately. A case of apples and oranges was included with the stores, and Alasdair and I took a little chickweed and sheep sorrel now and again. The crowberries ripened at the end of June and were plentiful for a month or more. We could pick a handful, crush them in the mouth for the sweet juice that was in them, and spit out the flinty seeds before their bitterness reached our taste.

Sea fish is a great luxury to us, though we live near the sea at Dundonnell. The fish come into the Loch late in the year and sometimes not at all, and there are not the men and boats to go far out in the Minch. We are in the position, then, of seeing herrings sporadically hawked on the West Coast from Dingwall on the East. Eilean a' Chleirich is well out, and the tangle grows thick round the island to form good cover for the lythe or pollack and the saithe when they come. We took our long bamboo rod, hanks of line and gut and a varied lot of white flies, spoons, rubber eels and plain hooks.

The question of contact with the mainland in case of emergency exercised us for a long time. We must have a boat of sorts, if only to fish from, and in which to poke about the inlets of the island coastline. A little nine- or eleven-foot dinghy would not be a big enough craft to cross to Scoraig or Achiltibuie in safety, yet anything larger than that could not be got out of the water at the island, for the landings are bad and there are no anchorages. We decided on a rubber or canvas kayak or canoe. These craft may look frail but they are easy to handle in the water, and because of their low centre of gravity and absence of keel resistance they ride the sea with a high degree of safety. The kayak is decked in also, and the occupant can be surrounded with spray covers so that the boat itself does not ship any water.

We bought this boat, the bell tent and several other oddments from Messrs Thomas Black and Sons of Greenock, and we shall not forget the delightful afternoon they gave us looking over the factory where, in an earlier day, sails were made for the Clyde clippers. Indeed, sails are still made there and a reek of wood, tar and rope is about the place. Colza oil lamps hang obsolescent in the windows, and dusty binnacles look as if they were forgotten. You could sense the continuance of hereditary craftsmanship as soon as you got inside the door. Each expedition since then has been helped by Messrs Black, and when we went to North Rona in 1938 they went so far as to accept the onerous duty of seeing a large part of our gear and stores aboard the cruiser. In the ordinary way, this is a task which every expedition should do for itself.

There was also the formal matter of getting permission to squat on Eilean a' Chleirich for six months. The proprietor had already given me his good-will, and when I asked the grazing tenant, Donald Fraser, I made a lasting friendship, for his desire was as keen as my own to keep the island as a sanctuary for the birds that live there. When I went round to see him that day he was rebuilding his house and was limited to one room which itself was stripped to the stone of the walls. He was busy and I had much farther to go myself, but we found the talk too good for work. It is the very spirit of our countryside that personal relationships and chance meetings are of greater importance than such practical work as we may be engaged upon. So Donnie and I sat before the peats for a couple of hours and his mother plied us with fly cups of tea.

It is one of the tragedies of this remote North-West that the fishing has declined along with other economic and social

conditions of the crofting areas. We are short of safe har-
bours, of boats and of men to make up crews. At that time,
the spring of 1936, there was only one boat on this lochside
with an inboard engine – a launch of twenty feet long which
was probably never built for work off this awkward coast.
This was owned by our friend Scoraig, who keeps the store
in the small isolated community of that name. I walked
down the track on the north shore of the Loch and found
Scoraig behind the counter of his shop.

Here in this little whitewashed building is none of your
chromium-plated shop fittings and aids to selling, nor has
Scoraig the air nor the arts of the counter-jumper. This is a
man's shop. You can buy butter and sugar there, and crockery and stuffs, buckets and girdles and rope and tackle. There
are shelves and benches of bare deal, hooks from the rafters
for stuff that will hang, and the stone walls and the window
are hygienically festooned with cobwebs to catch the flies. It
is such a shop as a man lingers in unashamed to discuss the
affairs of the world. I verily believe I could buy drapery in
Scoraig's shop without embarrassment.

Scoraig listened patiently to the scheme, and with a grave
face. He never raised an eyebrow in surprise, and naturally
he would not be telling me outright that he thought it madness. He merely commented on the earliness in the season
to be landing on Na Clerach, and indeed there would be no
eggs yet. That was so, admittedly, but in extenuation I said
there was as much to watch in bird life before the eggs appeared as afterwards.

'Ay, ay,' was all he would say to that.

Money is an awkward subject to discuss between gentlemen, more especially when the gentlemen are Highland.
Both Scoraig and I knew what would be a fair rate for the
ferrying, but good taste forbade our stating the sum baldly
thus early in the conversation. We never haggle here so
much as politely shuffle round a point, so great is the distaste
for the mention of money. We talked for an hour about
the sea, the island and the crofts, and as we were walking
out of the shop the awkward words stumbled from our lips.

We were in complete agreement, and that was a big fence over.

The packing for our shieling summer was quite as difficult as a total removal, for we had to pick and choose and eliminate drastically. There is always most trouble with those Last-Minute Things. We had to get the bell tent to the island, put it up and fill it with things not needed at home, such as my scientific instruments, bins of flour and meal, and some of the stores. March was a lovely month on our coast, but I was too busy with my work on the deer to leave for the island at that time. We feared for what April might bring, and sure enough the north-west weather came with the new month and put a great swell on the sea. It was difficult to be knowing what Scoraig was thinking of the weather each day, because there is no such thing as a telephone or telegraph down the lochside and there is no road along the north shore beyond Badrallach. I would go down the strath each morning to a place half a mile beyond the boathouse on the Loch and put my glass on the stone slip which is Scoraig pier eight miles away. Sometimes figures moved at the shore, and sometimes mirage and rain distorted the field and I could see nothing.

Wednesday, April 8th, was a morning of mist, rain and north-west wind. The Loch did not look good, but Scoraig and young Iain from Rhirevoch were at the boathouse with the launch at half past eight. It rained hard while we loaded the launch, but I was well pleased with Bobbie's packing of the stuff and felt there was no need to bother. Then Scoraig knelt before the engine and the ritual of starting began. I am one of those people who exert a bad influence over any engine or mechanical contrivance with which I come into contact. Animals I can charm, but to a machine my name is Jonah. I have sat on the verges of many a roadside and rolled in a boat on half the lochs in Scotland with engines which 'have never been like this before'.

'She wasn't coming too well at all,' said Scoraig.

I grunted.

He turned and turned at a handle, the shape of which

appeared to me to violate every law of mechanics and levers. Starting-handles are usually like that, hopelessly inadequate in size, shape and grip. I still have a scar on my chin from one of them which hit me ten years ago, and I hesitated about helping now. But Scoraig is elderly and he crouched lower in the boat to rest and get his wind back. I offered to take a turn, but the handle came out and hit me a sound crack under the jaw. It was a matter of knack evidently, and I left it to Scoraig after that. Iain sat in the stern and grinned all over his face.

Why engines do start, when previously they have refused to, is a mystery to me; this one did in its own good time, and the launch made a brave sweep and a white wake out into the middle of the Loch. The rain stopped and Eilean a' Chleirich shimmered in the sunlight and shower. This was fine; something getting done at last. But the engine, 'she was but firing on the one cylinder'. We put in to the Badluchrach shore, and John Macleod came down from the crofts. He tested the plugs by pressing his thumb down on top of them while the engine was running. I was silent in admiration of this Spartan method. Then he brought out the inevitable bit of string and tied wires here and there. We got under way at half past twelve, firing on two cylinders, which happily was the total number.

The swell was more evident when we came to the mouth of the Loch and it was considerable by the time we were out past Cailleach Head. We looked forward and backward until Eilean a' Chleirich looked nearer than the mainland. Then we looked back no more.

The sky became leaden, and when we turned in to the east bay of the island, Acairseid Eilean a' Chleirich, the swell was beating up white on the rocky coastline. The cliffs are sheer below Ard Ghlas and there are spiry stacks of red rock standing off from the land. They looked threatening today and the thud of the swell echoed between the stark walls of the bay. On the northern side there is a hole running into the cliff, and with this heave on the sea, and in this state of the tide, the hole filled with air as the swell dropped. Then the air was greatly compressed as the sea rose, so that a cloud of spray was shot out each time with a tortured scream of sound. An otter ran down the tiny shingle beach into the sea. Who were these people coming into his world at this season of the year? Beds of tangle appeared and disappeared in the water in an oily, secret way in the rise and fall of the swell. It seemed alive, and once I saw a long tail come out of the water and return, slimy and silent. A catfish. The swell was as much as ten feet; far too much to think of landing.

We had trouble starting the engine again, and the quarter of an hour lying about on the swell did not make me feel better within. Forward motion in a small boat in a rough sea is a fine thing to experience, but lolling about from side to side in a deep swell is the finish of many a good man's equanimity. We came round the south shore of the island and tried the west landing, but the swell was just as bad there. To the north-west high waves were breaking over a point of rock, and it is only when you are at sea-level in a small boat that you can judge the height of the waves at their true worth. Scarts and cormorants flew over us in clouds and settled on the rocks sloping up from the sea. They were ruffled at our intrusion, and their behaviour added to the sense of remoteness and aloofness which the island bears from the sea.

In the meantime the engine had stopped.

The next half-hour of swell and stench of spent oil broke down the reserve I had maintained until now.

We tried the south landing by the cave, just for the sake of trying, and we were becoming hopeful when a big wave nearly put us up the beach. We pushed off as hard as we could and made for home – after another quarter of an hour's prostration before the engine. Scoraig was as patient as ever. What was time to him? Iain grinned widely, as he always did. It was a miserable task unloading the boat at Scoraig's pier, and as I came home to Dundonnell I wondered if we should ever go to Eilean a' Chleirich. Good days were few now, and before we could go ourselves this first load must be landed.

Saturday, April 11th, came in sunny and fine, and I

thought it a good day to walk down to Scoraig and arrange for another try to the island on the Monday. But the Loch looked so calm and inviting that I went along the south side as far as Badluchrach in our old car. John Maclean ferried me over a dead-calm sea to the north shore. Scoraig was filling bags with seed oats when I walked up his pier at nine o'clock. Yes, he was thinking to be trying it in the morning-time but now he was thinking not. Would I like to try? I said yes, so we launched the boat, loaded up, fiddled about and had a cup of tea. At five minutes to eleven we were in the boat and starting away. Mistress Scoraig came running down to the shore and called in Gaelic. Scoraig's face became a little longer as he turned to me.

  'A party was saying we shouldn't be going today.'

  'Well, it is your boat,' was all I could say.

  'Och, och,' said Scoraig, 'we will be getting out of the Loch and seeing what Cailleach is like.'

He shouted back to the Mistress, and it was the long face was on herself now; then we were soon out of the Loch and rounding the point. There was a fine breeze by now and the sun shone to make the sea a deep blue. The spell I had ex-ercised on the engine earlier in the week had passed, for the launch went forward without a misfire. We sat back to enjoy the sea, except for an occasional turn of baling because the planking was not just too close-fitting. We watched the guille-mots skimming the sea and the dinghy we were towing, which pulled at the painter like a young horse on a halter. We were under the island in little more than an hour, making for the west landing. The anchor was dropped two hundred yards from shore and we began lifting cases from the launch into the dinghy. Three trips should empty her. The swell was bad enough as we drew in, and the little boat bumped badly on the rocks.

It was good to have my feet on the island again. While Scoraig and Iain went back to the launch for more gear, I carried loads over the boulders and up towards the ruins of the old shieling. The sea had begun to whip up white; I knew Scoraig would be anxious to get back as soon as he could, and as I was not staying on the island this time, I had no wish to linger after the warning we had been given.

It is not always easy to put up a tent of any size in the West Highlands. You may find a flat place, but will it be dry enough? If there is a flat and dry place, will it be sheltered, and is there depth enough to take the pegs? I was thinking of such things as I made my way to the place of the old shieling, which would be the most likely to provide a site.

But my eyes were here, there and everywhere, not wishing to miss anything of the island's life. A flock of purple sandpipers scurried over the barnacle-covered rocks at the sea's edge, and when I came in sight of the ruins twelve grey lag geese rose from a patch of green grass. Eight more were swimming on Lochan na h'Airidh. A snipe flew out of the rushes and rock pipits undulated in flight round about me. The sun was brilliant, making the lochan a deep blue. The goat's-beard lichen clung to the rocks, a dull pastel green, and the grass was a dull parched green as well. But the patches of crowberry were a darker and livelier green, and as a background for all of them the rocks showed a bright red in the sunlight. I wanted to drop the gear and look at everything, but beyond the lochan I could see the blue expanse of the northern ocean flecked more thickly with white wave crests. And there was work to do.

I chose a position on a little knollie that was flat and dry, from which we could see the lochan and the sea. It was not as sheltered as I should have liked, but there was nowhere else as good and dry. Iain helped me put up the tent. We left the guys fairly slack because of probable rain before we came for good. Then we ran back to the shore, where Scoraig was having to hold the dinghy off the rocks and having to take her farther and farther out on the receding tide. Had he not done this, she would have been lying among the big boulders and we could not have got her afloat until the next tide came in. He was wondering what on earth Iain and I had been doing all this time, though we had worked as fast as hands could.

The north wind was strong now, but not too strong to

prevent us having the sail to help the engine. We were going at a good rate, and I believe we should have covered the eight miles from Eilean a' Chleirich to Scoraig in under the hour had not the tow rope of the dinghy broken. Running before the wind was fine, but turning back to catch the dinghy and make her fast once more was not so good. The engine took a quarter of an hour to start, and I was thankful, if the boat had to pitch about, that I could get the wind in my face.

When we got under way a kittiwake followed us, coming within two or three feet of our heads. How easy the flight of those grey wings! How white and round was her head and how wise-looking her black eyes! Scoraig watched her for a long time and turned to me.

'Man, is she no bonny?'

Then he asked me how old I thought the bogwood was. In an unguarded moment I answered as truthfully as I knew – about eight or ten thousand years. A look of doubt and some sorrow crossed Scoraig's grave face. I knew I had uttered heresy by indirectly questioning the time scale of the Old Testament, and not needing to be told twice that I was on the edge of dangerous ground, I changed the subject.

Strings of guillemots and razorbills passed us, flying with swift wing strokes close to the water. Sometimes a puffin flapped by in his own clownish way to make us smile.

There are some animals that always amuse us, and the puffin is one. I remember Hector Morrison saying to me one day when I was looking into a tree:

'It's a squirrel you'll be seeing now.'

'Yes,' I said. 'How did you know it wasn't a bird?'

'Because of the laugh on your face.'

Scoraig and Iain put me off on the Badluchrach shore, and I was back home at Dundonnell in time for tea.

CHAPTER TWO

THE JOURNEY

FROM MONDAY MORNING, April 13th, we had to hold ourselves ready to start for Eilean a' Chleirich. We were dependent on the state of the sea and what Scoraig thought of it. We would be up fairly early each morning to run up the brae behind the house and throw the glass over the Loch. Was it calm? Was there a sharp line across the mouth of the Loch, which meant that the sea was much rougher outside in the open Minch? Was the surf breaking in a white line on the shores of Eilean a' Chleirich?

Monday and Tuesday were no good at all, so we let the hens loose and did not pack the Last-Minute Things. Wednesday seemed good and I went down to the boathouse. Soon the wind got up and it rained hard. I came home and let the hens out once more. By this time the food problem was growing troublesome at home, for you cannot be in a state of indecision about moving from a place for three or four days without your resourcefulness being taxed. We are ten miles from a shop at Dundonnell and only dry goods can be bought there. Now, four years later, we know that three or four days of doubt are nothing at all. We have waited in that hand-to-mouth state for as long as a month.

Thursday morning was good at half past six, as spring mornings often are but at nine clouds were gathering. Scoraig was to be seen coming up the Loch at ten o'clock. When I got back to the house the henhouse door had fallen open and the hens were running free. We got busy with a landing-net, and Kennie McLennan worked them with his dogs.

Bobbie had most of this job to do for I was taking stuff down
to the boathouse. The bantam cock and one hen refused to
be caught and they had to stay at the Brae House. There
they remained all summer, and seemed well enough when
we returned in October.

We had enough small baskets of oddments which had to
go out of the house with us, but these things, apparently,
were of little importance compared with the stuff Alasdair
suddenly decided he must take with him. His lonely life and
the fact that he had never been to school were the reason,
probably, for his keeping his early childhood's toys. There
was Willum, the cloth-stuffed squirrel, a tiny cairn terrier and
a spaniel in a model dog basket, several varieties of small
boats and a broken antique camera which was a treasure re-
trieved from a lumber room during his recent visit to Edinburgh. These things had to be stowed with the utmost care in
the car and in the boat, for be it known that stuffed squirrels
breathe the same air as you and I do and their emotions are
similar to ours in that they must not be crushed, turned
sideways-on or upside-down. But the car did get us and our
gear to the boathouse eventually.

Scoraig had a load to land at Badrallach. We saw him put
in there, but mist and sleet showers soon hid the other side
of the Loch. The north-west wind was increasing. It was our
good friend Hector Morrison who suggested we should go
down to Scoraig anyway, and if it was good weather we could
go straight away from there on the next day without the de-
lay of the boat's journey up and down the Loch. Scoraig
thought it was a good idea also, when he came across from
Badrallach, and away we went in the rain and sleet. This
shower did not pass as others did, and the wind freshened
again. It was magnificent going, nose into the rough sea,
but that day we were not out for the blow. The goats were
wet through in the bow of the boat, and the spray drenched
us all sitting abaft the engine. Bobbie looked at me and raised
an eyebrow. Yes, we were both thinking of the drying out of
bedding and so on when we got ashore. But we had no wish
to spoil the fine sense of well-being of the moment. Alasdair

was enjoying it too, and he cracked jokes with his new friend Iain.

When we came to within a mile of Scoraig the sun came out and the wind slackened; and in the way of this country our clothes were blown dry by the time we drew up under the concrete pier. Scoraig suggested we should put our animals in his warehouse-cum-barn; and for this we were glad because it was obvious there were more stiff showers to come from the north-west. The goats munched some oat straw and the hens were put into a large packing-case, for the building was not bird-tight. We did not want another hunt on the morrow like we had had that morning. The canary, which was now singing very loudly, was hung high in the rafters because of the rats.

It was our intention to find a bieldy place and put up a small tent which we had with us. Scoraig would have none of this. There was a room empty in his house, he said, stripped in readiness for repapering. We could have that in the meantime. Now this was kindness in two ways. A roof and four walls would be better for three of us than a small tent in this weather, and yet, the room being presently bare, we could accept the hospitality without feeling we were being a nuisance. Bobbie and I are a bit fussy over such points. As it was, Mistress Scoraig made us a great fire of peats and some tea, and we were able to dry some of the clothes from the suitcases which had got wet in the launch.

Scoraig and its headland seem very much out to sea after Dundonnell, where the hills are close about and the beautiful peaks of An Teallach are our southern horizon. Bobbie and I walked along the short turf by the shore and went to look over an empty croft we had thought of taking. The land is easily worked and the good drystone dykes round the ploughed ground make it a desirable place. The house has almost fallen in, and because that is a woman's first concern I could arouse no enthusiasm in the place from Bobbie.

'Perhaps if it was morning-time and a sunny day I could be thinking of it more,' was all she would say.

To me the little croft was full of interest, and though the

sky was louring before another squall, the sun shone to me
from the furze bushes which were breaking into flower. Here
in the open fields we heard the skylark for the first time that
year, and the sound was good. We cannot keep our larks
throughout the year; they come in April to the fields of the
crofting townships on the coast and by September they are
away again. Thrushes were perching on the more prominent
rocks, lacking trees for a stance, and singing of a new spring.
Life presses upwards against the weather, as it were, at this
time of year. But spring comes late to this north-west country,
and undue haste on the part of living things in their efforts to
reproduce means tragedy. The year before, I had seen the
frog spawn killed and thousands of mother frogs as well by
the frost. Our immigrant birds, therefore, must learn a
patience against which their bodies rebel.

I rose early the following morning to look at the sea. It
was calm and the sun shone, and yet I could tell the sea was
not settled. An occasional burst of surf showed white on
Eilean a' Chleirich. Scoraig rubbed his chin and thought
he would wait and see 'what like was the day'. So I milked
one of the goats and put them out to graze for the morning;
they, philosophical creatures, concerned themselves with filling their bellies. There was one hail shower before midday,
and the wind freshened, though not enough to bother us.
Scoraig decided to go at half past twelve. We reloaded the
launch and got under way, goats, hens, canary, bedding,
child and all.

We were barely out of the Loch before the wind increased.
Before we were off Cailleach Head the weather was a
thoroughgoing squall. Rain, hail and sleet beat down on us
under the force of the wind and we were drenched with
spray from the bows. The little launch would rise over the
crest of a wave and come down with a terrific slap into the
trough. She was not a heavy craft, and the force with which
she struck the water each time made the water spurt up
through the seams. One or other of us was baling all the
time. One goat lay down philosophically on the boards; the
other stood all the time and shivered as the spray broke over

her. The hens sat huddled together and did not express their emotions. I was most sorry for the canary, for although we had put him where he would get least of the weather, some of it was reaching him now and he and his cage were wet with seawater. He crouched over his seed trough, his little wings drooping low. Bobbie did not smile at me now; yesterday was a joke coming down the Loch, but this was not funny. Alasdair was amused yesterday; now he was cold and wondering, looking very much like the poor animals.

I began to feel my responsibility heavy upon me. There were those who thought I was wrong to take a wife and child to an uninhabited island at this time of year, and to live in a tent at that. Were they right and I wrong? I looked at these two and these animals under my care, and all looked unhappy. I asked Scoraig to turn back if he could and to try later. Scoraig said he was not wishing to turn the boat just now and would rather keep her nose into it. Obviously he was right and we kept going for the shelter of Bottle Island. The slap in the trough of each wave was monotonous and we dared not go fast.

I fell to wondering what would happen if the engine failed. At that moment it coughed and spluttered and I jumped forward to the carburettor lever to oscillate it violently. It was not my engine, but I was more nimble than Scoraig and I was frightened at the idea of it stopping. Then, looking forward, I saw that the screw cap was off the paraffin tank in the bows. I climbed over the gear to look for the missing cap. Happily it was down on the boards and had not been left on the small decked bow, otherwise it would have fallen off into the sea long before now. These chugging old Kelvin engines will stand a fair amount of ill-treatment, but a good dose of salt water would make anything mechanical splutter in justifiable complaint. Scoraig was at once surprised and relieved. So were we.

We were now lying under Bottle Island, and Scoraig asked me if I would rather wait a while before striking across to Eilean a' Chleirich. I wondered. If we did wait I should be soon no man at all lying around on this dreadful swell, and I felt there was a lot of work ahead of us. The worst was over, so I asked him to go ahead for the south cave, for it was obvious that neither the east nor the west landing would let us in today. Since we have lived on the island and I have known this stretch of water better, I have seen how with a north or north-west wind, the sea bores through between Bottle Island and Eilean a' Chleirich. From the summit cairn you can see a great semicircular series of deep waves riding through the two-mile strait. The launch had now to cross these. We did not ship nearly so much water from the long deep waves as when we were heading up from Scoraig. Each wave as it came across us seemed to climb up the gunwale, but they never came nearer than two inches of it, for I was watching most carefully. This to me is one of the mysteries of boats.

We were soon under the south-east point of Eilean a' Chleirich, and Bobbie and I will not easily forget the relief of being on a comparatively calm sea. Back where we had come were the white-capped waves, and here, close under the land, there was no wind at all. And when we anchored off the south cave and stopped the engine, the silence was sheer luxury.

Scoraig thought he, Iain and I should go first to try the landing before the Mistress. So we loaded the dinghy not too heavily and pulled over. I jumped into the surf and held the stern of the boat while Scoraig and Iain got out the stuff. I carried the gear over the clean rounded boulders of Moll na h'Uamh to the cave while the dinghy went back for Bobbie and Alasdair. When they came I lifted each of them through the surf.

'I don't care if we live here for ever now,' said Bobbie.

And apart from the particular satisfaction of that first moment, we have not felt very much that we wish to reverse that sentiment.

The goats came over on the last trip; their heads looked expectantly over the gunwale of the boat to the island and they seemed as keen as we were to be ashore. The sun came out to make the surf sparkle as it crashed on those round boulders. This little pocket of the coast was quite out of the wind and we felt actually warm. We took the goats to the flourish of grass above the cave, where they began grazing immediately. Here on the islands, and on the south side particularly, the grass is earlier than on the mainland, and this green bite was a treat for the animals. The canary, being a thoroughly hardy bird, was put down in the sun to dry. He preened his feathers and within ten minutes was singing in that great voice of his which experts tell us is much too loud for a canary. Here it sounded well and the sun cheered us all.

There is but one thing to do for people of our country after this kind of experience – to make a cup of tea. I climbed over the big ridge to the nearest lochan for water while Scoraig and Iain got a fire going with heather shaws and driftwood. Bobbie found food from among the Last-Minute Things and it smelt good. Alasdair began exploring as soon as he had settled all his treasures into the cave. He has a remarkable memory for locality, for on this island where he had not been for two years, and then only for a day, he was able to point out places near the caves where he played and had found things which interested him.

Scoraig, refreshed and rested, looked over a much calmer sea to Little Loch Broom. It was four o'clock and time for him to be moving. He gave us a warm farewell and we could see he had misgivings about leaving us alone on this 'wild island'. He had called it that from time to time, but today he had climbed to the ridge while the kettle was boiling and had looked down over the maze of little hills and lochans.

'Man,' he said, 'I like the feel of this place. I'm thinking I could have lived here had I been younger.'

Now he shook hands solemnly and I pushed the dinghy through the surf. We watched him kneel at the engine, looking meanwhile for the tell-tale puff from the exhaust which would show it had started. There it was now, and Iain was standing in the bows hauling in the anchor. They went away

with a waving of hats, and we waved handkerchiefs in return
from the sea's edge till we could see them clearly no more.

'This, you might say, is where we start work.'

As we looked at each other we realized suddenly and forcibly
what there was to be done by dark. Our first load consisted
of the hens, the white goat which had kidded earlier and was
agile, and a basket of ready-to-eat food. This was the beginning of a back-breaking job, for the climb from the cave
to the ridge is two hundred and fifty feet and very sharp.
From the ridge we passed down a rough and stony way to the
strip between Lochan Iar and the sea. There was the sea
pool to walk round, and over two little ridges until we came
to the old shieling and the tent by Lochan na h'Airidh.

The one-time inhabitant of Eilean a' Chleirich was an
outlaw, put out here by the people of the mainland under the
old clan law for sheep-stealing. It has always struck me as a
most sensible thing to have done with that man. Here he had
to work out his own salvation, and from all accounts he
became a reasonable member of society. He brought a wife
here and had children. They grew up, married and had
children also, and as far as I can find out, it was this third
generation which left the island about eighty years ago. The
family was now accepted by the crofting community of
Lochbroom and was under no stigma. Descendants of the
Eilean a' Chleirich family still live in the parish of Lochbroom, and one of them came over with Scoraig and the
mails one day during our first summer. It was his first visit
to the island of his forefathers.

Well, on this stormy April day of our landing, when we
had carried two or three loads from the south cave to the
camp, we were able to imagine vividly the feelings of the
outlaw when he was planted on Eilean a' Chleirich. Perhaps
he had carried things over this ridge to the place where he
had built the little house in drystone, but I am certain the
folk would not have set him down with as much gear as we
had. From the ridge to the foot of Lochan Iar you can see
that boulders have been rolled out of the way and that

places have been built up with stones to make a very rough track down the steep brae-face. Now, through disuse over a period of nearly a century, the path is difficult to see under its covering of grass and crowberry, but it is the way you would take instinctively to cross the ridge. All the gear from the south cave came down the outlaw's path on our backs. We made four journeys the first night, and it took us four days more to get everything over to the tent.

Morag the little brown goat was very heavy in kid. It would have been cruel to walk her that mile to the tent, so I made her comfortable by the cave where, with the wind in the airt it was, she would have the most shelter. It was dark before ten o'clock, by which time we had put the things in temporary order at the camp and I went over to the cave again to see that Morag was all right. She had started to kid. I waited with her a while until the white, drop-eared male kid was born and getting to its feet. Morag, it seemed to me, had a better place for the night than we had ourselves. I left her lying down and content, and as I came over the ridge in the darkness I was cheered by the triangular shape of light which was the tent. Bobbie's shadow moved to and fro as she busied herself making comfort for all of us.

We slept solidly because we were dog-tired, and when I woke at seven o'clock it was to think immediately of the little brown goat. I would get up and slip over to her before breakfast, but I fell asleep again until half past eight, when Alasdair was awake and anxious to be up and doing. What with one thing and another it was nearly ten o'clock before I reached Morag. She was lying chewing her cud in her own quiet, untroubled way exactly where I had left her, but there was no sign of the kid until I looked about and found a hole in the rocks six feet away. He was down there and dead, and another one, a nanny, had gone the same way, though she had wedged by the neck nearer the top. She was still breathing as I lifted her out.

I blamed myself then for not coming immediately when I woke first at seven o'clock. This is the sort of occasion when reason does not order behaviour. We had brought the goats for milk, particularly for Alasdair, and the decision was made long before that we must kill the kids. We were, indeed, short of milk and we could not have kept this kid, but now when the little mite was cold and in such dire straits I could do nothing else than put it inside my shirt to try to warm it back to life. I was half successful and brought it to the stage of sucking when I held its head to one of Morag's teats. I was angry with myself. Morag would not walk a step back to camp and I had to carry her all the way. When I say she would not walk, I mean that she would neither drive nor be led, nor even stand. First I would carry the kid for fifty yards, vainly hoping she might have enough maternal feeling to follow. Then I carried her as far as the kid, and so on. Her motherly sense had evidently not been excited, and she made things harder for me and added to my irritation by going downhill each time I went forward with the kid.

Morag thrived and milked well for a goatling that summer, but the nanny kid lived only through that night. I was both sorry and glad, for we should have been sorely put about had it lived. Nevertheless, I was left feeling that tragedy had visited us at the beginning of our venture and that it might have been prevented if I had been more careful.

Our days were busy thereafter making things shipshape. It is a thought which appals any research worker if he suddenly asks himself how many hours he devotes to his actual research. They are extraordinarily few, because research not only demands its own routine duties of recording, reading, getting things assembled and so on, but there is the irksome business of caring for the physical body which even the most intellectual of folk must continue to carry round with them. This becomes all the more apparent when research workers embark on expeditions into places where there must be some battle with the environment. The body will stand hard treatment for a week or two and perhaps be the better for it, but for a trip of several months you must make up your mind to the necessity of being as comfortable as the conditions will allow.

In those early days I was itching to be exploring and to be

watching the birds which were so tantalizingly close. Sometimes I did snatch a couple of hours, though I felt as if I had
gone on strike by doing so. The fact was that the weather,
having barely let us land on the island, gave us a fortnight
of all kinds of unpleasant stuff. On our second night we had
a north-westerly gale; then a northerly, and some terrific
hail-storms. We woke up to two inches of snow two mornings
in succession, a rare enough thing out here. Rain and south-
west weather followed the cold, and we had several nights of
gales when we were out to tighten or slacken the guys or give
pegs an extra security by resting big boulders on them. There
was a fireplace to build, a trench to dig round the tent, a
table to make from driftwood, some sort of shelter to make
for the goats and hens as the weather was so devilish, and
there were all those things to carry over from the south cave.
We lived hard those days and felt we were getting top-side
of things. We even went the length of building a turf shelter
as a place of retreat should the tent blow down. I put the
canvas and rubber kayak together one afternoon, trying to
follow the instructions, which said the job would take twenty
minutes. It took me two and a half hours and a lot of hard
work. I was so impressed by this business that I never took
down that portable canoe any more. It went about with us as
it was, and finished its days on North Rona in the late autumn
of 1938 when the seals broke it to matchwood.

The first day of May will long remain in my memory, for
to begin with it was gloriously calm and mild. When you have
had a long period of wind and wild weather and it is followed by a perfect day, activity seems to be frozen and all
you can do is to lie about and heal your battered self in the
quiet of it all. This morning had brought the welcome sound
of common sandpipers to the lochans, that long-continued
piping which is as moving to me as any music Pan himself
might make. The sun shone through the canvas of the tent
in the early hours, and I lay basking in it and listening to
the sandpipers before I rose. This, I thought, was spring at
last, and I let my imagination play with the picture of that
active little mite standing on a stone at the edge of the sunlit

water, his head and beak nodding and tail flirping, and then the ecstatic, vibrant flight over the lochan with a paean of his piping.

This was not all, for the eider ducks had come on to the freshwater lochans and were courting. To me the wood-pigeon-like croon of the eider drake is a sound of the north and of spring. 'Ooh-*ooh*-oh' calls the drake with a lift and drop of his head; 'ooh' answers the duck with little more than a chuck of her beak. I lay there listening and content, and would not have changed places with anyone in the whole world.

How lazy I was that day! I rubbed my chin and realized that I had not shaved for a fortnight.

'M'm, suppose I really ought to shave today; can do it outside in comfort.'

'Well, you'll look a bit less of a mess if you do, certainly,' was the compliment from Bobbie.

Oh well, there was no hurry anyway, but it was placed on the mental list of things to do. We were sitting over lunch when I heard what I thought was very much like a human voice. Impossible. No, not quite; there it was again; good God! I think you have to have lived alone for a long time to appreciate the primitive terror which the unexpected sound of the human voice can bring. At that moment the roots of my back hair tingled, and possibly it rose a little as the novelists tell us it does under the stress of circumstance. Anyway the lunch went dead on me and I keeked out of the tent door like a frightened rabbit. There were two men and a boy a hundred yards away walking towards the tent; I sat down again and murmured the news. We heard them go to the edge of the lochan and begin talking loud enough that we should hear them, and only then did I go out to greet them. I was grateful for such a charming way of calling on a household where you cannot knock on the door. There was nothing to do but make the best of my face and remember it was only one of three. Our visitors were neighbours from Loch-broom and had come over in their yacht on this first good day of spring.

When we had had a cup of tea altogether, had been aboard with them and then waved them goodbye, Bobbie and I thought we would take the kayak through to the east side where the sea was calmest and try the fishing. This meant carrying the boat from the camp to Lochan Fada, paddling the length of the lochan and carrying it to the sea at the other end. The three of us were packed in as we travelled along the lochan, and then came the second shock of the day. Figures appeared on the knolls of the eastern skyline and came towards the shore of the lochan. One was a woman. I could see that the man expected me to pull in and speak, but my nerve had gone completely and I did what I have always since regretted – turned the kayak down the main arm of the lochan and disappeared from view of the visitors. Once ashore at the east end I knew this behaviour simply would not do, and face or no face, we must turn back and meet the strangers. Bobbie and Alasdair went on foot and I paddled, but somehow we missed the people altogether and all we saw of them was rowing back to a yacht in the dinghy. It was two years after this incident that I heard who were our visitors that day, and only then could I make a late and somewhat lame apology. It seems that our surprise at seeing them was almost equalled by theirs at seeing a canoe and three people paddling along an unexpected loch on a remote island.

All that remains to be said of this disastrous day is that we caught no fish. I had also learned my lesson; while the wind kept blowing I could go unshaved, but the advent of calm weather meant I must attain to a certain decency of appearance. Decrepitude of clothing never embarrasses me, nor its possible singularity if it happens to be fitted to the job I am doing, but it takes a better man than I am to carry off a half-beard successfully, the dark, dirty-looking sort of mess which will degrade the best of faces. There is no doubt about it, whether your expedition is just a wee thing like ours or an honest-to-goodness Polar show, beards are definitely bad form.

Our next visitors came a fortnight later and were of quite different type. I was walking along the coast to the

north-east of the island one unpleasant rainy afternoon after
a cold spell of weather of which that first day or two of May
had been a false harbinger. I was surprised to see a forty-foot
East Coast type fishing-boat lying offshore and a launch
from her shooting lobster creels. This was something new
indeed, for there is no such outfit on our coast. There was a
definiteness about the behaviour of the men which seemed
foreign to the leisurely way we do things here. The launch
and I reached positions where we could hail each other.

'Where are you from?' I yelled.

'*Bluebell*, of Wick. What are you doing in a place like
this?'

'Staying here for the summer and doing a bit of work.'

'Well, there's been no summer yet, by George! Where can
we come alongside and give you some crabs?'

I pointed to the east bay, Acairseid Eilean a' Chleirich,
and ran round the cliffs towards a place on the north side of
the bay which is known as the Exchange. This is a very
interesting and puzzling phenomenon. At this point you will
find that the swell does not break and does not rise and fall
with the same depth and suddenness as elsewhere. It is
usually possible for a man to get ashore there from a boat or
for goods to be thrown one way or another, but it is a long
way from the habitable part of the island and we could not
have got our heavy gear ashore there when we first came.
Nevertheless, it was an excellent place for the East Coast
skipper and me to exchange greetings. Here was one of those
grand Scandinavian types of men to whom the sea is a foot-
path and to whom physical conditions make very little
difference. Times were bad on the East Coast, so four of them
had made up a crew and were trying this new venture of
lobster-fishing on the West. They were a fortnight out from
home and had come in this little boat through the Pentland
Firth and round Cape Wrath. He threw up to me four big
cock crabs and I asked him to come ashore in the evening
and take some hens' eggs back with him. He said he would
the next day when he came to lift the creels.

Bluebell lay in the west bay the following evening and I

paddled out to her in the kayak. What men, I thought! The
boat was never fitted out for more than overnight fishing, yet
these fellows under the stress of the times had improvised
bunks and cooking arrangements and were doing a month's
trip in waters they had never visited before. This was the
first time out and lobsters seemed scarce. Paraffin, also, was
$8\frac{1}{2}d$ a gallon over here and only $6d$ in Wick. Doubtful if the
trip would do more than pay its way, but it was better than
doing nothing at home. And yet when the skipper and two
of his men came ashore they brought some little soles for
Alasdair and small lobsters for us, and it was with difficulty
we were able to persuade them to take some eggs back with
them. They were sure we should need them all, living so far
away from things.

The skipper was particularly anxious to hear the shipping
forecast at nine o'clock, and as he sat on a packing-case with
a mug of coffee and a biscuit in his hand, and the cultured
tones of the announcer came through, he exclaimed:

'Well, now, this is the first touch we've had with civilization for a fortnight!'

And as I take it civilization really boils down to folk being
on good terms with each other, his statement was right and
complimentary.

The claws of cock crabs are strong and immense. That afternoon I brought them over from the Exchange they were
dropped near the tent for a while until we had got a fire
going and a bucket of seawater in which to boil them. The
poor things waved claws and legs and lay quiet, and waved
blindly again, and as I was reflecting on the sufferings to
which we put living things in consuming them, the strange
movements of the crabs attracted the attention of Blanquette the white goat. My reflections were for the moment
impersonal and then they became more personal, and I went
on watching.

Blanquette is the epitome of all that is caprine. Horns,
beard and mischief. Her horns are satirical and her face is
an inquisitive travesty. The amber eyes with their long pupils

sometimes convey a withering superciliousness and quality
of poise and experience. You can tell from the ears that she
misses nothing, and the lips and beard are a continual
mockery, just as her tail is. Blanquette is a strong and mus-
cular goat with a voracious appetite for string, brown paper,
leather and the bark and foliage of young trees. It would be
quite wrong to say I hated Blanquette at that time, but I
was under no delusions about her. She had been kept by a
woman until I bought her for a pound that spring, and I
found her as thrawn a creature as you would meet in a long
while. I happen to be a very good milker and cows take to
me at sight, but Blanquette would lead me a dance every
morning and evening. And then she began sharpening her
horns in Alasdair's ribs. So I took hold of Mistress Blanquette
in cold blood and basted her ribs pretty thoroughly and gave
her one more round when she objected to being milked. The
effect was all that I could have desired, for after that she
never caused me the slightest trouble. Her behaviour altered
completely in that she sought my company on every possible
occasion and would run up to be milked, standing quite still
without restraint all the time this was going on. Her devo-
tion to me became embarrassing. If one has to take sides in
any discussion of the necessity for corporal punishment in
dealing with animals, one must be against it, but in private
practice I know quite well that there are occasions when one
sound tanning does much good. When Blanquette and I had
our showdown we gained a new respect for each other upon
which our later friendship thrived the more.

When Blanquette became interested in crabs we had not
achieved our *rapprochement* and I felt that her inquisitive-
ness about the tent had better receive its deterrence by con-
sequences, if such were to be. The ears came forward and the
lips made little nibbling movements as they hovered over the
crab. A waving black claw was not considered by her at its
true worth. Black claw and white nose, followed by satirical
horns, galloping legs and a mockery of a scut, were a long
way from the tent before I could reach them and effect a
parting. This, also, was all to the good between Blanquette

and me, for though she could hardly divine that I had wilfully let her get nipped, she did know that it was myself who relieved her from the pain. She did not try nearly so much to eat the guy ropes and tent fabric after that. Morag the little brown goat seemed quite incapable of ever doing anything wrong, and this seemed strange in a goat.

We had one other accident with one of our animals that spring which taught us a lesson we have scrupulously observed ever since. There was a hen called Greenshank who was far too tame, and because she was a decent, trusting sort of bird we did not chase her out of the tent every time she came in. The poor thing seemed under a compulsion to lay her egg on my bed and would walk around the tent in obvious discomfort if not allowed to do so. Bobbie and I were lying in the sun in the lee of the old shieling one evening when Alasdair came running down crying:

'Fire in the tent. Quick.'

The tent was closed and full of black smoke. When I crept in, the Valor stove was overturned and burning fitfully as it was short of air. A cushion was also on fire and a packing-case smouldering. Bobbie fetched water from the loch, and I, suffocating within, damped the fire. Then we opened the flaps to let out the smoke, which had made a mess of everything. We had been very wrong in leaving a stove alight with a kettle of water on it; Greenshank had climbed in over the bottom flap and had overturned the stove, and there is no doubt if the tent had been open and provided a better draught of air much of our stuff and the tent itself would have been burnt. We counted our blessings in very much the same way that Crusoe did, and made a firm resolve then and there that we would never again leave a stove alight in a camp.

CHAPTER THREE

EILEAN A' CHLEIRICH

LEAVE THE CAMP and its life for a while and let us explore the island.

The south cave is as good a starting place as any other because it was not only our depot on landing in 1936, but it was where we first set foot on Eilean a' Chleirich some years before. The name of the island means the Isle of the Priest or, more correctly, of the cleric. This name goes back to pre-Reformation times because Sir Donald Munro, High Dean of the Isles, mentions 'Na-Clerache' in his famous manuscript of 1549. He is not very informative, unfortunately, and merely says, 'Northwart fra this ile (Gruynorde) lyes ane ile callit Ellan Naclerache, ane haffe myl lange, guid for gersing and wild fowls eggs, perteining to McEnzie.' Probably the island became a retreat from the religious establishment on Isle Martin at the mouth of Strath Kannaird, and was thus used from a very early time. Some day, perhaps, we shall find some tangible evidence of clerical occupation, but as it is unlikely that the place would be very suddenly relinquished, artefacts will not be found easily.

The south cave above the little boulder beach of Moll na h'Uamh is wide-mouthed and not very deep. It is fairly dry and the floor is covered with a very thick layer of powdery earth. The whole floor is in the nature of a kitchen midden and we have dug into this inquiringly for things of interest. Bones there are in plenty and even bits of antlers of red deer, but no artefacts. Miss Margery Platt of the Royal Scottish Museum, Edinburgh, has kindly identified some of the bones from a bagful we sent, and gives the following list of species: grey seal, ox, sheep, red deer, pig (which is most surprising, especially as there were relics of two pigs, one with a milk molar in the lower jaw), dog; and of birds, oyster-catcher, song thrush, skua (unidentified species), guillemot, lesser black-backed and herring gulls, shag and fulmar petrel.

This list is really thrilling to anyone working on the birds of the island and interested in the present distribution of birds in Scotland. Guillemots do not breed on Eilean a' Chleirich or anywhere in the neighbourhood, but they are common on the sea in spring, so perhaps they were obtained from the sea rather than from the breeding ledges. All the same, I have not heard of these birds ever being caught on the water and it would need a fairly crafty fellow to do it. There are no skuas in this area now, though I cannot see why. And lastly the fulmar petrel: before 1878 the only certainly recorded British colony was on St Kilda; after that date the most completely recorded colonization has taken place and a few years ago the birds came in small numbers to Eilean a' Chleirich. Yet it seems at the time of the kitchen-midden folk fulmars were obtainable.

Sometimes, as I have scratched about in that cave, I have wished it possible to call up visions of its long history. If I could but speak to those old folk who fed on seals and skuas and fulmars I could make some useful contributions to the natural history of this countryside.

Eilean a' Chleirich has two wild mammals apart from the grey seal – the pygmy shrew and the otter. The island is an otter's paradise, for there are not only innumerable small caves about the coast in which they can lie, but there are the eight freshwater lochans and many dry cairns of rocks where they can breed in peace. The dry, powdery mould of the south cave often shows the claw marks of the otter and the furrow made by the long and powerful tail. Naturally I like otters, but a population of twenty or thirty of them can do a lot of damage to the avian inhabitants. The birds I have seen affected happen to be two of my favourites – the grey lag goose and the tiny storm petrel. There are not many

geese, and that makes it all the more serious when an otter
puts a goose off her nest and takes the eggs. The little stormies are numerous and the otter seems very clever at catching
them. He bites off the head, and the tail with the legs attached,
eats the body and leaves the wings. Each year you will find
remains of one or two newly killed storm petrels in the south
cave.

The climb from the cave to the summit cairn on the ridge
at two hundred and fifty-two feet is a steep one whichever
way you take it, but it is always worth the effort. The character of the island can best be seen from there and the distant
view is the finest I know. This is an easy thing to say – the
finest I know – but I have now lived on other islands with
magnificent views and the West Highlands are very well
known to me. The view from the summit cairn of Clerach is
the finest I know. As you cannot see all ways at once, it
would be better perhaps to say there are two main views –
to the east and to the west, the mainland and the Hebrides.
Seven o'clock of a fine June evening is the best time to see
the mainland, for the sun is behind you and still high enough
to shine into the corries of the high hills. The whole range
from the Reay Deer Forest to Torridon is visible and those
hills nearest are among the best – Quinag, Suilven and Stac
Polly, with the rough coastal foothills of Archaean gneiss in
the foreground; Ben More Coigeach and the magnificent
range of An Teallach; you can see the summits of that great
country round Mullach Coire Mhic Fearchair, Ruadh Stac
and the Maiden; and continuing southwards Slioch and
Beinn Airidh Charr. It is a fine picture, but better still when
you happen to know the individual corries and slopes. I have
lain on the summit cairn of Clerach and lived earlier years
over again.

When the sun had at last fallen on this same evening it is
well to turn about and look upon the long, purple line of the
Outer Hebrides. It is hard to tell where Lewis disappears into
the sea where the sun has gone already, but after the thin
line of that northern peninsula the Forest of Harris rises a
bold shape, topped by Clisham. Farther south again, North

Uist is just visible beyond Rhudha Hunish, which is the northern point of Skye. Here is none of the detail lately seen in the mainland hills; just the remote, violet, swelling and fading line with which the imagination can run riot.

Eilean a' Chleirich itself is seen to consist of two main masses cut by a principal glen running slightly south of west to north of east. The southern mass consists of the ridge on which is the summit cairn. The climb was steep from the cave, but the slope was gentle compared with the northern face of the ridge, which is sheer in many places. The rock of which the island is formed is Torridonian sandstone, but the complex out here is smoother and redder than that of the mainland. The strata are tilted to form rugged cliffs on the northern faces, and the southern ones slope unbroken into the sea here and there. This northern face of the ridge is of extreme beauty, especially when seen of a fine March evening, for then the sun is low and throws the fluted columns into sharp relief, and the redness of the sun makes the rock-face shine an amazing vermilion. It is in this cliff that the peregrine falcon has her eyrie, alternatively with a place over the sea. She also has eating places at several points, and I, clambering about, have found many remains of little auks left by the falcon. We do not see these little birds on the coast every year, but there were large numbers in the winter of 1936–7.

The eastern end of the southern half of Clerach opens to form two low corries ending in steep boulder beaches to the sea. The floor of each corrie is a flat peat bog of several feet thickness. I, the farmer at heart, the man who has always had the urge to carve out a new farm, play with the idea of starting from scratch on Eilean a' Chleirich. These two flat areas, well-sheltered from the raking west and south-westerly winds, should become my cornfields. I would run surface drains to the boulder beaches, burn the herbage in the dry days of March and April, bring boatloads of shell sand from the beaches of Tanera Beag and spread on the charred surface, then plough and, by whatever means I could, get muck on to it. 'But it wouldn't pay,' screams your up-to-date expert. No, it would not *pay*. What a debt we must owe to the men who

first broke the earth's surface! Probably they had not brains
enough to realize it 'wouldn't pay'. Modern agriculture follows the enlightened dictum of the man from the Middle
West who said, 'Posterity never did nothing for me.' And for
all my brave talk, those fine flat bogs of Clerach will continue
to grow their sour crop of sedge, interspersed with cross-
leaved heather and a clump of common reed where the
water gathers.

The slopes of this southern half of the island drain easily,
and being covered with good black peat they grow fine
heather. Rowan and birch trees would grow in many places
if the sheep gave them a chance. Think of this island as it
must have been when the first man landed on it – a tiny
Highland world of hills and wooded glens and lochans to
mirror the green fringes. Two shallow lochans cover part of
the floor of the main glen and end westwards in a narrow
boulder beach running to the sea. They are the least interesting of all the lochans, and rarely are any birds to be seen
about their shores other than the common sandpiper. Some
time I hope to see whooper swans come there, for since I have
known the island these lochans have come to grow a wealth
of *Sparganium*, and one day I shall take some water-lilies
there to plant. The fringes of these two lochans are lined
with otter tracks constantly used. There is also a cairn on the
southern edge where the animals breed; a patient observer
prepared to wait all night on the rock a hundred feet above
may be lucky enough to see the family gambolling on the
grass in the early hours.

North-west of these lochans is another little range of hills,
and at their northern foot is the longest loch on the island,
Lochan Fada. This stretch of water is of exceptional beauty
and interest whether you see the large view or the tiny. The
water winds before you, and the hills either side frame the
distant view of the mainland – high, rocky mountains with
white specks of crofts at their foot. Several beds of flags grow
on the edges of this lochan, and here and there the banks are
too steep for sheep to climb down and nip the aspen poplars.
Some of these little trees reach a height of ten feet, and iso-

lated though they may be by miles of sea and moor from
others of their kind, their leaves are grazed each year by
caterpillars of the poplar hawk moth. At the foot of the trees
and at several points around the loch are large plants of the
luxuriant royal fern *Osmunda*, and what adds further to this
sub-tropical place in the senses of the foliage-starved islander,
the honeysuckle climbs about the trees and shrubs of willow.

There are times when we, as island dwellers who have
known hidden, tree-shadowed pools in softer places, wish to
turn away from the wildness of the west wind and the tortured sea, and it is then that the beauty of Lochan Fada has
great healing power. I have never known a July without
great gales and rain from the south-west, just the time when
the honeysuckle is sweetest. How little do we use our sense of
smell for the enrichment of experience! Wild hyacinths or
bluebells grow in a patch of vivid green halfway along the
northern shore of the lochan, and many an idle quarter of an
hour have I spent there in late May when the flowers have
added another blue to those of lochan, sea and sky.

As I have lain on the hillside above this lochan I have had
a glimpse of the haven it must be to some birds. I have seen
a solitary shape fly in from one of the other islands two miles
away, a grey lag goose weary from a long spell on her nest.
Her wing-beats sound rhythmically as she circles and de-
scends into the quiet air over the lochan and between the
hills. Then with a final rush of water against the feet and
feathers she comes to rest on that still surface. There is beauty
in the way she sips eagerly at the fresh water, leans into it
and throws it over herself. Rarely have I seen a bird unconsciously express the feeling so vividly, of refreshment
which must have flowed through her. She rests content on
the water for a quarter of an hour before rising again to
return to her long vigil. These are the moments which give
me the most pleasure in bird-watching, moments of spontaneous and revealing behaviour which carve deeper into
the mind than hours of observation *ad hoc* from a hide. I
should like to share them with all men, so that wild geese
would be no longer creatures to be thought of in conjunction

with guns and punts and chilly dawns. This is noonday and this one goose is without suspicion.

Mergansers breed along the banks of Lochan Fada and enjoy its quietness. They are extremely wary ducks on the sea near the mainland and wherever they are found ashore, but on Eilean a' Chleirich they seem aware of the sanctuary the island offers. I can walk by the lochan without disturbing them, and with comparatively little effort have managed to get photographs.

There are five more lochans on Eilean a' Chleirich, each with its own charm and marked individuality. Lochan Bheag, set high in the little range of hills north of Lochan Fada, gives exactly the impression you get from coming suddenly to an unexpected loch on a high moor. It is quiet and unfrequented except by a pair of common sandpipers in the summer. Sometimes I seek it for its upland character when the sky is very blue and dotted with sharp-edged white clouds. North again and a little eastwards is the Hidden Loch and I call it that because its discovery is my one small addition to the body of geographical knowledge. It is by no means the smallest loch on the island, and even the One-inch Ordnance Survey map shows all the others. But the Hidden Loch is not shown on any map except mine. It is one hundred and forty yards long and eighty yards wide, roughly tri-angular in shape and eleven feet deep at its deepest (sounded by illustrious discoverer when messing about with kayak). The lochan is enclosed by little hills, and if you were making a circuit of the coastline and plotting a rapid survey from high points, as the surveyors did, no doubt, the loch would be lost entirely. An otter lives there, but it is rare to see any birds swimming on it or working its steep shores.

Lochan Tuath, or the north loch, is not far away but is of quite different character. This loch lies high, gets a lot of wind and does not give the impression of quietness. It is beloved of the eider ducks in spring and summer, and most of the eiders' nests are round its shores, hidden in the heather. The wild geese commonly come to Lochan Tuath, and it is practically the headquarters of a colony of lesser black-backed and common gulls. When the young birds appear, the lochan is in the nature of a thoroughfare and a training ground for flight. And, of course, there are the ubiquitous otters and common sandpipers. It is the kind of place where something is always happening. The lochan is twenty-one feet deep in one place.

Lochan Dubh Medhonach, the little black middle loch, lies westward of Lochan Tuath and twenty feet below it, taking the overflow from its big sister. The special beauty of this loch for me is that it gets very little wind, and as you lie quiet and sheltered in the heather by its shore you are quite out of sight and sound of the sea. You are in a little cup of the island's hills, and from the south shore of the lochan there rises a sheer bluff of rock about forty feet in height. A thick green willow bush reaches forth over the dark surface of the water. Seeing what there is to see in scenery is something of a practised art; a painter concentrates your attention on his picture by framing it, and if you look over a limitless scene you will find it difficult to fully appreciate any single part of it. You must look at the small scenery sometimes and have it framed off from the outer world. Thus the beauty of the little dark loch, where I love to watch the tiny breezes crossing its surface in rapid shimmering patterns of silver. No far horizons lure the eye from this play of water, air and light.

When this lochan has water to spare, the overflow falls another fifty feet to Lochan na h'Airidh, the loch of the shieling. I called it that because of the remains of the outlaw's little house at the southern end. Here is another hub of the universe, a stretch of water much frequented by herring gulls, black-backed gulls, eider ducks, oystercatchers, grey lag geese and cormorants fishing for eels. It is also the loch from which we take our water supply. Little bays and points make this a happy playground for Alasdair and his kayak. From this flagship he inspects fleets of driftwood boats and dockyards of original if not orthodox construction, and from its southern margin he can see the great ocean to the north and the sea bounded by the sands of Mellanudrigill to the south-west.

It is near to the heart of the island and a happy place. This lochan provides the deepest sounding of any on Eilean a' Chleirich – twenty three feet – under the steep hill on the east side. One or two royal ferns are beginning to grow on the shore of this loch and we have transplanted a few more because we like them, but I believe your pukka plant ecologist surveying the island would frown on this. Suppose I suggest to him that he should consider the whims of elfish folk who love little islands as an ecological factor affecting distribution of species? That factor would also account for flags growing in the tiny burn which runs from Lochan na h'Airidh through a little green flat below the shieling, and then loses itself among the stones of the storm beach above the west landing.

The place of the shieling, the burn and the little green flat are the heart of the island. You would not think seriously of living anywhere else. The outlaw chose aright, but he would not be the first man to build in this area. When, in preparation for our second year, I drained that acre of ground, the foundations of an earlier building appeared from the grass at precisely the spot where we were going to put our hut. These were nearly twenty feet long, pointing east and west, and we have wondered if it may have been an early chapel used by the clerics in retreat. The doorway was evidently at the west end, a queer position for any ordinary human dwelling. As I dug those parallel open drains to the burn I cut through what had obviously been a made roadway of shingle about seven feet wide and leading from the building now gone.

The Scottish naturalist Harvie-Brown paid several visits of a few hours each to Eilean a' Chleirich, and the place fascinated him so much that he wrote some pages about it in his *Vertebrate Fauna of the North-West Highland and Skye*. On his first visit he saw what he thought was a stone circle on the west bank of the burn and in the little green flat. He found it had disappeared next time he was there and, imagining it to be of too great interest to be lost, he returned with an excavation party. The stones had evidently sunk into the turf, which had become much more boggy than on his earlier visit. He dug them out and replaced them in circular form on the east side of the burn where the ground is firmer; they lie there still, and as the sheep graze over them, the stones do not disappear. The hole made by Harvie-Brown's party in excavation became a little wet place with a clump of rushes, much beloved of the snipe. As we lay in our tents thirty years after Harvie Browne's bit of fun, we used to hear the snipe coming down to that hole, 'chick-chacking', every night at about five minutes past ten. So do our deeds live after us; Harvie-Brown would have liked to hear this, but he has been studying the natural history of Elysian Fields these many years.

A botanist would divide Eilean a' Chleirich into two main zones by drawing a line from the south-west point to the north-east point. Heather is dominant to the south, but to the north and west it gives way to a wealth of crowberry, sheep's fescue grass, buck's-horn plantain and sea-pink. This is a herbage floor of great beauty for the senses – the crow-berry is kind to the foot, and aromatic scent rises from it, and its darker green against the grass is pleasing to the eye. How can anyone write of the profuse growth of sea-pink flowering in late May and in June without lyric fervour? Clerach is a fairy garden of colour, blowing in a heedless world year after year. That north-western half of the island is gay by the end of April when the dwarf willows are in flower. There are several species present of this numerous family, and each flowers profusely. The bumble bees come to the golden heads shining from the drab herbage and give a breath of summer while it is yet far away.

One day in that first summer on the island a brown-sailed boat came into the west anchorage, and like an animate figurehead leaning over the stem was a laughing child, her eyes the colour of sunlit sea and fair hair streaming in the light breeze. She disappeared into the island when she first landed, but in a quarter of an hour she was with us again with the island in her hand, at least its distilled beauty. She had gathered with an unconscious art which made me gaze in wonder. There was the bright green and red of bearberry, the three purples of bell heather, ling and rinze heather; there was a sprig of white heather, a flower of the golden bog asphodel, and from somewhere thus late in the season she had found a silvery head of bog cotton. A rich posy of colour in the hand of a child chosen by the seeing eye of a child from what is called a barren island.

Eilean a' Chleirich repels from the sea but invites from within. Let us see the different world of its coasts. Six miles of coastline round half a square mile of island seems impossible at first thought, but there it is, and exploration of every cleft and sea cave has taken a long time. Some of those caves can never have been entered before by man, for alpine rope is a relatively modern production and the men of past times left the cold reaches of dark sea caves alone. There is one cave running into the cliff from one of the little boulder beaches to the south-east, hidden from the sea and easily missed from the land. It shows signs of human occupation in that the boulders inside are built into the form of a small circle. The cave is a narrow, eerie place – water dripping from the roof in one place to form an ochreous stalagmite, ferns growing in the dank floor with their light-starved fronds reaching piteously to the opening; and when I shone a lamp into the rickle of stones I saw three toads sitting there like statues. Small eyes gleamed in the strange light and their throats pulsed every few seconds, the only signs of life.

This cave was, I believe, a store for smuggled whisky in the bad old days of not so long ago. Many a nostalgic West Highlander in Glasgow has sipped the raw spirit distilled on Eilean a' Chleirich and imagined he has felt the breath of his home air. The cave may have been the store, but the actual distillation took place by the tiny burn running from Lochan na h'Airidh to the storm beach. The broken iron 'pot' of the smugglers is still there, but the 'worm' is somewhere in Lochan na h'Airidh lost for all time probably. The legend of the capture of the smugglers is funny.

These men had some sheep on the island, and the attention paid to the animals was remarkable. Every week or two the

smugglers would be going over a dangerous stretch of sea
in a small boat to look at the sheep. One young man got himself married and, like all women of the West Coast, his wife
looked anxiously to sea those times her man was out. When
a squall blew up and the boat disappeared in the murk this
new wife was frightened. She was panic-stricken when it did
not show up again after the sky had cleared. She called out
the men of the township, excisemen and all, and they rowed
the eight miles in the longboat. There was no boat drawn up
at the usual landing and no sign of the men. The crew began
rowing round the island and then saw the small boat hauled
up and neatly made fast in a tiny bay of rounded boulders.
A nod was as good as a wink to the gauger, who leapt into
the surf, went into the mouth of the cave and found the
gentle shepherds far tasted in their own brew. Even the most
indulgent and understanding of excisemen could not over-
look that.

Indeed, this sort of whisky is raw stuff. A pedlar with
whom I talked one day in Uist described it to me in a phrase
of delightful restraint. Stricken with a cold, he had begged
a night's rest in a widow woman's byre and she had given
him half a bottle for a cure.

'You will understand,' said he, 'that in the light of that
dirty lamp I couldn't be seeing the colour of it whatever, and
believe me, I could not get away under three days.'

There is a narrow inlet between sheer walls of cliff on the
south side of the east anchorage. The water is deep and a
rowboat can go in quite well if the sea is very calm. A cave
goes westward into the cliff, strikes north again and comes
out to the sea in a narrow fissure. It is a big cave but not very
interesting, and its best thrill is got by climbing down to it
from above. I have done that once, and for the last time I
hope.

Some way north of the east anchorage there are two dark
geos. It is a bad place for a swell in there, and it is doubtful
if you would persuade anybody to take a rowboat in. A kayak
is much better. The light fades as the walls of cliff steepen,
and once the cave proper is reached you can paddle on for

fifty yards to reach a boulder beach. You wait for a slackening in the swell, which pounds with a frightening roar in here, and then quickly in you go, jump into the surf and lift the little boat high before she breaks herself on the boulders. Eyes are now getting more used to the dim light, and you see, as you climb up these round boulders every step resounding like a shot, that the high roof and narrow walls converge to an arch about fifteen feet high. Once through, the cave opens again into another large chamber thirty or forty yards long. You see with amazement that spring tides have been right up here and there is a large unpicked assortment of timber. I have all the delight in beachcombing generally attributed to the shore dweller, and on my first visit of discovery I greedily loaded my kayak with wooden rollers and towed spars round to the east landing. I never went there again during our first year, but in 1937, when Kenneth McDougall was with us, he and I went in together for a fuller exploration. He is a bolder fellow than I am, and when he found a hole through which he could creep at the far end of the cave he must needs go down it and I followed. All was quiet and dark, for we had brought no torches, but still Dougal must continue and strike occasional matches. I meekly follow.

After hands and knees for fifteen feet we found ourselves in another chamber, and on again to still another and much larger one. Here we were indeed in the hollows of the hills. The matches did not burn well and they were getting few; and to be frank, I was wishing myself out of this place. I got the fright of my life when we went up the wrong hole and found it a cul-de-sac. Damn adventurous folk who go caving with a box of matches, and that not full! We retraced our steps, if they are steps on hands and knees, and found the right hole. Thank goodness!

When we got back again to the outermost cave, where the dim light was ineffably welcome, it was to find the swell much increased. We had to wade a good way out to get the kayak launched again. Two days later found us in the cave once more with torches and a ball of string. We measured the cave as being one hundred and thirty-four yards long – quite inconsiderable to a pot-holer or speleologist, but exciting enough for me. When those terrific spring tides had entered the cave, how long, long ago we do not know, they brought oak timbers through to that farthest hall of Pluto. Years and years of that still, dank air and the complete darkness had wrought a strange change in them. They were spongy and tough, like india-rubber.

Dougal and I would never have mentioned it to each other, and would have deprecated it as unwise anyway, but there was no doubt just the merest trace of rivalry existed between us in finding new caves. He found a beauty on the north side of the north-west point which necessitates a nice climb down the cliff to sea-level first. Once down, you can go through a narrow fissure a long way, to come out on the west side of the cliff. But more of this cave later. Bobbie did all these caves with us because she would not be outdone by a mere couple of fellows, and yet she suffers from claustrophobia.

But one day I scored a mean triumph. There is a long slit in the cliffs running in from the north coast of the island, and even when the sea is moderately calm the water bores into there and crashes dully far in at the head of a sea cave. It is a horrible place at the best of times. This morning was the calmest I ever knew, and I had been fishing successfully in the Cauldron, as we call that northern bight of Eilean a' Chleirich. I would just look into the mouth of Geodha Fada. By George, how calm it is! I believe I could get a bit farther. Too narrow to use paddle now. Pull kayak along by putting hands out to the side. The sky disappears, but good light yet. Here was I in a large cave floating on a floor of deep water. I could see dim corridors leading far away inland and no beach anywhere. And then, right up there where I could not see, there was a horrible deep boom. I could not hurry out of here, but the way out to the dear, kind light of day seemed endless. No boat could get in, for, as I said, I had to pull the narrow kayak through with my hands; and no one could climb into the place on a rope. I had looked where no man had looked before, and I do not think it is myself that will be going again. Dougal listened to the story and said nothing. The sea had changed after lunch and he could not go. The weather never attained to that calmness again, and now Dougal is three thousand miles away. Who knows? He may come back yet to chalk off this point, and I am not alone in wishing he would.

There are a few more caves on the west coast of the island, but little worthy of mention. A rock arch goes through the north point and can be navigated on a calm day with a kayak. But just south of that, and opening to the east side, is a terrible place called Toll an Chleirich – the priest's hole. Shortly, it is a sea cave of undetermined length, in the roof of which a large chunk of rock has sloughed away to form a sort of skylight. The sea in this cave is never calm – at least I have never seen it so in two years. It seems to gather, gather, gather in the mouth of the cave and then rush forward into it in romping fashion. Several seconds later you hear a dull boom, smothered by the length of passage. When the seas are big the boom is like a cannon shot and the rock upon which you sit trembles palpably. There is no place on Clerach I like less than this. God made me for the daylight, I have decided, and to enjoy the sunshine. The fair face of Eilean a' Chleirich is good enough for me.

CHAPTER FOUR

THE EVEN TENOR

THE WINDS and bad weather of May, 1936, did not give us very much peace, and when the time came for Scoraig to pay us a visit and bring the mail we felt nervous for him. Much better, we said, that he should wait a few days rather than attempt the journey. But Scoraig was feeling he had a responsibility and must see those three folk were all right. We saw him coming from the top of the hill, on a day that was bad enough. There he was in the field of my glass, a little white launch bobbing up at what seemed a perilous angle and disappearing in the trough of each wave. This north wind would be on his beam, and I could imagine the baling he and Iain would have to do. Evidently it was not very pleasant, for I saw he tacked southwards past Stattic Point as if he were making for Gruinard. Then he turned full into the wind and in the direction of Clerach. When I saw about three-quarters of the bottom of that launch and the bow in the air, each time it seemed he must have been going bows under when he was out of sight. I thought of that leaky planking and the pounding it was getting, and the temperamental engine. The boat was not big enough for this sea.

The launch was now in calm water under the island and came to anchor in the west bay, a hundred yards offshore. Scoraig was silhouetted against the sea taking a long draught from a bottle of water. Drinking water when he knew there would be tea in plenty as soon as he came ashore! They were drenched with seawater, yet they could sit and drink cold water from a bottle! We shook hands with them in a spirit of thankfulness for their safe journey, but Scoraig was

obviously concerned only to know that we were all right.
That seemed such a superfluous thought to us. If you are
lying snug in bed of a wild night when the rain sounds like
pebbles on the window-pane and the wind screams about the
roof and guttering, a tent on a remote island which has little
shelter strikes the imagination as a poor sort of place. If you
are actually in the tent you may be aware of some discomfort,
but you cannot help but feel how much worse it is outside,
and you count your blessings of a warm and dry sleeping-bag.
Scoraig had evidently been thinking in terms of his own bed
and fireside.

The north wind was still blowing in June, and especially one
sunny afternoon when we were lazing in the sunshine in the
lee of the old shieling. It was cold if you put your nose up
into the wind, but June sun is always hot anyway if you can
eliminate the wind, and we were basking in it to the point of
semi-consciousness. The West Highland June draws living
things to abandon, whether they are human beings taking
the sun or the yellow flags blooming on the lochan's edge.
There is enough of wild weather in the year to keep the
crofter folk battling with it one way or another, but the
prodigality of June sunshine calls a lull. Southrons remark
on those lazy West Highlanders sitting around in the sun
when they should be cutting peats. This is not laziness but a
therapeutic necessity. A materialistic civilization considers
doing nothing a social crime. On the contrary, it is an art
which reaches its aesthetic zenith in the sun and laziness of
the northern June. For the nonce, all is right with the world;
we have reached the higher indifference.

Is there any light quite like this June sun of the North and
West? It takes trouble out of the world. I remember one
June evening walking along the white sands of Iona after
watching them all day as I had trudged along the weary road
of the Ross of Mull. I found a boulder on which were daubs
of pigment from an artist's palette – grass-green with the
yellow of horseshoe vetch in it, a brilliant blue with a touch
of violet in it – and I felt with the artist who could not believe

his eyes. For in these splashes of paint on the pale grey rock was no exaggeration. They were not brilliant against land and sea, and when I had picked a handful of marble pebbles from the white sands, there were the colours all over again in small compass. What better, then, should we be doing than lying in the sun, talking of the affairs of our world or lapsing into silence? The sun makes the warmth of the heart.

Then we heard voices, and round the knollie which hides the west landing came Scoraig and Iain and our friend Kenneth McDougall. We had expected no boat today and were completely caught out. The big fair head of Dougal was all smiles and white streaks of dried salt from the spray they had shipped on the crossing.

'Absolutely magnificent,' said Dougal, 'God, what a country!'

'The point is, how long can you stay?'

'Best part of a fortnight.'

It seemed the best of all possible worlds at that moment. Who was more welcome than Dougal? He was not only the friend of Bobbie and me, but the personal possession of Alasdair, almost.

Lily came into our lives that first evening when Dougal came. We were going to the summit cairn for a general look round when I heard an awful to-do in the neighbourhood of the lochans under the ridge. The wind had dropped and the loud, raucous cries of birds which we now heard sounded worse for their echoing in the glen. I ran along by myself to see what was happening and saw the unpleasant picture of two grey lag geese standing back to back with tiny goslings at their feet. Each goose was facing a heron, and these piratical wretches were trying to get the goslings from under the parent birds. The geese were doing the right thing, standing back to back, but the herons were very cleverly trying by feinting tactics to make the geese both turn one way, and one of the herons would make a quick dart with that javelin of a beak in an attempt to steal a gosling. I did not watch this for long, for the geese had only three babies left of their brood, and these were the very birds of the island in which I took most pride and wished to preserve.

The herons flew up with that deceptive slow flapping of wings which hides the speed of their movement, and were gone. The geese turned to what they considered a new enemy, and I found myself in a quandary. If I just left them alone I knew the herons would be back before long; if I took all the goslings to rear I should bereave the geese. I compromised and took two goslings, but I have always regretted since not taking the three, for the parents did not manage to rear their one child.

Two wild goslings fresh from the egg are an enormous responsibility. I looked at these beautiful mites of green down which I must now mother as well as their own parents, and put doubt aside. I gathered eider-down from old nests, put it in a box with a hot-water bottle for the night-time, and in the day I carried the goslings inside my jersey. Bobbie had the good idea of cutting grass small and floating it in a shallow dish of water, and this started them grazing on their second day of life.

Geese have a faculty of becoming 'fixed' on a foster-mother in a very complete manner. All were kind to the goslings, but they took little notice of anyone but myself. I learned much of child behaviour from them in that first fortnight of their lives, and I saw things which I never should have done in the ordinary way. Sometimes I would take them to some fresh grass at the head of Lochan na h'Airidh where I would lie silent as they grazed about me. It was revealed to me then how other birds were taking an interest in these babies. On one evening alone there came a rock pipit, a female wheatear and a snipe. The pipit and wheatear hovered above the goslings, not in any animosity, but in interest. The snipe walked up to them, her beak and head extended inquisitively. The goslings took no notice as the snipe walked round with short, quick steps. I would be wrong to say that bird expressed wonder, but that is how she looked, and because of my relations to the goslings I felt that for the moment I had entered a world from which we are nearly always barred.

One of the goslings died at a fortnight old through having picked up what I did not know we had in the place – a drawing-pin. This placed an even greater responsibility of companionship towards Lily on my shoulders, for I was beginning to realize that if you rear a gosling in this way you make it human and deprive it of kinship with others of its tribe. As time has passed this has become the more plain; Lily is a personal person, not a goose any more. She takes no notice when other geese fly over, nor will she associate with other tame ones we may have about the place.

The bond of utter dependence on me as a mother slackened suddenly at eight weeks old, but not the joy of my companionship, which she sought on all occasions. She would sit on my lap each evening after a supper of bread and milk and run her beak through my hair. The anecdotal Reverend F. O. Morris in his classic work on British Birds mentions the preoccupation of a tame goose of his acquaintance with its master's hair. The delight of Lily's friendship with me has made me decide that when I can settle for a long period in one place I shall rear a whole brood of grey lag goslings from the eggs and carry out a minute study of the social relationships which will ensue from their special contact with me as a mother goose. Such a study would take some years to complete, but I believe at the end of it we might have a valuable story of a species which has reached a high state of mental development.

I believe it was while Dougal was still with us in June that we seriously thought of spending another year on Eilean a' Chleirich. Supposing we got the fellowship for which we hoped and were to build a hut. We could then come earlier in the year and record the very beginnings of the seasonal influx of the gulls to their breeding grounds, and make a more valuable study than we should have this year. Were Dougal to come as well, we could do a parallel study on the cormorants. He said little then, but he joined forces with us before the year was out.

Everything seemed late in that spring of 1936 and it was not until the beginning of July that the fish were about the island in any quantity. We began then to supplement our feeding very largely with fish and were glad of the excuse to get out in the kayak in the late evenings. Nevertheless, 1936 was not a good year for fish and there were many unsuccessful hours spent working the west coast of the island where most of them seemed to be.

A few ewes and two- to three-day-old lambs were brought to Eilean a' Chleirich from the Coigeach shore about the middle of May. The ewes were poor and had lost the wool from their bellies – a sure sign of a bad time in a hard winter; the lambs were poor and had very little coat. These were Cheviot sheep, a breed not suited to this poor section of our West Coast, and the whole stock in this area is of poor quality. If the Cheviot is kept in a country unsuited to it, the lambs soon show the fact by having a very poor birth-coat. The lambs of old ewes also tend to have a poorer birth-coat than those of young ones. A breeder of Blackfaces looks askance at the nakedness of these misplaced Cheviots on the Torridonian sandstone, which is one of the poorest rock formations in Britain, as far as the soil is concerned. Old and poor ewes were the ones brought to Clerach, the ones which might not survive if left on the mainland. I learned between that time and September the truth of Dean Monro's words of 1549 that Clerach was 'guid for gerssing'. Ewes and lambs improved at an amazing rate, and I realized how well the lambs looked only when I returned to the mainland in October and saw the miserable sketches which were probably better, and certainly not worse, than the Clerach lambs at the time of their birth. As one old man put it to me:

'Clerach is the hospital of this country. Everything does well here in the summer season and this is the only place that will cure the liver fluke. If you put a fluky ewe here she will recover very soon and fatten.'

Sheep do fatten very quickly if they overcome an attack of fluke, for the liver seems to be stimulated, but there are few places with a reputation like that of Eilean a' Chleirich for surely effecting a cure.

Eilean a' Chleirich has unfortunately suffered with the rest of the West Highlands in the recent invasion of the green-bottle or sheep blow-fly. It is hard to think of anything more devilish than for animals to be eaten alive. Several blow-flies gather together at one place on the wool, often in the area of the saddle, and lay their eggs in close mass. These hatch in two days' time and the maggots feed on the secretions of the skin which are held in the wool. Their own secretions irritate the skin of the sheep and then the maggots begin in earnest to feed on the flesh of the living animal. It seems that the maggots have a poisoning effect on the victim, for the sheep do not die because of the actual wounds and amount of flesh eaten, but from a general toxaemia which intervenes after a certain time. The good shepherd watches his flock with extreme care from June to October, and especially in July and August when they are most likely to be struck by the fly. The stricken beast tends to go alone and lie under a dyke or a rock. It shakes its tail frequently and takes quick glances round at its own flank. This wretched fly has been my enemy since early years when, at the time of the Great War, men were few and there were some wet, close summers. The fly seemed to get the top-side of us then.

The sheep of Clerach have no shepherd seeing them every day or at frequent intervals. If they are struck by the fly they die or get over the attack themselves. And some of them are learning to rid themselves of the maggots. They go to a peat hag and rub the affected part against a dry and preferably overhanging surface. Maggots and wool are rubbed away to a certain extent, but a fine, crumbly lot of peat is diffused through the wool as well, and I believe this has some value as a prophylactic measure. It is practically impossible for a sheep to rub all the maggots away, but my own observations lead me to believe that a fair concentration is necessary for their continued growth and existence. A very few left together or just singly soon die. There is a fortune awaiting the man who can produce an effectual preventive dressing for sheep blow-fly. Australia has been invaded now, and the fly is having a serious effect on sheep-farming in that continent.

It was obvious I should do what I could for the sheep during the months we were on the island. We had no collie and there was no enclosure where we could bring the sheep for inspection. When I did see a sheep struck by the fly I had to run it down myself or jockey it into a place on the cliffs where there was no escape. I would then bring the beast back to camp over my shoulders, in which position I could hear the seething of the maggots in their fiendish writhing on the back of the sheep. Then I would dress the skin and keep the sheep on a long tether until a scab had formed on the wound.

I know that we had many a wild gale in that summer of 1936 and that I was often out slackening or tightening guy ropes and looking to see that the child was all right in his little tent. What can sleep like a young thing? I have been amazed and grateful for the power that kept Alasdair asleep and unconscious of the tumult round him, and free from the anxiety we have sometimes endured in the night hours. Though we can remember these times, the impression remaining uppermost in our memory is of sunshine and long hours idly looking over the sea. There were days when we could explore the coastal cliffs intimately in the kayak; rare days those, of absolute calm and broiling sun, but they have so filled our minds that they are not rare now. How lovely it was to be in the kayak at low tide on such a day, seeing the wonder of the strange world of the cliff foot. We would have to pull our way through the glossy tangle now half exposed and giving off that strong tonic scent which you can sometimes smell in iodine. There are shiny masses of red and gold sea-anemones, and tiny, silent seas caught up as pools in the rocks for the few hours of the ebb tide. How grateful we were always for the sun! Island sun tans darker than the mainland sun, and we have been so deep brown that people have grinned when they have met us. It is doubtful whether any other place in Britain gets more actual sunlight than we do in June, or May and June together. Eight and a third hours a day average for a month is a very high figure – half the total possible sunlight for this latitude.

You may think I write a great deal about lying in the sun and doing nothing; and when exactly, you may ask, do I do any work? Well, if you would hear the birds singing their sweetest it is not in the hot sunlight of the afternoon you would be listening. That is the time when the birds are least active, and so are the seals and the deer. I follow their example and take a siesta whenever possible. But in the dawn-time and at sunrise and in the forenoon I may be found at work; and again when the heat of the day is past and I am soaked in sun and sloth you may find me becoming active until the darkening. It is remarkable how much outdoor work you can accomplish in our country after ten o'clock at night in June. All the same, says your practical man, it seems to me you have a jolly good time of it, and it all sounds just what I should like myself if I didn't have to chain myself to the serious things of life. Of course I am having a good time of it, for the simple reason that I am doing the job in which I am most interested. You've been lucky, says the man in the bowler hat, I should like to live on that island free from all care as you seem to be. Perhaps. I did not get to this island and this job of work just by saying I would like to go. There have been sacrifices to make somewhere.

Most people do seem to demand a reason, or at least an excuse, from the man who lives on a small island without human neighbours, for he is apt to be deemed asocial and is failing to be regimented in the countless small ways which make life possible in a country seething with people. Freedom seems to be playing a losing battle these days, and we who love her must be prepared to make sacrifices, to see clearly and with single-mindedness. The bowler-hatted fellow may say my love of islands shows frustration, or even fear, and that my desire for quietness is really a veiled attempt to escape from reality.

Look at the question this way: personal sincerity must be the standard of action unless self-respect is to be lost. I, the complete egotist if you will have it so, feel that the way and surroundings of my own life are of immense importance to me, and consequently, but to a lesser extent, to my fellow men. My wish is to serve, to give, to seek and interpret. I find truth in the wilderness, though another man may find it in the press of humanity. In my view humanity spoils when it packs, and I find myself moving to the fringe. Natural scenery is spoiled as well, water becomes unfit to drink without treatment, animals which give pleasure disappear or are exploited for profit, and everything takes on a soiled, second-hand character, all of which is unpleasant. On an island I can be scrupulous about these things without having my efforts rendered void. There is a cleanness about things here which means much to me, and I can respect cleanness in my comings and goings about the place. If I make the birds tame I can do so without wondering if I am increasing their chances of getting shot.

It is not only the physical evidence of large numbers of people which makes ugliness. Minds that neither seek nor find solitude soon become afraid of it. They lose their intuitive faculties and soon become insensitive, which makes for un-beauty in endless small ways. What am I to do, then, if I am to be sincere?

There is a strong spirit of revolt in the younger generation of us against the increasing complexity of our civilization, and some feel we must make a move towards simplicity. Conventions and petty luxuries which soon become necessities can absorb much of a man's earning power and leave him little to live the life he might have chosen. Unfortunately, there are many who cannot be as simple as they would wish, for the world has got hold of their bodies and their existence depends on their remaining a drop in the vortex. Every move towards simplicity demands a greater personal ability in doing things with head and hands, and on a coordinated strength of the organism as a whole. The type of simplicity I seek – hard living by mountain and sea – is not everybody's choice; obviously it could not be without general famine and starvation, but it is one form of friction on soul and body that they shall not rot.

It is not frustration, then, which makes me seek an island, but a refusal to be frustrated. This way of living is not an escape but a goal which has been sought. To this end I have sacrificed money and comfort. I must admit, all the same, that I cannot enjoy comfort for long before I am yearning for the wilderness again. Now, with worldly goods worth about a couple of hundred pounds, I find myself one of the few really successful men. But what about your wife and child, says the bowler-hatted fellow, are you so wrapped in your own conceit that you have no thought for them? Bobbie can answer for herself, and she says that life is altogether fuller since we came back to the field to do our research and left the laboratory. A child of ten or eleven can answer for nothing but the moment – in which Alasdair himself is happy. I have a feeling that the island years have given him a background which in later life he would not be prepared to trade for the pounds in money I might otherwise have left him.

The fact remains that I draw many good things from the civilization I question so severely, and while I continue to do so something must be returned. There is such a thing as ethical economics which demands service to his fellows from every man. Unless you walk out naked and alone into the jungle and live on what you can catch, you are partaking of the goods and services of society. If no service is given in return, the conscience is soon bankrupt.

To this end I sincerely believe in the cultural value of work which reveals the ways of life in animal societies. When man can look upon animals as sentient beings, often with vivid personalities, he will consider them less as material to be exploited. When life is respected in lowly forms, our human society will be a better one in which to live. It is not killing that is our sin, but killing thoughtlessly, needlessly and for fun. And now, Mr Man-in-the-bowler-hat, shake hands with me, please, and let us part friends. If you should ever get the length of Tanera Mor, there is usually a fly cup of tea going. You have not really had a fair chance to answer me back.

That first summer wore on seeing us become more and more
adapted to our island life, and anxious to come back to the
island at the end of January, 1937. News came in one of the
mails that we should have a research fellowship for one year
at least, but with any luck, for three. We were quite agreed
that it would not do to face the worst part of the Highland
winter – from January to the end of April – in a tent. Not
only would the nights of wind be too trying, but cooking is
far from easy in a gale. Bobbie had to lace up the tent tight
if she was baking bread in a high wind or all the heat went
from her oven, but that confinement of the heat within the
tent made for her very great discomfort.

We designed a sectional hut ten feet by eight feet, with
plenty of headroom for tall folk like ourselves, and it was
made for us by Messrs Cowiesons of Glasgow. It was to have
a deep shelf running the whole length of the hut above the
window; half the window was to open inwards from the top;
there was to be a rain-shedder above the window and door,
and a shutter to the window. That order went away in
August and we began to prepare the site.

I have already spoken of the little flat beside the burn
running from Lochan na h'Airidh, and of the shelter provided there from all airts except the south-east. It was a little
meadow at one time, but in 1936 it had degenerated to bog
once more. There was no doubt it had been drained at one
time and I could drain it again now. I dug half a dozen
open parallel drains to the burn, with immediate and surprising effect, and a circular ditch round the place where I in-
tended to transfer the tent. From this a drain led into the
main drain of the system. We pulled all the grass from the
patch where the tent would be, and left the site to dry off
for a while.

We shall not easily forget those first few days of September
when we moved the tent to the new site alongside where the
hut would be. One night brought a south-easterly gale, a
dry one, which gave us no sleep at all. We decided to go

down to the new and sheltered place the following afternoon, for the wind had dried the ground beautifully. We looked at the weather and said it would rain in two hours. Could we move all our gear about seventy-five yards in that time? It was worth trying anyhow; come on.

The work took us exactly two hours going as fast as we could, and the rain began in about two hours and five minutes. So we had five minutes to get tea ready in a very delightful atmosphere of calm and security. The rain came softly with no wind, and gradually increased in intensity. By nine o'clock we said it must stop soon; can't go on at this rate. I was improving the drainage from the circular tent ditch to the main drain at ten o'clock and was working in the nude, for I should have been wet through in no time in clothes, and things are such a nuisance to dry in a tent. Wear nothing, and you only need a towel to dry your-self when you come in.

I think it must have been about one o'clock when I dug a deep, narrow hole in the floor of the tent so that we could bale out as soon as it filled and thus keep the bedding more or less dry. But it still kept on raining.

We were tired from the last night's gale and slept from sheer exhaustion and because the monotonous patter in-duced sleep. It was still raining when we woke in the morn-ing, but not so hard. I rose to see what our island world looked like after such a flood. My highly successful drains were working like millraces, and there was some kick to be got out of that. At the foot of the burn where it disappears into the high ramp of the storm beach there was a loch of about half an acre in extent, complete with gulls swimming on it; the burn itself was running like a real burn and the sound was pleasant. The overflow from Lochan Dubh Medhonach into Lochan na h'Airidh comes down a rock-face at one point, and this was now a rushing waterfall audible from the other side of the loch. The goats looked utterly miserable, for they are dry-weather animals for preference.

There was a certain pleasure in measuring the rainfall in

a gauge – over two inches in about sixteen hours. Another inch fell that day, but a mere inch of rain in a day was not enough to maintain the temporary lochan, which fled through the stones of the storm beach and washed into the sea our one little patch of shell sand in the west landing. Rubbish such as small trees, heather and a good deal of hay drifted over the eight miles of sea from the mainland and littered our coasts for a long time. I realized then what an effect such a flood as that might have on the distribution of plants from a mainland to islands offshore.

We were lucky to get off with two inches of rain that night, because they had five inches at Guinard House, eight miles away. And they were not at the centre of the cloud-burst, which seems to have been on Druim na Fuadh, the road leading from Gruinard to Little Loch Broom. The waters there reached such magnitude and velocity as to wash away the road at half a dozen places and make a jagged furrow several feet deep. A large part of a field at Muncastle became a shingle beach. And then the weather cleared up for a magnificent September.

September was a time of ease. The birds were going away and there was not the same necessity for close watching as before. We entertained visitors from the mainland, indulged in a good deal of talk and erected the foundations which would take the hut when it came. I also used the turves which I had carefully cut from the drains to build a turf dyke round the encampment. While the weather remained so good and we had plenty to do, everything was pleasant, but as soon as a touch of wind and louring weather came along we felt a sense of anticlimax. It was because the birds were going. Human beings watching a large number of birds cannot help being excited by the almost ceaseless activity they are witnessing. Then comes August and the flight of the young. The gulleries have lost their shining newness of spring and look decrepit places. No birds singing except the in-defatigable wrens. A happy season was drawing to its close.

Shortage of food is a most unpleasant thing to experience on a small island because, first, your appetite is large and nicely whetted, and second, there is no way of getting a supply quickly, nor does the uncertain state of the sea allow you to say when you will get it. We had planned our amounts rather carefully in that last month because we did not wish to carry much back with us.

Imagine, then, the sudden advent of a young man we hardly knew, from the Continent. He jumps ashore and shakes hands and turns about to tell the launch to call for him in a week's time. That young man started with a severe handicap. I might have helped him up with his gear to the camp, but I noticed with some apprehension that he was travelling light. He was one of your real open-air boys, the rough stuff. Had he brought food with him? Not much – half a loaf – he was going to eat whelks and *Boletus* fungi; that was what was so extraordinary about the English, they didn't understand the wealth of natural food going to waste around them.

Oh!

Tent? Yes, here it was. He had cycled through Scotland, but do you know the Highlanders were so hospitable, the tent had not been undone from the parcel in which he had bought it. I showed him the place I would like him to use for his tent and began helping him put it up. The material was like a coarse butter muslin and the poles rather thicker than a match-stick. The neat little price label still hung by its slip of thread and flipped in the breeze; a real lightweight this. We let him have one wet night in it and then gave him Alasdair's tent. Alasdair came in with us and could not help being the nuisance any third party would be in a tent, even if he was our own bairn. I explained to the visitor the peculiar set of circumstances under which people lived on a small island, and that to avoid personal frictions as far as possible we made a point of taking our siesta quite alone. The idea never got through; he talked to us in his monotonous drone every afternoon. The British have never learned to be sociable.

The whelks and winkles were never in danger, and the

population round our shores continued to creep about the barnacled rocks and among the seaweed. The *Boletus* fungi waxed into their short period of ripeness and waned into glutinous blobs.

We saw the butter disappearing and the flour supply going low. We learned that indigestion was a myth; what you should really do was to get your belly tight every meal; never get up from the table with an appetite.

Oh!

Fishing became sheer necessity and the sea was kind. We caught lots of large, oily mackerel. Now then, thought Bobbie, I'll just feed these into the hopper and see how the machine will take them. They were grand mackerel, weighing a pound apiece and more as they came from the sea. Now, I am considered a biggish fellow, carrying fourteen stone when I am lean, but I cannot get further than one large mackerel. Our visitor consumed three, completely and with relish and half a dozen raisin fritters as well. We stared in admiration and with a new respect. I expect the British simply have not got the digestions.

The boat did come a week later, and though a big swell was running we bundled our friend into it somehow. He wrote us a charming bread-and-butter letter afterwards; it had been one of the best holidays he had had, and never had he been better fed.

For some days after that we were actually tightening our belts against hunger for Scoraig had not come with anything for us. Supposing this calm weather suddenly stopped and we had a week of gales. It was September 30th now, and October is one of the stormiest months of the year. I felt justified in going the eight miles to Scoraig in the kayak.

The sea was flat and calm, with trailing banks of mist drifting about in the early morning. I paddled all the way at my best pace and did the journey in a little over an hour and a half. Scoraig was away to Dingwall for a day or two, but Mistress Scoraig fitted me out with bread, butter and a jar of jam and one or two other oddments. It was still calm as I set forth on the return journey, but a north wind began to blow when I was half way; not a serious wind at all, but enough to frighten me. The muscles of my back seemed about to crack as I paddled without ceasing, and I wondered how much way I was making. The north point of Eilean a' Chleirich and the south point of Ghlas Leac Bheag gave me a good bearing. As long as I was seeing less and less sea between them I was getting on. There, they joined, and Clerach seemed to creep along the length of Ghlas Leac. And now Clerach was giving me some shelter, the fear was gone and I felt exhilarated. Bobbie was delighted, and after some mackerel we simply gorged on bread and butter and jam. The butter was Mistress Scoraig's own make, full-flavoured and tasting its best, as bread and butter does when eaten out of doors. On this occasion we followed our recent visitor's advice in not getting up from the board with an appetite.

We felt autumn coming upon us and that we should be glad when the hut came. When that was erected and all stowed inside, our season's work would be done. My present neighbour, James Macleod of Tanera, brought it one evening laid across the decks of his big teak launch. Donnie Fraser was with him and in a state of tearing eagerness for work. It was a ticklish job getting the sections ashore, especially those of the roof and window; one dunt through the felt would mean the rain coming in and a great deal of trouble repairing the damage. It was nearly dark when they left, but all the sections were down at the site and if the weather would let them come two days later we could get it up and return to Dundonnell.

The weather fortunately continued good, though autumn was subtly making itself felt in other ways than the departure of the birds. The bracken was not growing green, uncurling frond after frond in the June sun; it was browning and falling back to earth. The bents and deer's-hair grass browned also, and the wind whistled in a different way through the wilting swords of the flags at the lochan's edge. A swell would come on the sea with little provocation and took a long time to go. Now if the skies and seas were grey we could not feel, as we did in the spring, that the weather would get better soon; there would be no improvement, nights would draw in and lengthen the time we should be confined to the tent. Life would be harder for the child and for us.

That little wooden hut with its rigid walls and roof would be the acme of luxury. How surely had the climate shriven us and found us humble before it. Bacon said that man conquers Nature by obeying her, and that is our own attitude when faced with a stern environment. We do not hate and fight and lose as we might cutting a way through the rain forest of the Amazon, though we have to spend a lot of time achieving a moderate comfort. Our contention is friendly, we love the wild weather at heart, and what is more, we have acquired a patience to endure, a spirit of acceptance which must always be one of the lessons of each individual's life. It is best to treat Mother Nature as a foster-mother and accept her discipline; only a topsy-turvy world treats her as a serving wench.

James McLeod and Donnie Fraser came in that first week of October, but not alone. There must have been eight or ten of the lads and lasses from Coigeach all ready to help and all primed for a good day's fun. The hut shot up into position, the lining was fitted and the wires slung over the top and suspended with boulders. We put what we could inside, and the rest was carried to the landing by the willing hands. The goats were excited, and Lily, not being sure if she liked all these strangers running about, would be happy nowhere but on my knee. It seemed as if we should never get off that night; when we were all aboard, James found that his exhaust was leaking into the boat, and that meant going back to the hut for tin and wire to bind round a pad of cotton-waste. No one wished to spoil the general sense of well-being with a consciousness of time, even if we could not get to Dundonnell boathouse by dark. What was that floating on the sea a quarter of a mile back? Round we go to pick up a worthless fruit crate and add it to the present congestion of folk, goats, hens, canary and so on. Gaelic songs rose to heaven all the way, and I could not help contrasting this happy journey of fulfilment with the one in the spring when the weather seemed against us and so much had yet to be learnt.

Our homecoming was the more pleasant because our friend Elsa Graham Dow had taken possession of the house a week or two before, and now she had a meal on the table and a cheerful fire in the grate. Kenneth McDougall had cycled in that very evening, and he had come to stay for a year or more, he said. Sure enough then, we would get that grey seal job done now. Alasdair went to bed as soon as we could get him there, and we should have followed soon after. But the sweetness of good-fellowship was deep upon us all until the early hours of the morning.

CHAPTER FIVE

THE BIRDS OF CLERACH

1. Those of the Land

THIS BOOK is no treatise on natural history but a simple tale of one way of life and of things seen, in which you would not thank me for a bare list of birds seen by us on Eilean a' Chleirich. Better that we should crack over the peat fire and be anecdotal, showing the birds in their personal relationships to ourselves as other members of the island fauna.

The raven is a personal sort of bird, and as he is first on the British List he might as well come first here. The raven used to breed on Eilean a' Chleirich in the high central precipice, but the birds were dissuaded from this course many years ago by the grazing tenant, who was convinced of their rascality in pecking the eyes from sheep. The Summer Isles are many, and eviction has not bothered Mr Corbie, for he and his like are to be seen every day about Clerach and they breed at several other places within a few miles. The ravens come about Clerach as foraging parties, and sometimes I think they come with the express purpose of annoying the peregrine falcons, which have three eyries in all that central ridge. It is one of the familiar sights and sounds of the island which we used to have as a breakfast- or tea-time entertainment – the warfare of the peregrines and ravens. The falcons were irascible always, and obviously in a heat of fury when the ravens came scouting along the cliff. Stooping time after time, the falcons would attempt to drive away the ravens, but our black friends flew nonchalantly on their way to and fro; only at the last split second of each falcon's stoop did they turn sideways in the air to present that remarkable wedge of a beak which would impale the falcon were it to continue its wild descent. But the falcon knows its match and does not strike an adult raven, though it may kill a young one which has not acquired the traditional agility of its race.

Both peregrine falcons and ravens display at the breeding season by much indulgence in aerial acrobatics. They are magnificent to watch, these stoops, spins, somersaults and steep zooms, and it seems to me that here we have an example of display having practical evolutionary value in everyday life. These very movements are of value in defence and offence, and, as it happens, between the two species in which they are such striking characteristics of courtship display.

On April 29th, 1937, our colleague Kenneth McDougall went in the kayak to Carn an Iar and Carn Deas, two islets joined by a shingle beach at ordinary tides. They lie just over two miles east of Clerach. It was a fine sunny morning, and though we hoped for his return before night, Dougal took food enough for a few days and his little Tinker tent. A strong breeze from the west came along and caught him up almost before he was ashore on Carn an Iar. Later in the day the weather turned still rougher and very cold, and I, taking a last scout round the north cliff of Clerach before darkness fell, could see through my telescope a disconsolate human figure mooching about the bare summit of Carn an Iar.

'Tough weather for making a census of the cormorants there,' I chuckled stonily to myself.

The real satisfaction of seeing him there was that he was there, and evidently not intending to come back over the rough sea in our flimsy kayak.

Bobbie and I were having breakfast next morning when Dougal opened the door of the hut, grinning all over his face at the surprise he had caused. Then he sat down and began with deliberation to unfasten the box of food he had taken with him the day before. The knots came undone and the

cardboard flaps went back and two big hands brought forth
a young raven. Dougal was delighted with himself, and I
with him for bringing it, but Bobbie and the raven looked
glum. The raven, after all, was concerned with what appeared to be his present adversity; Bobbie was thinking of
past and future.

Years before, I had brought a young raven home from
Shetland, and this bird had led her a pretty dance, pecking
Alasdair's year-old toes, winding wool intricately through
the rose bushes, and croaking, for ever croaking. Now, on
Clerach, she was thinking of the certain revival and surge of
spirits which would occur in this small black fellow's breast.
A little later I even began to think that myself, but there
was some pleasure ahead for me, and if righteous wifely
wrath fell upon the camp as a result of the raven's pranks I
should see Dougal get the brunt of it and I should feel rather
a good boy for once.

But things did not work out quite so easily in the end.
David grew so strong in his affection for Dougal – David
the raven was called because Dougal said he knew ravens
came into the Old Testament somewhere. That was all right
as long as there were plenty of fish-guts for the bird and
Dougal was about to look after him. But Dougal had a call
from his people early in June, as they were expecting to
move their household, and David had to stay with us.

What were we to do? Two months hence we should be
on the move ourselves to the Treshnish Isles, where we were
going to study the grey seals. We should have to pare down
equipment for that expedition to a minimum, and it was obvious David and his keep would be a needless complication.
It fell to Bobbie and me, then, to reconvert this humanized
raven into a wild one again, a wild and able one which would
have every chance of subsequent survival. This was a thank-
less task if ever there was one. We gently clammed him
down to one meal a day, then to one in two days, and in the
latter part of June we had a spell of bad weather which made
it impossible for me to get fish, which meant David had to
starve perforce because we had little to spare. His constant

croaking got on my nerves badly, and if ever I have cursed
my good friend Dougal it was then. The bird was very
hungry, and yet I had seen a good sign, that he was tending
to join with the other ravens which came about the island.
One Sunday morning we were feeling extremely sorry both
for David and ourselves, when we found an unlooked-for
harvest in a crack of rocks at high-tide mark. Two cruisers
had been into Loch Broom during the week, and on passing
Clerach had heaved overboard several wooden packing-cases
and – one carton of preserved shrimps.

We returned to camp in triumphant mood with this deli-
cacy, throwing it to David with prodigal abandon. He
pounced upon the carton and made off. We saw no more
of him for three days, and by this time it was evident he was
becoming more independent. He annoyed us little except
for stamping on the roof of the hut every morning for a
minute or two at five o'clock.

I was lying in the cliffs one day soon after that when five
ravens came along. I croaked to them and found one of them
to be David. He came out of the bunch and walked on the
ground near me, and this appeared to intrigue the others
so much that they also overcame their usual wariness. The
wave of curiosity brought them croaking volubly to within
twenty-five yards of me. Then they flew to a knot of ewes
and lambs and thoroughly inspected the wool of these animals. Starlings are the usual birds to be found perching on
the backs of sheep, but here were the great birds supposed to
be the mischievous persecutors of them. The sheep continued
to graze unperturbed.

So David went wild again, though we knew he was about.
He came down one day to some visitors who put ashore from
a launch and he took two beautiful pennies from them and
hid them in a cranny of the cliff. We ourselves tried to make
him not very trustful of human beings, a hateful job to us of
all people, and yet we felt responsible for his later life when
he might meet someone not so amiably disposed to ravens
as we were at heart.

During the summer of 1939 on Tanera we have had the

ravens about us most days, and two of them are so tame and given to jovial croaking as they have passed overhead that we have wondered if one of them might be David. I should like to think it was.

One of the most interesting things about having several animals of different kinds running free round the house is the interplay of their personalities one with another. A raven is dynamic in any society, and a promoter of many vivid situations. We had a pair of Chinese geese at the time which had succeeded in bringing off one gosling. That goose was an undoubted fool in motherhood, and that one gosling would not have survived had not a hen gone broody and insisted on sharing incubation with the goose. The goose was so hopeless after the gosling had hatched that the hen took charge of the poor little thing, mothering it with an excess of care and tenderness which was fully justified in face of David's interest.

This poor hen was called Doormat because she was lowest in the pecking-order of hierarchy of hens on Clerach. Utterly abject in her own group, she was now a Boadicea in defence of a puling and foolish-looking Chinese gosling. David would spar about, teasing the little bird, and would flap nimbly away when Doormat made a rush at him. He soon learned to treat her with respect, for she could make the feathers fly if she caught him. The gosling grew and ultimately joined its parents; Doormat was taken back to the other hens a quarter of a mile away, there to resume her former lowly position in avian society.

During the days we were 'tapering off' the food given to David he learned to follow us over to the hens when we fed them with fish-guts in the evening. If he was lucky he would get a trifle after we were gone. Poor Doormat was repeatedly pecked away from the food by the other hens, and perhaps we were in a hurry this one night that we did not stay to see she got her share. We left them all feeding hungrily, and when twenty-five yards away saw David fly down among the hens. They scattered in frightened confusion, but before David had picked up one mouthful he found himself bowled over on to his back and being given a rough house by Doormat. He made off croaking and dishevelled, whereupon Doormat began feeding again, only to be driven away by the other hens which now ventured to return.

Animal hierarchies are often criss-crossed in this way. Doormat the raven-chaser could not realize that she had put to flight David the hen-flutterer and should therefore be their equal at least. No, after her deed of valour she was once more Doormat, just the lowliest member of a pack of scriddy hens.

There is one pair of hooded crows on Eilean a' Chleirich, but in the years I have been about the island I have never found their nest and do not believe they do nest there. If all hoodie crows were as innocent as I have found these two birds, the tribe would be less persecuted. They appear to have been most decorous birds whose worst crime has been to steal a few lesser-blacked gulls' eggs. I wish I could speak as well for their numerous brethren elsewhere.

On the other islands upon which I have lived since Eilean a' Chleirich – Lunga of the Treshnish, North Rona and Tanera – there have been resident flocks of starlings, but on Clerach these birds were rare visitors, and then only two or three would be seen at a time. There is no large expanse of true grassland on this island, which bears, as I have said, a sub-Arctic vegetative complex in which grass plays a subsidiary part. Both Lungà and North Rona have a herbage floor of fescue and bent grass, and Tanera, in addition to having recently crofted grassland, has the ruins of our old herring factory, which are a starling's notion of paradise.

The same remark applies to the lapwing. I have seen this bird only once on Clerach, whereas on the Treshnish Isles they were constantly about the stretches of rich grass mixed with the starlings. A few were usually to be seen on the green ground of Rona, though they did not appear to be resident.

Perhaps the skylark should be mentioned here as well. I saw a flock of less than half a dozen on April 13th, 1937, on Eilean a' Chleirich, and they were gone within the hour.

Lark song was one of the things I missed there. Yet the birds are common on the green areas of Tanera and on the crofting ground of the mainland, and we saw them on the Treshnish Isles as well. Agriculture may mean restriction of range to some birds, but it means the chance of life to others. In a countryside as little tilled as ours, it is easy to see how the avian fauna could be enriched and not made poorer at all by the extension of arable ground and making the type of husbandry followed a little more varied.

Clerach has given me an excellent example, in the years I have known the island, of the effect on bird life which man can have by some act which appears to him of little consequence at the time. The island was burned in 1935, not a strip of old heather or dried bent grass here and there, but practically the whole island. That year saw an almost complete absence of small birds such as stonechats and twites. The twites were back in numbers in 1936, though not so numerous as in 1937, and it was 1938 before the stonechats were resident again. Thrushes were back in 1936, but there were more in 1937. The cuckoo was absent still in 1936, was heard once only in 1937, then evidently on passage, but was a summer resident again in 1938 and 1939. There was one willow warbler seen on passage in 1936, and it was 1938-9 before they were to be seen regularly once more.

Such heavy burning is much more devastating to incipient tree growth than the normal grazing of sheep. For when small patches of heather on a brae-face grow very long, rowans and birches grow within them and the sheep do not care to fight through the long stiff heather to nibble the shoots of the little trees. A large number of trees would soon grow on the precipitous slopes of the central ridge of Clerach if burning were strictly controlled. Trees bring about changes in the soil conditions below them and in the insect fauna of their immediate neighbourhood, and this added habitat on Eilean a' Chleirich would mean more birds. The shelter the trees would provide for the winter population of sheep would be wholly to those animals' advantage. These are early days to speak more than hopefully, but I surely have hopes of seeing a wood beneath those crags well within my lifetime.

It is characteristic of the bird life of these little islands to find very few members of the finch tribe. The twite has been mentioned already as being present where there is abundant heather, but few others of the family pay even flying visits. There were no others on Clerach except the snow bunting in late winter, and on Lunga we saw only greenfinches, feeding for a few days in late November on the rich store of seed provided by a forest of burdock plants below the eastern cliffs.

The short and cheerful cries of rock and meadow pipits are as much island sounds to me as the wail of gulls. These little birds are everywhere, and one of the delights of late spring and summer is the frequent discovery of pipits' nests. A sudden flirp of olive-green wings as we pass some stone or bunch of heather, and there for the trouble of kneeling and delicately parting the herbage with our hands we see a perfect, round nest of smoothed fibres and four mottled, olive eggs. The wonder of the first nest we ever saw is there anew each time. Happy and welcome little pipit! In our island winters you have become tame and graced our doorstep, and only we can tell you how grateful we are, for the island dweller in windswept places can have no fun from watching tits and robins and exciting newcomers at a bird table in the garden.

Pied wagtails are birds which come where men dig the surface of the soil. These universal friends live on Tanera, but nowhere else in the Summer Isles. We saw only one, and that but for a moment, near the camp on Eilean a' Chleirich on June 7th, 1936. The next year a white wagtail passed through in early May. How different from North Rona, where hundreds of white wagtails passed through the island in spring and autumn on their long migration between Iceland and Northern Africa! Harvie-Brown in his *Vertebrate Fauna of the North-West Highlands and Skye* (1904) pointed in his usual forcible style to the comparative poverty of the Minch and its adjacent coast as a faunal region for birds.

This is unfortunately true, but, as Harvie-Brown said, its true faunal value lies in its isolation. The region lies between the great migratory routes, and thus we in the Summer Isles partake of none of that immense excitement of certain other island dwellers at the migratory season. We can see nothing to equal the spring and autumn wonders of North Rona, Fair Isle, Isle of May and Skokholm, and it is doubtful if our winter visitors are as interesting as those of the East Coast. Nevertheless, we have some very rare birds, and some that do not appear in many places elsewhere in Britain. Where else in the same day could you see three species of divers, grey lag and barnacle geese and greenshanks? This has been one of my experiences in the first week of May, when some of the birds have just come and some not yet gone.

Eilean a' Chleirich, for all its lochans, is no haunt of many ducks and wading birds, and in early summer its cliffs are not seething with a million birds from the sea. Yet one of its interests to me has been that the twenty-seven breeding species have been in such numbers that I have been able to know most of the individuals of all these. Our small access of summer migrants has made for a time of pleasure in which we were not kept at a high pitch of excitement, but rather when we could reflect upon each incoming group or individual.

Bobbie and I were traversing the south side of Eilean a' Chleirich one early June evening in 1936 when the weather was calm and sky and sea leaden. It was not a pleasant evening for such a time of year, but the dullness suddenly went out of it when a swallow flew near us. We watched its slim beauty in entrancement, for we had not seen a swallow for some years. The bird perhaps recognized us as being of the species under whose eaves it was accustomed to breed, for it came back again and again, flying within three feet of us. Then it was gone.

Next year, when we had the hut and a wireless aerial led across to the top of the outlaw's ruin, two swallows came for a space and rested on the wire, twittering a soft song from russet throats. Would that our hut had a deep eave and a

Blanquette, the goat, on Eilean a' Chleirich

Tigh an Quay, Isle of Tanera, where this book was written

The author with a young seal which he played with every day from its birth until it was 28 days old

Alasdair and a shag exchange courtesies, North Rona

Bobbie at the peats

Lochan Fada, Eilean a' Chleirich

A fulmar petrel in the ruined village, North Rona

Puffins on North Rona

The camp on Eilean a' Chleirich

An Arctic tern

The Great West Cliff, North Rona

A 'ringed' guillemot and a plain guillemot on North Rona

A gannet looks out from a high perch, Ailsa Craig

support for a swallow's nest, and that we had a small patch
of clay to give it the material for building!

The wren is a bird which to me is an inseparable part of
the West Highland scene and of the little islands offshore.
This small person also happens to be ornithologically important, for he is a species of which several distinct races have
been identified within a comparatively small area of the
earth's surface. There is the Hebridean wren, the St Kilda
wren, the Shetland wren, and even the Fair Isle wren is a
little different from type specimens, and if I ever took the
trouble to make detailed comparisons I am sure there would
be a Clerach wren. Our wrens seem to me to be of a wonderful rufous colour, and darker than the mainland form
even so near as Dundonnell. The note is very loud and wild,
a characteristic which some of our visitors have noticed also.
But I am not entirely satisfied that the note is truly louder,
because I have noticed the same apparent increase in volume
and wildness in the voice of the song thrushes of Clerach.
May it not be that in still weather the large rock surfaces
and bare type of ground throw back the sound much more
than the absorbent sylvan surroundings of these birds on the
mainland? It is sufficient for us in our island life to hear that
wild free song, persistent in good weather or bad. Our wren
used to perch on our tent guys in the very early morning and
sing; and Dougal the canary used to reply with a song as
loud and more varied. The wren sings throughout the year
and brings cheer to a snell winter's day. More strength to
your throat, *Troglodytes troglodytes troglodytes* (*clerachen-
sis*); may you continue to perch on our guys at dawn and sing
your song, and at breakfast-time flit in and out of the hut.
Most birds are welcome, but you and the wagtails and rock
pipits are as part of the family!

I have spoken earlier of the marked difference in the
character of the herbage in the north-western side of the
island from that of the south-east.The wheatears evidently
recognize the difference, for they come to the northern and
western parts and almost leave the rest of the island untouched. Their relatives the stonechats observe rather less

rigidly opposite habits of staying on the heather-covered ground. It would be impossible to pass through the spring-time country of the sea-pinks, where heaps of lichened stones add their saffron and green to the brilliance of the whole, without seeing the wheatears. They are brilliant also, and no bird more graceful. Would that their voice equalled their plumage! The characteristic dull smatch would be almost depressing were it not for its association with scene and season; only for a short period of courtship does the male indulge in a little cheerful song in the course of his short, vertical flight of display. The Gaelic name for this bird is beautifully descriptive; even the sound of *clachoran*, the little one of the stones, gives an impression of the little flights from stone to stone, the bowings and bobbings and the flirp of the wheatear's tail. The birds come in April and leave gradually in August, and on Eilean a' Chleirich we do not have the apparent second coming of wheatears which we saw on North Rona. There the native breeding birds left in August, the island was without them for a spell and then came the Greenland birds in September, pausing a while on their journey southwards. Some of these are to be seen as stragglers on West Highland coasts as late as November. The wheatear never does seem direct of purpose to our eyes.

I have no intention of mentioning every one of the sixty-eight species seen on Clerach, because this chapter is not a catalogue. And yet, though there seems little of interest to say about it, I cannot resist a word on the hedgesparrow. In the first place, it is a bird of song; and in a place where few birds sing, that gift and exercise bring this little friend of sober colour and quiet habit prominently into our lives. You may think my last phrase fanciful; indeed it is not. Our minds and bodies may be running at a high level of activity when we are living among the islands, but of human society we have only ourselves, and the birds are vested by us with personal qualities which seem very real, so that the birds about our doors become as children. The hedgesparrow is found on many small islands off these coasts as a resident, but the numbers are always low. I think there are three pairs on Eilean a' Chleirich, and the casual visitor may never see them.

The peregrine falcon is the only member of his Order resident on Clerach throughout the year, and is generally in evidence. Merlins might have been expected to breed with us, but I have never seen them about the island two days together. I have never seen the kestrel either, though the absence of all small mammals other than the pygmy shrew would reasonably account for that. The buzzard is fairly common on the adjacent mainland, where rabbits are common, but it is not seen on Clerach in summer. In defence of this bird I have always pointed to the incidence of rabbits in relation to its distribution. It is one of those birds which have been pushed to the fringe by persecution, and small, inaccessible islands might well be thought to give it sanctuary. So they do indeed – if rabbits are present and I have seen as many as seven at one time over the one hundred and seventy rabbit-infested acres of Lunga on the Treshnish Isles. Where the birds are recognized as being among the farmer's and landowner's best friends they become remarkably tame. My friend Captain Guy Beaver tells me that about his house at Muncastle, Gruinard, the buzzards sit on the eaves of the corn stacks, or even on the stooks in the fields, waiting to pounce on wandering rabbits, and remain unconcerned at the passage to and from of human beings. The buzzard is not averse to carrion or any easily got dead meat and will exhibit the same tameness when getting it as when rabbiting. There is a table-like rock less than ten yards behind the Brae House at Dundonnell, and at this place I was skinning the head of a hind one December afternoon. Something called me to the house for a few moments, and while I was there I saw the hens come round the corner in a rush and flutter. It was natural I should hurry to the back of the house again to see what was the matter, and there was the buzzard calmly picking up the small pieces of meat from the skull.

But these birds do visit the island occasionally in wintertime, whether in search of carrion or of small birds I cannot say. The winter birds which I have seen on Clerach and on

North Rona appear darker than the buzzards of the mainland, and it is possible they are representatives of the Scandinavian stock rather than those of the adjacent mainland.

It would have been pleasant to record the sea eagle from
Clerach, but that has not yet been my good fortune. Nevertheless, I have seen this rare British bird on two occasions on
the mainland coast less than ten miles away from the island.

The birds of a small island naturally group themselves in
the observer's mind into those of the land and those of the
sea. I am telling of the birds of the land at the moment,
though this means splitting up the family of the waders.

I have spoken already of the evocative quality of particular sounds and scents in the natural scene. There are so
many in this West Highland country that emotions of delight, thankfulness and love, and a distant sadness at the
passing years, well up time and again in the heart. Bird songs
and cries are among the strongest of these stimulations, the
more so when the note is seasonal and linked with one type
of natural habitat. The common sandpiper reaches Eilean
a' Chleirich on April 29th or 30th each year, and its presence
is known to us immediately by that constant note of its
springtime flight – pi-wi-wee, pi-wi-wee, pi-wi-wee. There
are eight lochans on the island and seven pairs of sandpipers;
the little birds are neither shy nor of retiring habit, and as
their movements have charm and grace they catch at the
hem of my interest as I go my ways and hold me watching
them.

The common sandpiper displays in a shallow undulating
flight over its chosen stretch of freshwater. The wings are
alternatively vibrated rapidly or held rigid, and that characteristic piping is uttered throughout the flight of fifty or a
hundred or as far as two hundred yards. The bird comes to
rest on a stone by the edge of the water or projecting above
the surface and then bobs its head and tail constantly. Its
note is no longer the rapid, vibrant piping, but a single pro-
tracted note, slightly rising at the end and oft repeated.
When the two birds display together there is a tiny strutting
and the wings are raised vertically above the back and

stretched as high as possible. The ecstasy of their emotion is apparent and the posture is one of great beauty in the eyes of a human being. That, I think, is a large part of the charm of birds for us; they and we have colour vision, and what they see as beauty is beautiful to us as well.

The snipe is a shy bird which rarely gives us a glimpse of its daily life, which is an absorbing interest for an inquisitive man. You frighten a snipe from the rushy edge of a tiny pool and with a thin cry it has zigzagged away before you can look at the bird carefully. Or you may hear it drumming in the daytime and by strained looking into the sky discern a small black speck flying rapidly hither and thither. But there is part of the bird's life which can be carried by the ear to the mind as a pleasant experience. Both the tent and our hut on Eilean a' Chleirich allowed us to hear the tiny noises of the world of night outside, and in the early spring we used to hear the snipe come down to their favourite clump of rushes by the little burn. The drumming far above would stop, and in a moment we would hear the birds' coming-down note of 'chick-chack, chick-chack, chick-chack'. They came down at the same time night after night, and all was quiet from then until the early hours of the morning, when we would hear them drumming again.

There were still more intimate moments in wintertime, both on Clerach and on Lunga, when our tents gave shelter to the little birds. 'Chick-chack, chick-chack', coming ever nearer until we could hear the snipe come to rest on the other side of the eave from where we lay, and rising early we would unwittingly start the bird sometimes from its resting place. The glow of candlelight through the whiteness of the tent never seemed to keep them away.

And yet again, there is the arresting beauty of the snipe a few hours after hatching. No young bird gives me a greater sense of wonder and breath-taking beauty; when the tiny forms crystallize in my vision from the pattern of the herbage, I do indeed hold my breath. The down is richer than velvet, the stripings of Rembrandt browns and black making a pattern more intricate than that of an Afghan carpet. The little birds' eyes are open wide all the time, minute beads of black, and their long, soft legs remonstrate gently on your fingers, as if these babies were saying 'Please, please'. It is quite a different experience from coming upon the nursery of an allied bird, the oystercatcher, at the same stage. The young oystercatchers certainly have a velvety down, but it is stone-grey and not lustrous as that of the little snipe. The young birds themselves are about twice as big as the baby snipe, and they act in a way that appears to us as sullen. Their eyes are kept closed, or at least half shut, and the bird sits close to the ground, head extended. Young oystercatchers are not sprites in our fancy as the little snipe are; and it is just as well they are not, for on the open ground of the oystercatcher's terrain undue liveliness would mean being gobbled up by gulls or hoodie crows. The young snipe must be active, for it has to make its way immediately through the dense forest of sedge and fast-growing June herbage.

Eilean a' Chleirich is now a sanctuary for the grey lag goose. This bird is not an uncommon winter visitor to Britain, but the number of resident birds is small, and few are left anywhere on the Northern Highland mainland. The Summer Isles race, therefore, is not one to be lightly prized and allowed to be lost through active persecution on the part of a few or the general inertia of the many. Happily, geese are long-lived birds and it is probable that the population is able to withstand an occasional raid on the eggs, but humanity is not the only predatory species and it seems deplorable in an age when man has no need to hunt these few geese for food that visitors from outside should come to steal the eggs. The people of the country are poor, and when some of them are offered a pound an egg by some monied outsider who will pay the expensive hire of a launch to go round the islands in spring, it is a temptation hard to resist. The law protecting rare breeding species is in an archaic state and difficult to enforce because the action has to be led and that is expensive. The egg-stealer should be liable to be handed into custody and restrained like any other common thief. The prevalent fashion of keeping wildfowl on an ornamental lake, en-

couraging those that will to breed, is a good one, and in the
right hands might do something towards replenishing stocks,
but the fashion does not vest the theft of eggs of a fast-dim-
inishing species with any appearance of right and proper
practice. The first place in which we wish to see the Summer
Isles race of grey lag geese increase is in the Summer Isles
themselves. Years ago there seem to have been nearly two
hundred grey lags in the group; now I doubt whether there
are more than thirty altogether.

Geese are amongst the most intelligent of birds, and to
watch the lives of these abnormally wary grey lags has had
a fascination for me. I believe now that I can see something
of a coordinated social system in this Summer Isles race.
Winter is the time when they are strong on the wing, strong
even in the hard month of March, and they fly from island
to island in flocks of six to a dozen birds, grazing on the
sheltered green places near the sea where growth seems rarely
to stop completely. If they should be startled at such times
they are up with a great honking and away to some other
place, possibly two or three miles off. There is no circling
overhead and returning to the same place if the originator
of the disturbance should move on with no interest in the
geese. It is not usual to come close upon such a grazing flock,
for there is generally a sentinel posted on some higher knoll
and all the geese raise their heads occasionally to look over
the country.

The breeding birds from these small flocks split off in pairs
at the end of March to take up their chosen breeding sites in
the heather, and yet I have seen them rejoin and indulge in
a curious communal display at nesting time. There has been
a small ring of geese on an open patch of ground and a
gander has walked into the arena with lowered head and
open beak, as if in menace. He has walked and run across the
ring formed by the birds several times, and then he has re-
joined them to make way for another to do the same thing.
Observers for any length of time of wild grey lags at the
nesting season are few, but I would dearly like to know if the
kind of social display I have outlined has been seen by anyone

else. I have described it and other social displays in *Bird Flocks and the Breeding Cycle* (Cambridge, 1938), and it has been repeated in Witherby's new *Handbook of British Birds*, but as it stands it is a very lonely observation requiring more study before it can be accepted as a general type of display in the whole species.

The grey lag geese of the Summer Isles have two animal enemies which must exercise as great an influence in keeping numbers low as do human beings. These are the otter and the heron. The otter is troublesome when the goose is sitting in April and May, for sea fish seem hard to come by then and the otters of the island are scouting about for something warm-blooded. It was a great disappointment to me in 1936 to see a nest taken from the heather only two hundred and fifty yards from our tent. We ourselves had gone to considerable trouble to keep out of the bird's way, but when I had not been able to see her through my glass for two days I thought it time to investigate. There in a patch of soft peat not six feet from the nest were the tell-tale tracks of the otter, but no eggs and no goose.

I have already described the devilish patience of the herons in taking the goslings. When we see the herons poised at the sea's edge or on some river-bank we cannot help wondering at their patience and thinking that an hour or two is neither here nor there to them. But for those geese and the tiny goslings time has value; they must soon be on the move and getting something to eat, or at least the goslings want to be brooded in the warmth of their mother's down.

The geese shed their flight feathers in July, and the young geese are as yet unable to fly. It is a time of possible danger for the whole population, making it necessary for them to repair to some place of safety for their flightless period. The Summer Isles race of grey lags are fortunate in having the islet of Ghlas Leac Bheag as a retreat. This place lies a mile to the north of Clerach, and except for very few days of the year is inaccessible to human beings. The swell there will be high when everywhere else is flat calm, and as the landing place is a rock which shelves into the sea, it is always dangerous to take chances with a boat. One moment you may be afloat and the next find the boat lying dry on the rock and yourself tipped out. The herbage of Ghlas Leac is green and succulent and keeps the geese throughout August. Practically the whole population has gathered there by that time and feeds in peace until the new flight feathers have come. If someone does disturb them and is so cruel as to try to run them down, the birds have a second line of defence. They quickly take to the water, scatter and dive. Certainly they cannot stay under for very long, but their movements are sudden and beyond prognostication.

The other species of goose found in the Summer Isles is the barnacle, reaching our shores about October 21st and leaving during the first week of May. From the direction of the flight inward and outward at the time of migration, I am inclined to think our few hundreds come from Greenland, where this species nests in the country north of Scoresby Sound. That area happens to be one Bobbie and I have a great urge to visit, to see these geese nesting in colonies about high inland cliffs in company with the Greenland falcon, and to see the musk ox at home. Each year, then, when the barnacle geese come or go, we feel the pangs of being earthbound. They are exciting birds these, whether to see, hear or merely reflect upon.

It has been my good fortune to be on the little islands where they graze for the winter on several occasions of their coming and going in autumn and spring, and I have been impressed by the nature of their behaviour at these times. Here are some excerpts from my diaries describing their arrival at the Treshnish Isles in 1937, at which place there is better chance of seeing the whole movement than there ever is in the Summer Isles.

October 21st. Seventeen grey lag geese came flying southwards this morning, calling loudly; eleven more passed down later, and while we were at lunch we heard the different call of barnacle geese. We leapt for our glasses and went outside the tent to see two and five barnacle geese flying southwards. During the afternoon many more gaggles passed through, seventeens, elevens, eights, fives, and twos, nearly 160 in all, and since I have been writing this more have passed down in the darkness. This is one of the great days in the Highland naturalist's year; henceforth you may say it is winter until they leave again on May 1st. Are the geese coming in to Clerach today, I wonder? I am interested to see the geese arrive in small lots, not in the great numbers in which they leave for the north in the spring.

October 22nd. The geese have been excited all day long and we heard several lots coming through in the night.

October 25th. The geese are still very restless and have not yet settled down to their winter grazing. They have gathered into large flocks of from fifty to a hundred and fifty, and in addition to making several apparently pointless flights over the sea they settle on bare rocks on Sgeir na h'Iolaire and Sgeir na Giusach in dense masses; and there they stand and cackle. I saw another flock on the sea a couple of miles out on the west side this morning, and Dougal says he saw some on the water north of us yesterday. The barnacle goose is rarely seen on the water, and I have seen them there only at the times of migration. Eight grey lags came down from the west side today and I followed them through my telescope almost as far as Iona.

October 26th. A flock of twenty or thirty grey lags went south this afternoon in V formation and disappeared over the Ross of Mull.

October 27th. The barnacle geese have been restless all day and have spent much of their time densely packed on the bare rock of Sgeir na Giusach to the east of us. Occasional parties of six or seven, or even two, would leave the main flock, fly a long way out to sea, perhaps four miles, and return to the group with loud calling.

October 29th. The geese seemed to be settling down yesterday and today.

Thereafter I have nothing to say about the geese until November 15th, when there is the following entry:

'Bobbie met us [Dougal and myself] as we came off the sea at the Dorlinn and we went to the south end ... While we

were down there the Barra mail plane came from the west
and the pilot evidently amused himself by flying low over the
Dutchman and putting up the barnacle geese. I forgive him
because he gave us a fine spectacle, and me a few more data
I was wanting very much. The geese rose in hundreds into
the gold of the dying sun and we could see through our binoculars the long strings of geese across the sky. The noise
reached us over the two and a half miles of sea. After a few
minutes of flying high in the air round the Dutchman they
began to come our way. First a string of a hundred; half a
minute's lull; then three geese; then the main bunch came
by, and we reckon there were well over a thousand birds in
all . . . As this great concourse of geese went north-eastwards
we noticed that the flock was loosely composed of many well-
formed small flocks of twelves and twenties. The whole lot
was a population moving under stress of circumstances, but
the small groups were the feeding flocks, or possibly family
flocks, which we have found to exercise autonomy as regards
movement in the ordinary way. We saw the geese fly round
and round over Cairn a' Burg and eventually settle on the
high flat top of that island. We have not heard them on the
move tonight, but they may go back to the Dutchman in
the morning at sunrise, which is the time we seem to hear
them most nowadays.'

And now let us look at the barnacle geese on Eilean a'
Chleirich between the months of February and May. The
birds graze in small flocks of six or eight up to fourteen or
more, and from seeing these flocks every day I am practically
sure that they remain intact and discrete. They are much less
wary than the grey lag geese, and by careful stalking I have
often been able to come within a few yards of them. A sentinel is always there, gazing about more than the others and,
if suspicious, going away to some prominent knoll a hundred
yards or more from the flock. The sentinel flies back again
when it is satisfied the land is clear. If they are disturbed they
will not fly for miles but will probably come down on another
part of the island. Their tactics are always sound; one of
their favourite places to which they fly at such times is the

grass-covered knoll above the north cliff. A view of much of that end of the island is then well below them.

March is a hard month in the Highlands, and the barnacle geese feel it as much as any other class of grazing stock. They become weaker and weaker until the end of the month, when the birds almost become prisoners on whichever island they happen to be. Here is an excerpt from my Clerach diary for March 19th, 1937:

'I was interested to see flocks of fourteen, eight and four at the same moment, for the observation confirms my opinion that the flocks are definite entities and not changing aggregations. I see that the larger flocks are in better condition than the smaller groups of four and the odd ones and twos. It is harder to approach the larger flocks, and the ones and twos are most easily approached. When I say approach I do not mean stalk, for it is obvious that a larger flock would be more difficult to approach than a single bird. It seems to be largely a matter of condition just now. I remember from my deer work that if I found individuals going about alone for any considerable period, they were sure to be in poor condition.'

Some of the geese came to feed with our hens soon after this, and we were glad to give them the hospitality. There is another note in my diary during the week following the last quotation to the effect that the terrible northerly gales we had experienced had disorganized the flocks of barnacle geese, but that as soon as the weather abated there was a calling and getting together again.

The geese grew stronger at a surprising rate with the new grass of April and they were now beginning to gather in larger flocks and were always more ready to fly. A surging activity was apparent. I was spending much of my time in the hide above the big herring gullery during the latter half of April, and the hide happened to be near a favourite grazing ground of the barnacles. I felt extraordinarily fortunate in often having a flock within twenty-five yards. Their condition was now excellent and their plumage smooth and glossy about the neck and breast. My hide also allowed me to

look out to Ghlas Leac Bheag, from which island the barnacles were accustomed to take off on their northward migration. It was from my hide, one evening towards the end of
April, that I saw about a hundred barnacle geese on the sea a
mile out. They would mill together on the water, suddenly
rise, spread in a long thin line, split into echelons, mill
together again, and finally come down on the water. And yet
they were not leaving for good.

That time comes in the first days of May. All the barnacle
geese grazing among the Summer Isles are now in one flock
of two to three hundred. It is morning-time and they fly up
in one mass, circle and come down again, and repeat the
whole evolution several times. Then there is a time when
they come down no more but make away to the north-west
and out of sight.

My own view is that each migratory flight, southward in
October and northward in May, begins with the birds in
one dense flock, but just as it takes time to train a large
number of human beings to do something together, and especially some concerted movement, so do the geese have to
practise and train for their flight of two thousand miles. Two
thousand miles of the northern part of the North Atlantic, in
the line of the storm track! It is not to be wondered at that
by the time they reach their destination, whether it be
Scoresby Sound or the Treshnish Isles, they should not be
in that close flock in which they started, but in smaller groups
of birds which have kept company before the migration. And
then, having arrived, as we watched them in the Treshnish,
there is the period of reorganization of the vast flock, a social
need which it seems must be fulfilled before the birds can
settle to feeding. It is a beautiful and exciting story to try
to piece together, and if I do follow them to Greenland one
day, it will have been the barnacle geese of Clerach and
Treshnish that have prompted me.

2. Those of the Sea

The birds of the sea! The very phrase rouses a naturalist's enthusiasm because there is conjured before his mind's eye the many aspects of a tremendous surge of life which the birds of the sea express. A large rookery is certainly a place of constant activity, noise and industry, but I do not think this extreme example of gregariousness in birds of the land can compare with the exciting, stimulating quality felt by the observer of a cliff of sea birds. Stated generally and not particularly, the birds of the sea are much more given to a gregarious habit than are those of the land, and the limitations of nesting accommodation impose a gregariousness between species making for a temporary crowding which allows an observer to see half a dozen species breeding within a small area of cliff-face. And yet we see that crowding has not prevented each species occupying its particular type of nesting site, and what appears first as overcrowding is really a highly economical and efficient distribution of the available space.

Guillemots are massed on horizontal ledges too small for gannets. Kittiwakes occupy the tiny individual ledges which would not be large enough for the guillemots nor allow them to mass as is their habit. Razorbills nest in crannies a little above or among these other birds, and the puffins prefer to burrow in the soil and detritus of the cliff top. In such places as the cliff breaks into a patch of earthy slope covered with hard fescue and scurvy grass, the fulmar petrel shares this site with the puffin, the fulmar occupying superficial hollows over which droop the long, hair-like leaves of fescue grass. If there is a heap of tumbled boulders, or if the cliff should become brashy and allow boulders to lodge precariously, shags are certain to be found in their shelter with their great untidy nests of tangle stems.

There is the noise and abandon with it all, for the sea birds express their emotions with great intensity, and the discordant cries blend into a harmony accompanied by the deep voice of the sea. There is nothing else on earth like it; who has lain receptive by a cliff of sea birds has known wonder.

Eilean a' Chleirich has no guillemots, kittiwakes or puffins thronging her cliffs, and very few razorbills or fulmar petrels, and yet there is the same ecstatic quality to be felt among the colonies of gulls, at the cormorantries and on the shaded ledges where the shags build. Then again, there is that strange peacefulness expressed by the courting note of the eider ducks. The note of the eider duck is one of those nostalgic sounds which makes you tingle and fret if it comes out of the range of memory at some time when you are away from sunlit island coasts. The eider duck is preeminently a sea bird, yet here on Clerach, where the quiet freshwater lochans are so near the sea, the eider uses them as a courting ground and is usually the place where the young first take to the water.

I was lying under a peat hag one day at the edge of one of the lochans and I took a magnificent photograph of a group of eider ducks and drakes as they came close by me, all unknowing. What a wonderful chance that was! Two days later, when I thought this particular film seemed inexhaustible, I found it had come unhitched inside the camera and I had not taken any photographs on it at all.

The eider has a large kindly eye which I delight to see at close quarters; and for that reason I sometimes allow myself to creep up to an eider's nest and watch her for a long time. There is no doubt she is intelligent, but that beautiful eye makes her seem more so, and the rich brown plumage is entirely satisfying to contemplate.

The young birds are so beautiful as are all the youngsters of the goose and duck family. The white eye stripe against the dark brown of the down is arresting. Soon after hatching, the mother is faced with the task of getting her ducklings down to the sea, a perilous journey which is a frequent source of loss. The birds hatched inland on Clerach stay on the lochans for a day or two with their mothers, and this seems to me better than that early precipitation into a turbulent ocean. There are countless freshwater shrimps in the lochans, upon which the young eiders may be seen feeding by constant diving in search of them. Sometimes one of the four or five ducklings gets left several yards behind because of its active diving, but the mother always knows; she stops, turns about and waits for the little one to catch up, then on she paddles.

The eider duck is credited with getting the ducklings on to her back and flying with them to the sea. I have not been fortunate enough to see this happen myself, but a friend of mine in Shetland has told me that he once saw an eider duck collide with a telegraph wire as she was flying to the sea, and the ducklings fell from her. Once the duck and her brood are afloat they appear capable of tackling the worst seas. I have seen the youngsters swamped and tossed time and again by the tremendous surf breaking over sunken skerries, and yet continue diving in that very place as if that was what they liked most. I have also seen them trying to get out of the sea on to a skerry when the swell is very deep. They cannot swim to the rock and step ashore, for they are swept back again; instead they swim out a little way, wait until a wave is going in, and then paddle as hard as they can so that at the top of its course the little birds have acquired just sufficient momentum to scramble ashore.

There are usually several ducks about without broods when hatching takes place during the third and fourth weeks of June, for many eiders' nests are found and robbed by the black-backed gulls, and I suspect there is always a number of barren ducks in the vicinity of the breeding grounds. These eiders join up with those ducks which have broods and appear to act as aunties. Anyway, they take a certain amount of care of the youngsters and the group becomes a delightful one to watch. Ducks with small broods often join forces to make a sociable party and a stronger bulwark against the world.

The only other duck breeding on Clerach is that sawbill the red-breasted merganser. This is the commonest duck about the North-West Highland coast, and relentlessly harried by keepers and river bailiffs because of its toll of trout at the nesting season; I have already said how I found them very tame on the island lochans. It is remarkable how soon animals fall in with the idea of sanctuary, and the duck family seems particularly quick to realize it. Lord Grey often referred in his writings to the way in which wild ducks of various species would come in to his duck ponds at Fallodon and behave like his tame birds.

There is no more charming member of the birds of Clerach than the black guillemot or tystie. The little bird is classed as an auk, but it is the least representative of the family in type. It is gregarious on the sea, or at least given to making up playful parties, but it nests in private, deep in some cranny and not necessarily directly above the sea. Again, it lays two eggs instead of the characteristic one, which are not sharply tapering nor rough-shelled like those of the razorbills and guillemots. The voice is a high-pitched and plaintive 'Peeee', long-drawn-out and quite unlike the cacophonies of the rest of the tribe. There are between seventy and a hundred tysties resident about Clerach, and the birds stay throughout the year. Here is a contrast to North Rona, an island of the same size with a similar population of tysties and only eighty-five miles north of Clerach; the tysties do not stay on North Rona through the winter months. Only one degree of latitude farther north, but with a great difference in the severity of the winters.

Tysties are constantly playing games on the sea of the ring o' roses type. And when they come to the line 'all fall down' they dive below the surface, and from the cliff top you can see the lovely water-distorted pattern of the little birds swimming horizontally below the waves, executing another figure of the game; black and white of plumage and bright red of legs, in constant movement. If the peregrine falcon stoops through a flock flying above the water they save themselves by dropping like stones. They do not fly so strongly or nearly so much as razorbills, and if you watch them ascend from the waves they look anything but athletic.

Their form is tubby, and the little red legs have to paddle very hard to get them going into the air. I remember a boat-party of us being convulsed with laughter one day watching a tystie rise from near us in a steep sea. She managed to fly when passing over a trough, but she hit each wave-top, and this for several times, until one brought her down with a somersault into the water.

The common guillemot does not nest anywhere in this area, Handa and the Shiants being the nearest places, both thirty-five miles away. But the bird puzzles me somewhat because large numbers of them are to be seen swimming on the sea in spring, and some are about at any time of the year. Parents with young birds in down are also to be seen in August.

Razorbills are present, but few in number. There is a small colony in two or three cracks of the imposing rock on the west side of Clerach known as the Rudder. They came there in 1936, just half a dozen birds, but did not breed; next year there were more than twice as many, and young ones were reared. A few more inhabit another roofed ledge in a cave on the north side of Ard Ghlas. The largest colony of razor-bills in the Summer Isles is on Bottle Island, where they live in holes in the face of a high but shallow cave facing south-west. You may say the razorbills have an undoubted prefer-ence for a roof over their heads at nesting time, though this is not considered absolutely essential. For two years in suc-cession I have seen razorbills rear a chick on the shallowest of depressions on top of a tuft of sea-pink growing in the verti-cal face of the red column of rock in the west cliff of North Rona. It is utterly without shelter and nearly three hundred feet above the sea.

Razorbills also indulge in communal dances on the sea at breeding time, but the impression they make on my mind is that they are much more formal than the tysties and do not express nearly so much enjoyment. But the razorbill, after all, is not blessed with an expressive countenance.

The little auk which breeds in Greenland is an annual winter visitor to the waters of the Minch, but is much more common in some years than others. Thus the severe winter of 1936–7 brought in a large number of these birds to the seas about Clerach.

It seems surprising that the puffin should be so scarce in the Summer Isles when one of the great breeding places in Britain is on the Shiant Isles, a group which we can see from Clerach most days. A few do breed on Ghlas Leac Bheag, and from the presence of old burrows on the western cliffs of Clerach I gather they must have bred there also at some time. But now you may go several days without seeing a puffin. I believe, as I have stated elsewhere and in much greater detail, that among this close-nesting type of sea bird there is at work a principle of communal stimulation towards reproductive efficiency, making for an all-or-none effect in the distribution of breeding stations. It appears to me that a very small colony of this auk family of birds, budded off as a surplus from the main group, finds itself unable to breed. It must either wait a year or two until it recruits sufficient numbers or else fail completely, though other environmental conditions which vary from year to year may alter the actual threshold of numbers above which breeding would take place.

The fulmar petrels of Eilean a' Chleirich have given me more observations in support of this theory of social stimulation and a threshold of numbers for reproductive efficiency. The fulmar first began to haunt Clerach in the early 1930s, just a few birds flying about the northern cliff. I made accurate counts in 1936 and found eighteen birds at two stations – the north cliff and the north face of Ard Bheag. The birds occupied what appeared to be nesting sites and acted as if they were paired. They displayed in characteristic fashion, and in the common phrase – all was set for the party. But they did not breed and went early into moult, leaving the island altogether by the middle of August.

There were twenty birds in the colony at the north cliff in 1937 and I counted eight eggs between June 1st and 3rd. The other two nesting sites were hidden beyond my reach. The fulmars of the Ard Bheag station increased to eight in this year, but, as I expected, they did not breed. Fulmars were resting and flying about the high shallow cave of Bottle Island in 1939, where the razorbills are accustomed to nest.

These birds are so inextricably fixed in our minds with our island years that when we see them at sea we feel like saluting them. But the fulmar is a quiet bird whose face never changes its apparently benign expression; it neither fears us nor seeks our company, but goes its own way, gliding endlessly on straight-held outstretched wings.

The colonies of gulls are an outstanding feature of the avian fauna of Clerach. Six species of gull breed in Britain, and four of them on this little island of less than half a square mile. There are three colonies of herring gulls and occasionally a fourth; two colonies of lesser black-backed gulls, and within the last two or three years several pairs of this species have joined the herring gull colonies; there is one small and doubtfully successful colony of common gulls, and lastly, five pairs of greater black-backed gulls distribute themselves among the herring gull colonies. These greater black-backs thus observe a slightly different habit from their relatives only a mile away on Ghlas Leac Bheag, where the birds nest as a large flock of the one species.

The herring gulls nest on the tops of the cliffs in places where the green grass creeps in among the exposed strata of Torridonian rock. When the lesser black-backed gulls nest along with them it is always on the landward side, for these birds in their pure colonies are found nesting in the bracken and heather about Lochan Tuath and Lochan Fada. The few common gulls nest alongside the lesser black-backs, but always down at the water's edge of Lochan Tuath.

The herring gulls of Clerach nest in close proximity to each other on the uneven chequerboard of bare rock, sea-pink and short grass, and when eggs appeared in the nests from May 9th onwards I was much surprised to see that the pair of hoodie crows did not attempt to steal the eggs. Neither did the gulls mob these birds, which continued to hop about the gullery picking up scraps of fishy material left by their hosts. Was this some new kind of crow, I wondered?

Not at all. That same pair also visited the lesser blackbacked gulleries, with extreme circumspection, and I saw them help themselves to some of those lovely mottled eggs. Whenever they were seen by the gulls they were subjected to a severe mobbing until they were well outside lesser blackbacked territory. I should not like to suggest for a moment that this different behaviour to crows of two species of gulls is general. It just happened to be so here with these gulls and these particular crows. My own view of an interesting situation is that the hoodies realized the nests of the herring gulls are close together on open ground and any depredation of the eggs would be seen immediately. That would be a pity, to be driven off for all time, when, by leaving the eggs alone, they could continue to get a fairly good picking from the gulls' leavings.

The herring gulls gain an undoubted initial advantage in nesting in such close order, but when hatching time came along I found disadvantages were apparent. The chicks were concentrated in a small area, and, being inclined to wander, were apt to get severe or sometimes fatal worryings from other parents of their own species. Herons came and helped themselves to the downy chicks, and the greater blackbacked gulls which had nested within the colony were constantly swallowing chicks whole.

When hatching time came in the lesser black-backed gulleries the bracken had grown several inches higher and there was the large amount of heather for cover. It was difficult, indeed, to find many lesser black-back chicks, because they just disappear at a day or two old into the thick growth. The lesser black-back seems to have been a later comer to island gulleries, and I have often seen it written, from Harvie-Brown's days onwards, that the lesser black-back appears to be *driving out* the herring gull. I do not think there is any driving out at all, and certainly I have never seen a lesser black-back behaving more pugnaciously than a herring gull. The relations between the two species always seemed to have

been of the best. I feel the lesser black-backed gull suffers
very much from having a black back, even though it is
nothing like so black as his bigger cousin's. Gamekeepers and
most folk refuse to see any difference between a smaller gull
with yellow legs and the greater black-backed pirate with its
flesh-pink legs and feet. The lesser black-back is a handsome
and relatively harmless gull, and as it is with us only for the
summer months its total list of damage is probably less than
that of the herring gull.

My own observations, carefully made over two seasons on
Clerach, show that the lesser black-backed gull is more successful in rearing young ones than the herring gull. A colony
of 84–90 herring gulls reared less than 50 per cent of the
chicks hatched in 1936, and the same colony, swelled in 1937
to 130–150 birds, reared just over 40 per cent. This last
figure was so low because a great northerly gale washed
many chicks off the gullery. The lesser black-backed colony
of 72–80 birds in 1936 reared nearly 60 per cent of its chicks,
and in 1937, when increased to 120 birds, reared nearly 60
per cent once more.

I am also wondering in my own mind how much environment influences the behaviour of the chicks of the two
species. Some day I shall effect some changes of eggs and
carefully note the results. These two gulls are so much alike
in habits, and their eggs are practically indistinguishable; so
are the chicks immediately after hatching. And yet the
young herring gulls tend to be sluggish about their gulleries
and lie doggo at any hint of danger, and the lesser black-
backed chicks are active and soon swimming vigorously on
the freshwater lochans. Only rarely do the herring gulls'
chicks swim on the brackish pools among the rocks.

Their behaviour when learning to fly is also different, but
in this the difference in environment might easily be responsible. As they become fledged and ready to fly the young
herring gulls work to the edge of the cliff where an up-
draught enables them to essay forth on short flights and
return to the safety of the cliff top. The young lesser black-
backs learn to fly from the lochans. There are always gales

and strong winds in the latter half of July and sometimes in August, and the young birds hold out their wings as they sit on the water of the lochan and gradually take off into the headwind, hover there a while, flap the wings a few times and subside once more on to the water. It is all very easy and safe.

It was the gulls of Clerach that first gave me the notion that there might be at work a principle of social stimulation to reproductive condition. If ever a man was inspired to go to a particular island with a view to studying avian sociality it was myself, and if I have discovered a principle not known before (some say yes, and some say no), I must say I am extremely lucky in first being attracted personally to going to Eilean a' Chleirich.

A man of science is only human like the rest of folk, and a man as thrilled as I was with my idea naturally looks round other gregarious birds to see if his theory will apply. I thought of the cormorant, a species which bred on Clerach in considerable numbers, and I thought the theory fitted rather well. This is what I said in 1937, and let stand when *Bird Flocks* appeared in 1938:

'The cormorant is also a social nesting bird, but the group may be no more than a few pairs. I have seen cormorants nesting singly from time to time, but rarely with success. Sociality in this species is indeed close, and when numbers at an hereditary nesting site are rising or falling they are apt to change in sudden accretions or diminutions. A whole group forms a new cormorantry or leaves an old site ... I believe the sociality which has arisen from what may have been primarily a physiological necessity is of a high order in the avian world ... The cormorant has a much more developed sociality than its cousin the shag, a bird which is frequently social in nesting, but not necessarily so.'

I do not think there is anything grossly inaccurate in the above, but there may be an error in stress and interpretation when I speak of the sudden accretions and diminutions in cormorantries. Two more nesting seasons have passed since I wrote that passage, and in that time I have got a launch of my own, which lets me get about among the islands much more freely. The cormorants diminished as a nesting species on Clerach until 1937, when there were no breeding birds there at all. That in itself was a blow for us because a close study of the behaviour of the cormorants was to be Kenneth McDougall's part of the work that season. There was a large cormorantry on the western cliffs of Carn an Iar in 1937, and on the occasion of Dougal's memorable visit, which I have mentioned already, he counted sixty-three nests. The great white patch on the cliff as the cormorantry appeared from Clerach was certainly much larger than it had been in the two or three years before.

The situation changed again in 1938. Comparatively few cormorants nested on Carn an Iar, but there was a large colony in the western precipice of Eilean Dubh, an island a mile farther north. A number of birds had also returned to Eilean a' Chleirich, but not to their old place on a wide ledge on the south side, nor to an earlier place they had on Ard Bheag. They now established themselves on the top of the north cliff, above the places where the fulmars bred. This new cormorantry had much increased in 1939, and those on Eilean Dubh and Carn an Iar had diminished to much smaller proportions.

My view now is that the cormorant is certainly a social nesting species, and is so probably of necessity, but that those sudden accretions and diminutions are not primarily concerned with success or failure as a breeding colony. The cormorants change their pitch every two or three years, and one island is not a sufficiently large area on which to study them. Here it is the whole group of the Summer Isles which must be considered and numbers carefully checked over a period of years.

The stink and mess of a large cormorantry is indescribable, and revolting to our noses in a way that a ledge of shags never is, though some people find them unpleasant enough. It takes more than one winter's rains to wash a cormorantry clean. Naturally, we cannot impute a notion of cleanliness and sweetness to the cormorants, but I think this constant change of site is a hygienic measure nevertheless. The cormorantry, high above the cleansing wash of the waves, is certain to be impregnated with the birds' parasites, and the change of position is surely one way of getting rid of some of them. The squirrel changes his drey from time to time, and probably for the same reason, because if you examine an old drey fairly recently occupied, it is found to have a large population of fleas, whatever other invisible parasites it may contain.

Many people seem unable to distinguish easily between the cormorant and the shag. Their general shapes are similar, but there are marked bodily differences as well as of behaviour. The cormorant is much larger, blue-black in colour and with a white patch on the flank in the breeding season. There is a bare, extensible patch of skin below the beak and on the throat which appears white from a good distance. This elastic skin, together with a hinged beak, enables the cormorant to do the apparently impossible in swallowing a flat fish much wider than its beak. In flight the cormorant is stronger than the shag, and its underline from beak to tail when flying appears almost straight. That of the shag takes a slight step upwards at the junction of the neck with the body.

The shag is green-black in colour and its throat is fully feathered. The crest worn at the breeding time is more on top of the head and is recurved. The shag is much more volatile in its movements than the cormorant. The two species frequently gather together on what I call social rocks, though at such places there are many more shags than cormorants. Shags build on ledges immediately over the sea on Eilean a' Chleirich, but there are other places where they seem inclined to go well back from the water. Harvie-Brown pointed to this fact nearly fifty years ago in describing Lunga of the Treshnish Isles. When we went there in 1937 we found also that the shags were nesting as far as a hundred yards from the sea's edge in some places. It is the same on North Rona; the shags are there rarely seen in the cliff at all, but among the boulders of the eastern bit of storm beach and at the foot of the great *sloch* or deep cuts in the cliffs which occur at three places round the coast. The Clerach shags conclude their infancy suddenly by one dive from the confined area of the nesting ledge into the limitless ocean, and they seem well able to cope immediately with this remarkable change.

The shag is another bird which suffers from being rather like another species which happens to have a bad name with gamekeepers and trout-fishers. As everyone knows, the cormorant will go far inland for his fishing, but the shag is never seen on freshwater. Shags are not exacting constant toll on fish desired by human beings but take a variety of things, of which eels are one, but those who want cheap 'sport', or wish to kill something anyway, do not trouble to watch animal behaviour carefully or determine feeding habits. Thus the Summer Isles endure each year the deplorable spectacle of visitors to hotels and boarding-houses – yea, and shooting-lodges as well – coming out in launches and shooting at these frightened birds as they fly from the cliffs. The carcasses are left where they drop. And yet I have met some of these very people and I know them for decent, honest folk of fine type. There is no wickedness in their shooting, just sheer thoughtlessness and lack of a point of view.

That other relative of the cormorant and shag, the gannet or solan, is common in spring, summer and early autumn about the seas of the Summer Isles, and they seem to fish off Clerach in rough weather particularly. These birds do not like passing over land, though we see them pass through the main glen of the island sometimes. The solans we see here probably come from Sula Sgeir, which is our nearest gannetry, eighty miles away as the crow flies and all the way over the sea. This is not much of a journey to a solan at this season.

I have already said that Eilean a' Chleirich has no sandy or pebbly beach. What beaches there are, never more than a few yards wide, are of large rounded stones, utterly bare and clean. It is not surprising, then, that the bird life of the island should show some marked gaps. Turnstones appear but rarely, and then only for an hour or two, yet they are common in winter on adjacent mainland coasts. I never saw a ringed plover on Clerach though they are resident on Tanera six miles away. The winter population of waders is indeed small – curlews and a few redshanks about the big gullery, but plenty of purple sandpipers about the coastal rocks.

These last birds give me a constant pleasure by their tameness, especially so when I think how few of the family allow close approach. The winter habitat of the purple sandpiper is the barnacled rocks washed by the waves of every tide, and there, apparently indifferent to the weather, the little bird quickly follows the receding wave, gathering small life unseen by us but which is caught among the barnacles. And then a short fly back again as the new wave breaks on the rocks once more.

How the ceaseless rhythm of the sea must have become part of the purple sandpiper, for in wintertime she is concerned wholly with the turbulent, changing strip of the intertidal zone. She chooses the little beaches of boulders as a quiet roosting place, and often when I have been there at night, whether on Clerach, Lunga, or Tanera, I have heard her cheerful 'Qrrrp' as she has flown a few yards farther away.

I close this chapter with mention of Britain's smallest sea bird, one which is more common than is generally thought, though confined in its nesting to islands of the western fringe. It is also a bird which not one in a thousand naturalists has seen, the storm petrel, almost swallow-like in build and no bigger.

I never cease from wonder at the storm petrel and its life. How does it manage to survive and increase? Think of a bird of such small size and slender build living from October to June on the face of the mighty ocean, never coming to land. Perhaps the very smallness of its bulk saves it from being buffeted, so that it walks the waves in freedom or sits on them as lightly as a cork.

They come to us about June 2nd and occupy the ruins of the outlaw's house, the cletts on the ramp of storm beach near the west landing, little stretches of dyke on the east side of the island, the tumble of fallen rocks below the central ridge and any rickle of boulders almost anywhere on the island which will give them a dry place. I have even found one in a crack of the peat in the middle of the island. The birds come in the night and only betray their presence by their churring song, which goes on and on, sometimes night and day as well. We have found this sound to have a restful and comforting quality.

One of these mites nested in an accessible place in the outlaw's shieling, so that we were able to take an occasional look at her and her egg. One large white egg, an egg often cold and taking five weeks to hatch; then a helpless chick, it also often left for a period of days without feeding and taking three months to fledge, a chick which receives no aftercare from its parents, but which is just left in the dark and bare cavern where it was hatched. It must come forth into the world of its own initiative and face the stormy environment of the ocean in autumn. What a tenuous thread is this for the survival of the species! We have no knowledge of what the death-rate may be during their life on the ocean; probably it is low, but each year that the adult birds come to land to breed is a time of danger and loss. On Clerach the otters take a grievous toll, and I often find a head, and tail and legs, lying in piteous relic near an otter's lair. These birds find their worst enemy in the great black-backed gull on North Rona, though I cannot understand how this wretch manages to catch them. You find the remains of the petrels in the casts of the black-backs.

If you take a storm petrel in your hand during the daytime it will lie quiet and seemingly half dazed by the unaccustomed light. Or perhaps it will shuffle away on its hocks into its crevice again. Its legs, though of fair length, will not support the bird in the upright position of a robin or sparrow. Like the rest of the family and also the auks, its is plantigrade.

The storm petrel loses all this apparent awkwardness at night to become a bird of amazing speed and dash. Often have I lain out of a summer night by the outlaw's shieling to hear and see the stormies. It is but a fleeting glimpse, for the birds are black and they do not fly until the night is at its darkest. Their aerial manoeuvres are not of the closely communal and intense type of those of Leach's fork-tailed petrel, but I have been spellbound by the terrific speed and energy of the little birds in their nocturnal flight. The loud swish of wings as they come near gives the impression of power and of much greater size. It will be a grey day for me when I know that never again will I go to sleep to the churring song of the stormies. It, like many other bird sounds, dwells deep in the mind.

If some readers think I have dwelt too long on the birds of the island instead of getting on with the story of our daily lives there, I would answer that the birds are part of our lives and experience to a much greater degree than if we lived in the world of men, busying ourselves with affairs many of which clothe themselves with a mock importance. We see these birds as brethren in the complex of living things.

CHAPTER SIX

SECOND YEAR

WE HAD CONFOUNDED the Jeremiahs by August, 1936. We had neither come home after the first fortnight on Clerach, died of rheumatism or pneumonia, nor had we said 'Enough is as good as a feast'. On the contrary, we had made new friends and welcomed old, got some first-rate research results and gained a fellowship which would greatly ease our financial condition for the next three years.

Kenneth McDougall had decided to throw in his lot with us for a year, a factor which made us all the more eager to get back to the island. He stayed at the Brae House and cared for the hens, goats and Lily while we made a trip south. It seemed as if we would never get home again, but we did get back by the middle of January and were actually ready to go to Clerach by the end of the month. We live in a country, however, where human decisions are not the final ones; they rest with the weather and the sea, and it was upon the moods of these arbiters we had to wait for another month.

Waiting is the hardest job I know; inactivity, uncertainty, inability to get going, not because you are not fit and ready but because other factors are holding you back. Each day during February we used to go up the back of the house with the telescope to look as far as Clerach. What else did we see but a great surf breaking on the cliffs of that island? One day was reasonably calm, it was the 17th of the month, and we felt sure James Macleod and Donnie Fraser must be coming to fetch us. We looked out and – yes, there was a boat in the mouth of the Loch; but our wild hopes sank within us when we got the boat focused and saw that it was not the one for

us. It speaks well for the characters of Bobbie, Dougal and
Alasdair that none of us was sharp-tongued in that time; I
know I felt irritable enough sometimes.

And then I found something to do which took the sting
out of waiting from day to day, something I had never done
before. I am one of those people who itch to be able to draw
and paint but seem congenitally incapable, or is it lack of
application that prevents me? Anyway, I had a series of
good pencils and a packet of smooth Bristol boards, and on
these I began to draw birds, nervously at first and very self-
critically, but by giving the whole of my attention to the job
and forgetting about real islands in this projected dream of
them I came to find I could draw reasonably well. My two
masterpieces were quite the most difficult ones to do. Lily
grazing and a storm petrel in flight – and I think it
significant that they happen to be the subjects for which I
had perhaps the greatest love. My success was amazing me
and I began to have fancy ideas of illustrating one of my
own books but I have given it up now, for as soon as the
strain of that month of waiting was over, my new-found
ability quite disappeared. I gathered some goose wings from
dead birds when we got to Clerach and thought to draw
these in a sketch-book for future use, and believe me, I made
a most childish hash of those drawings. Nevertheless, I know
now that my hand has drawn something presentable, and if
the need ever comes again I shall make it work. Dougal,
meantime, had amused himself wood-carving and had
turned out some creditable bowls and spoons, some of which
we still have and treasure.

When the boat did come for us eventually we did not hear
until one o'clock in the day, when we had given up hope.
Now we were to go, the going was a nuisance; hot stew
on the table for lunch, and Bobbie's birthday plum-pudding.
We had awful indigestion for the rest of the day. Goats,
hens, geese, canary, bedding and a thousand and one things
had to be taken to the boathouse, and it took us four
journeys with the car, two of which were made before the
boat came. There were James Macleod, Donnie Fraser and

Donnie (Beag) Macleod on board, all in a cheerful frame of
mind. We worked as fast as possible, but even so it was half
past four when we got away, by which time the wind had
freshened from the east and was following us down the
Loch. Douglas was forrard, Bobbie and Alasdair aft where it
was warm, Donnie Beag took the tiller, and James, Donald
and I sprawled on the only other vacant place, the decking
over the engine amidships.

What a great length of a loch it is! I unconsciously noted
the landmarks showing the stages of the journey – the Ardessie point on the south side, then Cadha na Muic on the
north side; then Scoraig, where we saw the Macivers outside
their house waving to us. There was something warming
about that. When we got out beyond Cailleach Head we felt
the great swells coming down from the north, and Ghlas
Leac Bheag kept appearing and disappearing as we topped
them and fell into the trough again. Several little auks were
on the sea that day, and we realized their small size only
when some razorbills came by as we were looking at them.

The darkness was coming down as we neared Clerach, and
we could make out no details. The launch went round to the
west landing and anchored off because James would not take
her close in, seeing the swell licking up white everywhere. I
did not count how many dinghy loads came from the launch,
for I was busy getting stuff above the tide-mark on the pier
rock. I had come ashore with the first load, which had included the pair of Chinese geese in their crate. There was a
bit of trouble in landing them, but we looked at it in this
light: if we dropped the crate overboard and gradually
hauled it ashore, everything should be all right. For the crate
would float and the birds could swim. All the same, there
was considerable hissing going on as we got the crate on to
the rock. It was rather a nightmare pulling heavy boxes and
perishable stores out of the dinghy and dragging them up
the slippery seaweed-covered rocks in the dark. Obviously we
must let James and his crew away immediately the last
dinghy was emptied. That pier rock looked like the Cal-
edonian Market just then.

It had been our intention that Alasdair should go back with the launch to Achiltibuie to start school there, but we did not like the idea of his going off to new surroundings at that time of night, so we said no. Instead we put him down in the lee of the cliff, put some rugs over him and a cushion under his head and told him to lie quiet. Dougal, Bobbie and I began sorting the perishables from the non-perishables, making a neat heap of the former over which we could put a tarpaulin. There was no moon, but it was not a dark night, for Venus was very bright, throwing a golden path along the sea, and before she had set in the west Sirius was high to the south.

It was long past nine o'clock when we had finished; then we came up to the hut, which we were relieved to find in the same position we had left it in October. It had withstood one of the stormiest winters in years. We were all more than ordinarily tired, but I was thrilled, nevertheless, when our little friend the snipe rose from the bog before the hut and returned there within a few minutes. Two curlews also got up, and as we went to the loch for water there was a red-shank piping at the north end of it. What lovely sounds these were after the interminable weeks of waiting.

Bobby made us plenty of tea and we drank much with slices of bread and marmalade. The canary had his head under his wing and his feathers fluffed out – fast asleep; I know I envied him at that moment. We let the goats run loose, put the geese into the outlaw's shieling, and then the hens into the box in which the geese had been.

And now we could think about bed, which meant putting up the bell tent first of all on its old site alongside the hut. The circular, drained patch was good and dry, and I felt how simple it was putting up this tent on this night, compared with that day less than a year before when Iain and I raised it and Scoraig had been troubled holding the boat off the rocks in the west landing. Dougal and I slept in the tent that night and did not talk before going to sleep.

I was up at seven o'clock in the morning after a rather cold night and made tea for the company. It was very cold

now, with a strong and penetrating east wind, but I was
bursting with eagerness to get doing, and surely there was
enough to do this day. What a day of hard work! That
carrying of boxes of provisions and all the other stuff from
the rock is almost heart-breaking as well as back-breaking.
There were also the six panes of glass to put into the window
of the hut, for we had not had time to do the glazing when
the hut was erected the previous October. It was quite a long
time before we could find the putty, despite our careful
labelling of boxes. I felt it incumbent on me to do the hardest work, so I set Dougal down to the glazing. It took him a
long time to work the putty down with linseed oil, and he
got rather stuck up with it. Some had to be worked very soft
to bed the panes in; then the panes were tacked into position
and the rest of the putty 'run' round the outside of the panes
and bevelled off. There was I sweating hard at carrying cases
over from the pier rock, and here was Dougal at the hut in
the teeth of the wind getting colder and colder and almost
blue. So I took over the glazing for the last pane or two and
Dougal carried stores from the rock to get himself warm
before lunch. We finished all the carrying by half past three;
whereupon a raw-backed party enjoyed a reflective cup of
tea, the universal panacea for all ills in this countryside.
While we had still been carrying I had worn my binoculars
and had seen purple sandpipers on the rocks, some young and
old tysties in the west landing, and the winter remoteness of
the island was heightened for me when, in broad daylight,
I had seen a mother otter and her half-grown young one running from Lochan Iar to the sea on the western side. Now
I must have a quick run round the island before nightfall.

There is something attractive entirely in its own way
about this winter remoteness. The herbage is bleached to a
pale buff colour and the rocks stand out stark. The winter
birds, to one who knows them, have a direct effect on the
mind. There is a feeling of everything being closed down to
the lowest level of activity. It was but a short round I
made that afternoon, for I was too tired to go far and carefully. The fleshpots called and I was glad to get back to an

immense tea and the good-fellowship inside the hut.

We had been interested to see what the animals did with themselves on this first day back on the island. The goats, Morag and Blanquette, hung about the hut and tent just as they did last year and were constantly in mischief. The hens stayed about their new house, the goose crate, at the foot of the burn where it disappears into the ramp of the storm beach – all except the wretched Troggie (short for Trog-lodyte, from her habit of nesting far out of reach under rocks) who, always given to travelling, made her way up to the shieling and hut and hung around in her interfering way all day. I did not like that hen – she was so nosy and un-amenable to the course laid down; in fact, I came to dislike her so much for her strong personality, which was always running counter to our own affairs, that I came to the state when I knew I should never be unkind to her. If your dislike of someone is strong enough and you are honest with your-self, you know that you can never let go your spite; you have to make up your mind to be more decent than ever. Thus Troggie is still alive, having survived more island ex-peditions, and in 1939 she has managed to realize the dream of her life in creeping into a crack of the earth's surface without being seen and hatching out a brood of chicks.

To return to Clerach: the Chinese geese made their way to the foot of the burn and found it very much to their liking. Soft bog, shallow water and a bite of green made a fine place. Lily looked about her for a few minutes when I let her out of her basket. Then she took a short fly to the burn; after breakfast she held her head high and talked for several minutes – a sure sign that she was going to fly. And so she did; high and far over Lochan na h'Airidh to the north-west, round again, out to sea from the west landing, back and down by the Chinese geese by the burn. She knew quite well where she was. But Lily had become too human to stay with the other fowl and she soon returned to the hut, hardly ever leaving its vicinity afterwards. The call of her own wild kind flying overhead aroused no interest in her, nor would she associate with the Chinese geese.

We had made the hut a homely place within two days, though it was not yet painted inside. Both Dougal and I had been emulating each other in ingenuity of making supports for shelves. And now there were books on their own shelves, a shelf for the canary, hooks upon which hung telescopes, cameras and binoculars, the tools of our craft, and there was even a tablecloth on the table. At that moment I had reached the ideal kept in my mind since childhood, a tiny house with presses and shelves for everything, set down in your own fairy country beyond the reach of an external world. I had played and pretended this bit of escapism all my life, and here it was, as good as the pretending and perhaps a little better, for I had with me those I loved. As a philosophy of life I doubt whether my pleasure at that time would hold water, but as a moment in a lifetime it was perfect, reaching its apogee when a flock of barnacle geese came low in front of the window and landed a hundred yards away to graze at the foot of the burn.

Alasdair was delighted in these days. He was supposed to have gone to school and would thus have missed these early days of March on the island. And he seemed to grasp at the unexpected joy with almost the fervour of a man trying to keep time still for a moment. I took him stalking the barnacle geese, creeping within a few yards of them so that he could see their faces and the barred plumage of black and grey and white; and by himself he went round his own little haunts of last year, remembering his way among the maze of lochans and little hills.

We had been back about a week when on March 7th there dawned one of those perfect West Highland days; the sky cloudless, the water a deep blue, and you could see just as far as it was possible to see. The hills of the Forest of Harris on the Outer Hebrides showed up in their snow-caps, and the deep snow on the mainland hills made them sharply outlined in the sunlight. Dougal and Alasdair and I went to the big herring gullery in the morning to begin building a hide there, the still, warm air tempting us to take off our shirts while we were carrying stone. When this kind of weather comes in early spring its exhilarating power is remarkable; no work is too hard or too long, and mealtimes become the crowning joy of the day.

Dougal suggested we should start summertime henceforth, so we put the hour on during the afternoon. Alasdair asked if he might have the kayak launched on Lochan na h'Airidh, and there he had a grand hour or two coasting about and running the model motor-boat which Donnie and Alasdair Fraser had given him at Christmas. Bobbie and I carried driftwood to the gullery for roofing the hide. Lying there in the sun at the cliff edge we felt this was a day of days and all that wretched month of waiting was shed from us.

The work on the life-history and social behaviour of the grey seal was now firmly in our minds and we were busily planning ahead. For this reason we had brought an Arctic Dome tent to Clerach to test its reaction to big gales; the seal work would be a wintertime job requiring sound equipment. Messrs Thomas Black and Sons of Greenock had lent this tent to us, a second-hand one which had been with the Oxford University Arctic Expedition to Ellesmere Land. The tent was like a half-sphere with a little ventilation pipe coming from the top, where eight curved ash poles converged and were clamped. There was an inner wall as well, six inches away from the outer one, and this insulating layer retains heat within the tent. Dougal took up his abode within it, crawling in and out each time through a canvas funnel. Alasdair shrieked with laughter and had to be gently dissuaded from constantly going in and out himself.

But next day he was gone from us. Launches and men came to take away the hoggs which had wintered on the island, and to put ashore a few weakly ewes that would have a better chance of lambing six weeks hence than they would on the mainland where the hard winter had bared the lower hills and the grass parks as well. There was great commotion, for Clerach is a difficult island to gather, and once the sheep are together it is not easy folding them near the sea's edge while they are severally picked up and thrown to a man in the stern of a dinghy. All were aboard at last, and Alasdair went away with them in high spirits, for which we were duly grateful. He was going to stay with Donnie Fraser and his mother at Raon Mor. I think it was Bobbie who had the fears and heart-burnings, but she took comfort in thinking he would be back in a month or so for his Easter holiday.

We had some cold weather about this time, and we saw the unusual phenomenon of the lochans being frozen over after the thermometer had been down to 25° F in the night of March 12th-13th. But it was pleasant weather, warm in the sun when you got out of the north wind. That evening we heard of the blizzards on the mainland and heavy falls of snow. A Peeblesshire sheep-farmer spoke on the wireless of the trouble they were having with sheep buried in drifts and the country impassable. He had a rich deep voice, and his little talk in a clear, cultured Doric as part of the news was one of the finest performances I have ever heard over the air. How strong and real it seemed after the attenuated southern English of the announcer. Not that I am crabbing the announcer, but to us in the far north, where we speak English and not the Doric of the Lowlands, the speech of the southern Englishman sounds indescribably thin.

March 16th dawned another magnificent day, but the wireless forecast a south-easterly gale, against which we made due provision. This, perhaps, would be a good test for the Arctic tent. We worked on the little flat bog in front of the hut on this day, burning the old foggage from it, digging another drain through to the burn and building the turves into a dyke round the hut and tent. Then we raked moss from the grass after burning and spread some shell sand which we carried up from the little patch at half-tide level at the west landing. It was good and happy work, made happier for me because Lily sat on my coat all the time and chewed at the buttons just as if she had been a puppy.

It was blowing hard by dark that night, so hard that there was no hope of sleep. I went out at one o'clock in the morning to look at the bell tent, which was up all right, but every guy slackened completely. A dry gale means that the guys will not bind, and one with heavy rain means the ground gets sodden and will not hold the pegs well. If there must be a gale I like a few drops of rain periodically to keep fabric and ropes tight. This gale was very dry from the east, but when I went out at two o'clock again to see how things were the rain began, and I knew she would hold thereafter. Knowing Dougal's capacity for sleeping, I thought I had better have a look at the Dome tent, St Paul's Cathedral as Alasdair had dubbed it, and find out if Dougal could sleep through this screaming turmoil.

The tent was nearly down, and two of the curved ash poles were sticking through a rent in the roof. It was also tearing round the bottom flap where stones are laid to anchor it. I thought it best to let her down altogether and put stones over the whole thing to keep her flat. But where was Dougal? I dared not open the funnel entrance to the tent because it was on the windward side, but thought it wiser to crawl underneath from the lee. And believe me or not, there was Dougal fast asleep, the inner envelope of the tent draped over his person except at his head, which was kept clear by a sack of potatoes standing there by his bed. The man can't be human, I thought, and Dougal himself, waking so slowly, thought I must be a fussy fellow to be capering about at such a time. He changed his tune when he switched on a torch and saw the front half of me on the ground at the opposite side from the door, and the roof close in on him.

We had everything safe within the hour, and Dougal came back to the hut to drink tea and spend the rest of the night. Next day we let the east wind have its own way, keeping ourselves warm by fetching some sacks of guano from the south cave, taking the turf from a piece of garden and forking over the tough ground beneath. We spread the guano and some shell sand. It was back-breaking labour, but gladly undertaken because we wanted so much to see how new potatoes would do there. It was several days before we had got the peaty soil broken down and dressed with seaweed, and not until March 29th, Easter Monday, did we get the potatoes planted.

The sea had calmed and had only a deep swell by March

20th. I made up a cast of rubber lobworm and piano wire with a view to fishing from the kayak. Bobbie was nervous and derisive, but Dougal and I could stand a lot of that, and essayed forth hopefully. Dougal did the fishing while I kept the kayak moving in the places where I thought the fish would be. This helped me to keep my breakfast down, for I have observed before that porridge is not good stuff on which to go to sea. I was always better after tea, which with us is a solid and ample meal. This day we caught two good-sized lythe (pollack), and thus felt able to return to Bobbie with a proper air of masculine superiority. We passed a flock of nine tysties on the way home:

'Will they fly or will they dive?' I asked Dougal.

Eight flew and one dived, and when he came up again he looked most surprised at not seeing his fellows.

Two days later we woke to a great northerly gale which shook the very island. We could hear and feel the boom of the waves in the Cauldron as we lay in bed. Dougal and I went there after breakfast to enjoy the spectacle of flying water; spray from each great wave came down into Lochan na h'Airidh (our drinking water), which is itself about thirty feet above sea-level. Gulls and fulmars were enjoying themselves in the up-draught against the north cliff, on top of which we lay ourselves. A wild sea of green and white, a great sound of water and of crying gulls and the blessed sunlight withal. Dougal and I could not have heard each other speak, but when we smiled across at each other we knew how good it was to be alive. It was on that day we picked up an exhausted barnacle goose and brought it back to camp in the hope of it recovering. But it was so tame I knew it was done.

It was blowing a north-westerly gale two days later when in the evening we listened to Clemence Dane's play *Granite*. It was grand, and we wondered if anyone else was listening to this macabre story of Lundy Island in such appropriate surroundings as ourselves. We enjoyed every minute of it.

Easter was early in 1937, and as the weekend came near Bobbie was eagerly looking forward to Alasdair's home-

coming. But he did not come, and though Easter Day itself
was one of brightness, made the better by the good Easter
hymns which came over the wireless, I knew Bobbie was a
worried girl. I took Dougal into the great east cave in the
kayak, but there was far too much surf to allow of a landing.
As it was, we got pooped by a wave as we came ashore on the
east side. I happened to be in the stern and got the lot round
my ears. Dougal, being forrard got only his seat wet, and his
laughter was quite immoderate as we carried the kayak up
the shingle onto Lochan Fada for the short cut home.

The good days came and went, and bad days followed and
still neither Alasdair nor the boat came. We were short of
paraffin and butter, and yet our appetites seemed almost to
increase. Dougal and I built a little tin oven into the bank,
using all our cunning to make it conserve and concentrate
the heat; and once we had got the fire hot, Bobbie cooked
some currant scones which were pronounced successful at
tea-time. But she did not seem much cheered, pointing out
that our outrageous appetites had ruined any sense of dis-
crimination we might have had in food. Once we get
paraffin again, we thought, we shall not use this contrivance,
because one baking uses up nearly a year's supply of driftwood. There is no doubt that if you are reduced to this kind
of thing you must give up the civilized notion of baking and
depend on frying, stewing and boiling, and let your bread be
girdle scones.

On another day, when we were getting rather desperate,
we saw the Altandhu boat shooting lobster creels on the east
side. We hurried back for our large packet of outgoing mail
and then hailed the boat, which was manned by four old
men. One of them rowed over to the Exchange rock to take
the letters, and looking round, he saw there was not a dry
spot in the dinghy, which was leaking visibly. So the old man
continued to hold the letters in one hand and rowed the boat
with the other, using the oars alternately. Then another
great hand reached down from the big boat and stowed the
mail carefully along with the lobsters. These four old men
with their worn tackle seemed to me to epitomize the social

conditions of the West Highlands at the present time. Old
men were carrying on a job here as best they may – the
young ones go away to earn money.

Alasdair came home on April 3rd, bursting with high
spirits, trying to tell us everything at once and coming out
with his Gaelic now and again. The school had not broken
up till last night; that was why he had not come at Easter.
Also, my eagle eye noticed he had a sniffle – oh yes, he had
had a bit of a cold, he said. Thereupon, glad as I was to see
him and to dig into a sackful of mail, I expected the worst.

This was the sort of occasion when we pay the price of our
isolation. Exactly forty-eight hours after Alasdair's return,
Bobbie, Dougal and I went down with cold, such colds as
townsfolk never know, for to isolated communities the
common cold can be a major illness. I have also noticed that
a cold caught from a child is far worse than one taken from
an adult, because the virus has been strengthened by passage
through the younger and less-hardened material. We were
simply wretched by the following morning, staggering about
with such sore throats as we had rarely known. How much
we sympathized with the old St Kildans who did not welcome calls by strange boats because of the round of colds
which inevitably followed. We had a feverish day or two,
made worse by a south-easterly wind, which we find is
always bad for any affection of the nose and throat. Then on
the following day the wind had swung round to the south-
west, driving away all the dull haze characteristic of south-
easterly wind and having an immediate effect on clearing up
our colds. Happily, a cold in this clean air is not complicated
by a long period of devastating catarrh.

Spring seemed to come suddenly about the middle of
April. A softness which had not been there before came into
the air, the grass shot forward, willows showed their flowers,
scurvy grass began to flower on the cliffs, and the foliage of
the sea-campion came thick and tender also. The geese were
getting stronger on the wing, and the ewes looked better
than they did a month before.

There is no doubt that Dougal's presence this year

helped us to do much more exploration of the island than if
we had been alone, exploration in this instance meaning the
caves which ran in from the coast and were not approachable
on foot, even at the lowest tides. I have already described
some of the little expeditions, which carried with them a
certain quality of emulation as well as cooperation.

One afternoon early in May, Dougal and I were on a knob
of rock near the north-west corner of the island. The impression when you were there was that the cliff went sheer to
the sea, but Dougal is a climber, and letting himself down
over the edge he found a good ledge of rock leading downwards to sea-level. He went down and came up again quickly,
all smiles.

'There's a big cave down there, more than I could see;
let's go and fetch the rope.'

So home we went to tea, and Bobbie came back with us to
explore the cave. The climb down was much easier than it
looked, because hand- and footholds were excellent all the
way; there is no danger whatever in climbing a precipice if
the rock is sound and the holds good and plentiful. In fact,
when I think of myself at the moment of writing these lines,
laid up in bed with a broken leg sustained on such an innocent errand as walking down the field to milk the cow, I
know that I could not possibly have sustained such an accident going down that fine sound cliff in bare feet unless I
had had a brain seizure and fallen off. So are the mighty
fallen; safety and danger should never be considered as
clear-cut states of being, when your very danger may be in
the illusion of safety.

We found ourselves in a narrow cave about fifty feet high,
the floor of which was strewn with immense sea-worn boulders. Here there was some danger stepping on these shiny
surfaces in the dim light. As it was, Bobbie slipped and found
herself up to the waist in a pool. We proceeded slowly,
finding this high corridor splitting into two passages and
light filtering in from somewhere ahead.

We explored each avenue, as the politicians say, until we
were checked in both of them by deep water. It was obvious

to us that these two forks of the main gallery were the two geos which we had entered already from the west in the kayak. The north-west corner of the island is, therefore, completely tunnelled through, and the sea passes from end to end, a distance of nearly two hundred yards, at high tide. I took a number of photographs in the course of this expedition, and we returned home feeling rather pleased with ourselves. We were agreed that this cave of the Gothic dignity was one of the best thrills of the island.

Dougal was always doing things which added to the general comfort of our island home. He made a lobster creel one day of driftwood and wire-netting, a prism-shaped affair it was, with a beautifully incurved hole in one end. It so happened that some of the Achiltibuie folk came in the afternoon to mark the lambs of the few ewes on the island. One old fisherman among them said:

'Well now, I wass neffer seeing a creel like that one pefore. She will not pe haffing much headroom whateffer.'

Never have I heard anything so artlessly damned as that creel of Dougal's, and Bobbie and I rolled on the shingle with laughter. But Dougal merely grinned and said he was content to judge it by results. Calum Macleod said wirenetting did not seem to catch lobsters very well, but that we should get crabs; he proved to be right. Devil a lobster did we see, but crabs were plentiful enough.

Dougal used the timber which I had brought from the great east cave to make a fine lean-to about four feet high along the back and one side of the hut, where we were able to store peat, driftwood and such things as did not need to be inside. He fitted a table and shelves against the hut just outside the door so that Bobbie could wash up there on fine days and keep her saucepans outside. It was Dougal who finished the turf dyke I had begun round the huts, and he hung a gate, built a piece of wall and planted stonecrop, scurvy grass and other little flowers on top of it. Indeed we began to wonder why anyone should ask for a house with more than a couple of rooms. Ours seemed so easily run and demanded little of the time one would have preferred to spend out of doors.

It is remarkable how much more work is made as soon as you have a house of stone and lime with doorsteps and fire-places and several windows, and when you have begun to collect furniture. We have reached the conclusion that the cure for the chronic state of monetary poverty in which we find ourselves while we insist on doing research which it pleases us to do and which cannot be conducted in a lab-oratory in the shelter of a university, is to simplify needs. Face up to the fact that much of the furniture and fittings, and therefore of indoor space, is quite unnecessary to comfort. Pare down continuously and avoid junk like the plague; be careful to see that such labour-saving devices as you install are not in fact labour-makers. We have never been more happy than in these wooden-hut days; if there is one fruitless consumer of good energy above another it is the eternal scramble to maintain or reach some false standard of comfort, social position or respectability. If you become sud-denly poor, cut your losses and climb down, and if you are chronically poor but doing what you most wish to do, then I repeat, simplify your needs with a bold, clear mind. The extra time given you by this means to continue doing the things you wish makes the effort well worthwhile.

These remarks are not offered as sage, sociological counsel for a whole nation; they merely apply to a fair number of people of my type and position. I should not like to see rich people simplifying their lives as we have done, for where would be the outlet for works of art and for much general labour? The islander inside his little shores, having solved to some extent his own small problems of life, must not become pontifical and offer gratuitous advice to the world outside; nor must he crab existing institutions outside his island which are certainly helping him at some point or other in his isolation. Islanders should never grow cocky, but the more humble and grateful as they are allowed to continue their life.

Just think for one short moment what was behind our

turning a knob on the morning of Coronation Day and
having Westminster Abbey brought inside our little wooden
hut. There was all the work and organization behind making
the set itself. There was the intricate organization emanating
from the hot and fevered atmosphere of Broadcasting House
(I have been there myself and wonder how they manage to
keep it up), and there were the King and Queen themselves
going through an ordeal, while we, a party of comfort-
loving islanders (living the simple life and all that), lay in the
sun at our ease and heard perfectly that wonderful service
and procession. It was magnificent and inspiring. We were
enjoying the fruits of an immense labour to which we could
hardly think we had contributed. No: if you are going to
crab civilization and extol your own simple life, you must go
back to scratch.

We were enjoying a lovely spell of weather at the time of
the Coronation, so warm, sunny and calm that it seemed
strange to listen to the accounts of rain during the Procession, increasing to a downpour in the evening. Clerach
was Arcady that day until late at night when a curious set of
local conditions somewhat spoiled our fun. The summit cairn
of the island seemed an unusually good place to have a Coronation bonfire, and during odd hours of earlier days we had
carried up to the cairn large bundles of driftwood and dead
heather shaws. It is extraordinary that when we get such a
good spell of weather as this had been there is often a wind
off the land at night which reaches Clerach as a half-gale.
Sometimes you see it happening even in daytime, and there is
a strip of rough water between Ben More Coigeach and Clerach, a strip perhaps two miles wide, outside which the sea is
quite calm. Why there should be this extremely local disturbance I do not know, but the nearer you may be in a boat
to Ben More at such times, the greater your danger. The sea
piles up short and steep incredibly quickly, and the velocity
of the wind is very great. A roar of waters greeted us when we
three came to the summit cairn that night. We knew there
could be no bonfire for us, because had we lit a fire it would
have spread immediately into the peat, which lies thin on the

ridge where the bare red rock is constantly peeping through. And with this good dry weather we had had the peat was parched and cracked; the momentary sport of a Coronation bonfire was no excuse for burning half the island and damaging it permanently.

So we had to content ourselves watching the blazes at Achiltibuie, Ullapool, Dundonnell, Gruinard and at Laide. We could even see a light in the Outer Hebrides. People at all those first-mentioned places, including Alasdair at Achiltibuie, were looking for our fire and we had to disappoint them. Unfortunately, they were not aware of the conditions which prevented our having it, so that, contrary to all our normal arrangements, some of them were a little troubled on this night because there was no fire on the summit cairn of Clerach. The heather and the driftwood is up there yet.

I found a dead ewe one evening about the middle of May, but the lamb was nowhere to be seen, and it so happened the next night that I saw a ewe wandering about and bleating. Her udder was a big one and packed tight, and I knew she ought to be caught and milked for she was in pain. It is always difficult catching an individual sheep, and as I have said before, harder still on Clerach. Bobbie and I had a pretty good run before we caught this ewe, but nearly a quart of rich milk rewarded us. We put the ewe herself on a long tether so that we could dry her off gradually and see that she was all right. The very next day the lamb of the dead ewe walked almost up to me near the north cliff. His eyes were sunken and his knees and hocks were knocking together. He gave me a good run, nevertheless, before I caught him. I brought him back to camp, thinking how providential it was that I had caught the milky ewe. She would have nothing to do with this lamb, of course, but we held her by the neck and it took lambkin no time to go to the right place. He sucked for a quarter of an hour and his belly swelled and swelled. After that he lay down and looked better.

We were able to leave this lamb with the ewe, but she would never let him suck unless we held her, and this we had to do three or four times a day. The lamb knew immediately what to do when we came along, and while the ewe was struggling as we took in the rope he would prance round her hind end ready to duck for his drink, as if he were saying, 'That's right, boys, hold her tight.' Eventually we had merely to go up to them and take hold of the rope, and Fortescue, as he came to be called, would dive under her and suck while she stood; but never would she let him suck without our being there. She was thrawn and starty as so many of these Cheviot sheep are.

Each year we had trouble with maggots on the sheep. It is my experience that animals rarely understand that man is helping them when treating them for any disease. They struggle nearly always and are bad patients. But there are exceptions; I remember a cow with which I lived, slept and ate for a week, and her gratitude was pathetic. Her eyes followed me everywhere and she would call softly all the time if I left her for a few minutes. Sheep are not like this, and yet, both in 1936 and '37, a ewe has come to the door of the tent and of the hut in an advanced stage of fly-strike and allowed me to treat her. The first one was too far gone, for as soon as I had cleaned her she went into the characteristic state of collapse and died. The second one was also far gone, but recovered after spending several hours in a collapsed state. What a pity they cannot learn to come for help before they reach this stage of being eaten alive!

We were getting fish regularly all through the second year, fine fat cuddies, occasional large lythe and some mackerel. The offal was boiled for the hens, and Bobbie cooked the fish in a variety of ways so that we never got tired of them. Sometimes she would fry them, sometimes steam them with milk, and one favourite way we liked cuddies was to roll the fillets with mixed herbs and bake them. It was amazing the amount of fish we could put away these days.

Dougal was fisherman more often than I was now, for I

was almost constantly busy with my birds. He thoroughly enjoyed the job, amusing himself now and again by stalking whales and basking sharks. I well remember one evening seeing him streaking down the west coast of Clerach in the kayak after a school of four whales. He was quite unaware that a fifth whale was less than fifty yards behind him and following. Then one of the school jumped from the water and there were signs of the whole school becoming playful. Brother McDougall knew when discretion was the better part of valour and left the arena.

He took the kayak out another day for sheer sport just after a gale of wind from nor'-nor'-west. Bobbie and I were on the Rudder, about a hundred feet up, watching him, and though he did not go more than five or six hundred yards out he often disappeared behind the waves. One broke right over him, but he had all the spray covers on and bobbed up again like a cork. There is something extraordinary in the pleasure of these slight rubber boats. You are not so much *in* a boat as you have a boat-like attachment instead of a lower half, and you bob on the water like a sea bird, able to go close in to a cliff, even when the swell is climbing up it in a spectacular fashion. They are most dangerous when there is a strong wind without much sea.

June 8th, 1937, was not a very happy day for Bobbie and me because Dougal went away to help his people pack up house in England. We should not see him until the latter end of August, when he would be joining us for the grey seal work on the Treshnish Isles, a job on which we had now set our hearts and which was in an advanced stage of organization. James Macleod had brought three cases of stores, two cans of paraffin and two bags of mail, so after despondently watching the launch go away from the Exchange rock we worked off our low spirits humping all this stuff over to the camp.

Four days later the weather was magnificently hot and calm, and I spent a good time finding shady and grassy places in which to tether the goats and the ewe with Fortescue. When I had got them all settled happily I tempted

Bobbie to come out on the sea. We paddled towards the south-west point, Ard Bheag, but a school of finback whales came by a few yards ahead of us, frequently breaking the water and blowing. Bobbie does not like whales in such close proximity and I was instructed to turn northwards. I obeyed dutifully, but imagine how I was tickled when less than fifty yards directly ahead of us there appeared the great dorsal fin of a basking shark. Bobbie does not like rubbing shoulders with these people either, so I had to take another point east-wards and landwards. And there another basking shark appeared. I turned sadly and with resignation to the west landing, but at this point Bobbie said she would be damned if she was going in if all the marine fauna of the Minch came sailing by. All well and good: I turned out again, but then I noticed my seat was getting uncommonly wet and thought I had better come in and get the leaks mended.

Those wonderful June days! If we did work at all it seemed play, and now only the good weather is remembered. The longest day was magnificent, and the sun recorder showed sixteen and three-quarter hours of bright sunshine. We built our peat stack that day and fetched in loads of driftwood from the little bays. Blue butterflies appeared for the first time this year, helping the illusion that summer was eternal. That illusion was soon broken, for I, sleeping that night in the heather near the north loch, was woken at four o'clock in the morning to find a smirr of rain and a cold north-east wind. I got up and ran back to the hut to get warm and drink some tea. Next day, the 23rd, was my thirty-fourth birthday, and the weather not much better. But I had work to do indoors, and there were surprise parcels to open and good things to eat, including a fine birthday cake from my mother. To be born on Midsummer's Eve is probably why I carry something of an elfish nature in an elephantine frame. It is my habit on this night to go forth and meet what may come; always it is something of interest. Year after year on the mainland I would pick up a hedgehog on the night of my birthday, but here on Clerach I saw the otters, and later the flight of the storm petrels about my head.

That last week of June was a dreadful time of south-westerly gales, reaching hurricane force at times. I went out on the afternoon of the 28th to find sheltered places for the goats, and my hands were blue with the cold. Torrential rain was driving horizontally from the sea. Then, when I came in again, Bobbie was listening to the Wimbledon tennis, and the commentator was remarking that it was a sultry day and the players were obviously feeling the heat. There seemed something exotic about cotton frocks as we looked forth from our window and listened to the blast.

The wind veered to north-west and then north in the night and blew a gale. I went to the Cauldron to see the seas and the big gullery the following morning. What tragedies were there! Many chicks were lying dead, and nearer the edge it was obvious many chicks and nests had been washed into the sea. A big grey battleship passed close under the island that morning, apparently steady as a rock in those great seas; and yet, as I watched her bows carefully through my glass I saw them dip under and the waves break over her decks.

We were utterly sick of this wind and our nerves were rather on edge. I know that I was getting in a bad temper by July 3rd when there was a fine calm afternoon and the mail launch did not come. I chafed and grumbled because I had corrected page proofs and indexed a book within a few days of the previous mail coming, and it had all been lying idle since then. Bobbie and I took the kayak round to the east bay in the afternoon and thought to fish from there in the evening.

We went through the island to the kayak just after nine o'clock, and my temper was not improved by the fact that a fresh north wind had sprung up. I could see a wicked jabble of sea off Ard Ghlas where wind and tide and rock-face were playing tricks with the water, but I thought we could get round it into straight water. Not so. The north wind catching us broadside drove us nearer the cliff round which the peregrines were screaming wildly, and into the choppy water which was of that unmanageable type where the

sea comes up in pyramids and a plume of white shoots
off the top. There is no rhyme or reason in this kind of
sea, and as we were getting too much of it breaking over
us for safety, I headed north into the wind and came back
into the landing under the lee of the north shore of the
bay.

This episode added further to my sense of frustration, for
I had nearly gone forward in anger. We carried the boat
through to Lochan Fada and paddled about under the
aspens and royal ferns which grow there. How calm was this
water, sheltered as it is from the north, after the noisy sea in
which we had just been! The bit of wind in the leaves of the
trees was a loved sound, and seen from the water these little
aspens looked bigger than they were, and very comforting.
The honeysuckle tumbled over the rocks to the water's edge,
scenting the air so that I was momentarily intoxicated by its
sweetness. How lush this bank on a bare island! To hear the
wind in these tiny trees, to smell the honeysuckle, to see the
noble fronds of the great royal fern and to feel the water of
the lochan lapping against my leg through the skin of the
kayak – all these after the stark red cliffs, the rasping cry of
the peregrines and the angry sea – assailed me with a sudden
wave of nostalgia for the kindlier country where the big trees
grow, and undergrowth and a wealth of foliage. But is not
this nostalgia part of the very joy this life gives? It is part of
that succession of contrasts, physical and intellectual, which
is the salt of life. On this north-western fringe of an old
world I reach an internal peace and occasionally experience
these sweet yearnings for trees and deep grass. If I go south,
the trees take on a heightened beauty and have a new fascination for me; but within a day or two comes the longing for
the islands and indomitable coasts of this country; and this is
no sweet nostalgia but a painful longing which does not pass.
There is a measure of asceticism in living here, though I
believe it is Epicurean. If it is, perhaps my Stoic philosophy
is not quite good enough.

Let that be; the man who pulled the kayak through the
yellow flags at the western end of Lochan Fada this night

was in a very different frame of mind from that in which he had taken to the sea an hour earlier.

I give you this as a little study of environmental impacts on one man's mind.

The weather improved after this; meadow-brown and blue butterflies became active, and the island flowers came forth with a new sweetness to make our world a gay one. The wild thyme made purple whole patches of ground except for the golden heads of horseshoe vetch. The asphodel was flowering in the bogs now, brilliant spikelets of golden flowers, each one like a star. The rinze heather was in flower also and some of the bell heather. Sometimes we wondered if we had ever seen the tormentil flowers so profuse or the golden suns of the hawkbit so abundant as this year. The purple orchis was still flowering and the sea-pink had not yet gone from the west side. That darling flower, the ragged robin, showed an occasional bloom here and there, on which we lighted unexpectedly, and the rock-faces sparkled with the pink stars of the stonecrop.

Alasdair was home for his summer holidays by this time, and had to amuse himself very largely for a week or two because his mother and I were busy typing out the draft of a book. But when we had finished we had picnics and did a lot of fishing with him. He landed a ten-pound lythe one evening on a rubber eel on piano wire. The same fish had earlier gone off with a white fly cast with which we were surface-fishing for mackerel, but by going carefully over the same piece of water again with the rubber eel we got fish and cast as well.

On the other days we would climb down into the cauldron at low tide and peer at the wealth of life in the pools, for Alasdair never tired of this pastime. They were good days, these last ones of July. One season's work was just about finished, and though we did not wish to leave Clerach we looked forward to our new job on the Treshnish – a new beast to study and new islands to explore.

CHAPTER SEVEN

TRESHNISH

WE LEFT CLERACH IN 1937 exactly a fortnight before we found ourselves on Lunga, the largest of the Treshnish group which lies a few miles west of that large Inner Hebridean island of Mull. It was little enough time to do all we had to do of final organization, but we were loth to leave Clerach before it was absolutely necessary.

By Sunday, August 22nd, I felt I had done all I could towards having new gear and stores waiting at Oban, cared for by the Stationmaster and Harbourmaster. These gentlemen had both entered into the spirit of the expedition and had given personal attention to our stuff, collecting it in a locked shed near the harbour steps. Our good friends, Messrs Thomas Black and Sons of Greenock, had done their best for us at the harbour there, which was the base of the ship which took us to the islands. We were receiving Government assistance in the matter of transport, for it was realized that our projected work on the seals had a practical bearing on fisheries problems. We were to go in one of the coastal patrol cruisers. I felt satisfied about arrangements ahead, but on this Sunday we were still at Dundonnell with the car to pack and three of us to get to Oban before nine o'clock the following morning.

It was a day of sweltering heat which we felt badly in the relaxing air of the glen after our many months on Clerach. More and more gear accumulated, so that I began to be a little anxious not only about its bulk but the total weight. Still, there was no alternative but to carry on, and by five o'clock we were ready to start, all the gear well tied and the last cup of tea inside us. Bobbie, Alasdair and myself were in the front seat of the Ford, and being well packed in we did not get out at Corriehallie where our friends the Morrisons came out to wish us Godspeed. That send-off did help, because we began our journey in a tired state.

The car was so definitely overloaded that I had to be very careful on any considerable bend in the road. Driving was undoubtedly a strain that day, made no less unpleasant by the large amount of holiday traffic on the roads. I never exceeded fifteen miles an hour over the terrible road of the Feighan, and rarely over twenty on the Dirie Mor, for that road is bumpy though metalled. Things were a little easier from Garve to the Kiltarlity turn just south of Beauly, which we took in order to by-pass Inverness and save fifteen miles. It is a bit of road of which I am very fond, from Beauly to Drumnadrochit, because the crofts look prosperous and there are plenty of trees. We got down the terrific hill into the village of Drumnadrochit by using the low gear only and the brakes not at all. That hill was a milestone past, I felt, and it was with relief we came on to the wonderful new road through the Great Glen of Scotland. It was possible for us to do thirty-five to forty miles an hour in safety.

We were immediately struck by the casual fashion in which youths strewed themselves across the road and would not move out of the way, and when we got down to Fort William we found them playing football in the streets. So much for the big new road, the manners of those living alongside and the decline of Sabbath observance. Once you are off these big arteries you find the people retain traditional Highland good manners.

It was dark when we stopped at half past ten on the north shore of Loch Leven. The night was utterly still, with low mist, very heavy dew and swarms of midges. None of us slept well, and I know that Bobbie and I were a little afraid of sleeping-in in our overtired state. Bobbie was up first before five and soon had tea on the go while Alasdair and I broke camp and reloaded the car, so that we were on the road again before six o'clock. The sun came out as we rounded

Loch Creggan, where the country has none of the starkness of the Northern Highlands. There are low hills, green parks and plenty of trees round wide stretches of sheltered water, and back of all the high, blue hills. We stopped for a quarter of an hour to have a wash, comb our hair and become human again. It was half past eight as we came into Oban, which time gave us five minutes to spare after we had garaged the car and stepped aboard SS *King George V* bound for Iona. We dived below to eat as big a breakfast as we could get; anxiety was past now and we were going to relax as much as we could for the next two days.

Alasdair went over much of the ship, finding her speed, tonnage, draught and other details which hardly bothered us. Bobbie and I were looking towards Mull where we have spent so many happy days. We picked out the places we know and love well – Lochbuie, Carsaig, and a big rock, almost an island, where we camped for a night long years ago. Nevertheless, we could not help feeling this country lacked some of that impersonal grandeur which belongs to that we have now come to call our own. I felt this and was pleased when Bobbie said, 'I'm wanting back to Lochbroom already.'

There is no doubt that Bobbie and I found ourselves shy of all people and felt awkward in a holiday crowd. I was also a trifle nervous about going ashore with a mob at Iona of all places. But our minds were taken from dwelling on ourselves by the sight of a large flock of Manx shearwaters skimming in gay fashion along the water – hundreds of them weaving in and out with the gliding, straight-winged flight of the petrel and shearwater family. The ship dropped to half-speed as we passed through the Torran rocks off the south-west corner of Mull. How red the granite showed, even at sea-level! And then there was the sudden change of seeing the greenness of Iona and its grey, gneiss hill of Dun-I an ever beautiful island.

Big longboats came out to meet us, and the ship spewed forth its mob, ourselves included. I was not happy just then – still less so when we got ashore and saw a fat blonde woman in beach pyjamas. This was Iona of the soul's rest vulgarized in a holiday August by fast transport. Last time I had come here I had taken a pilgrim's way, walking through the hill and then down the gruelling road of the Ross of Mull. I had rung a bell at Fionnphort and a boat had put across the mile of Sound, its crew a great Viking of a man and a dark woman whose raven hair streamed in the wind and rain. That was the way to approach Iona, and in the spring of the year, when the only people visiting the island were doing so in a spirit of pilgrimage and quietness.

Well, I had come to meet Ian Mackenzie, who rented the grazing of the Treshnish Isles and who would be bringing us mails from time to time. He was there on the concrete slip and came directly to us, picking us out from the crowd though we were previously unknown to him. Happily, the hotel was full, and he took us to stay in a tiny cottage which had no garden at all, but just rested on the grass near where a burn ran down to the sea.

We put Alasdair to bed after lunch, for he was dog-tired and had a hard time ahead of him yet before he would be on Lunga. We ourselves went into the island, lay down in the sun and went fast asleep for a couple of hours. Thus, we found ourselves refreshed and eager again after tea, and ready to visit the Abbey. It seemed quite untouched somehow by the number of visitors who must pass through in the year: even now, it was empty but for ourselves.

When we came out of the Abbey, Iona was Iona again to me, and later in the cool of the evening all its charm and beauty came back. We went to the white sands at the north end of the island to augment my store of pebbles of green marble and to bathe our feet. And lastly, before a welcome bedtime, we talked with Ian Mackenzie, who told us details of the landings on Lunga, the best place to camp, and where the water was – all good information which saved a lot of time two days later.

Next day after lunch we boarded the *King George V* again. The ship was lying off a quarter of a mile because there was a fresh southerly wind and a fair sea running. The longboats got rather knocked about against the side of the ship, and some of the passengers were drenched. Once aboard, we had half an hour to wait while further relays of people came in the longboats, so I amused myself taking flight photographs of young greater black-backed gulls which were hovering about the porthole by the galley. They were in a grand position below me, heedless of my attempts to photograph them. The results were good, and one of them I look upon as one of the six best photographs I have ever taken.* Two of the birds with wings outstretched came parallel with each other and diagonally across the field of the lens; every mark of the intricate pattern of the young gulls' wings is apparent, and below is the glinting, summer sea.

When we turned into the Firth of Lorne Bobbie and I began to get more and more excited and impatient to be ashore, for if everything were as it should be, Dougal would be meeting us off the boat and there should be signs of the cruiser. It was a lovely evening as we turned into the harbour of Oban, and there she was lying at anchor and looking rather remote in her battleship-grey. Lying near her was the well-known ocean-going yacht *Norseman*, and the masts of smaller craft reached skywards beyond these two ships. I cannot describe the kick we felt at that minute and the next one when we saw Dougal's grinning face in the crowd as the *King George* came alongside the quay. It was one of the great moments – a lot of fikey work now in the background, a rosy future ahead and this present meeting of good friends. We looked around for a teashop.

Dougal had been aboard the cruiser and talked things over with the Captain and First Officer, who, he said, were rather looking forward to this little trip with us, but that they wondered what like of folk we were. Dougal himself was not camping meanwhile but had got a room in a back-street pub in Oban. He had also checked over the stores and had interviewed Stationmaster and Harbourmaster. Excellent: and still better when he took Alasdair off our hands to sleep with him in his attic. This meant that Bobbie and I

*Reproduced in *Wild Country*: Cambridge, 1938.

could manage a rough camp for ourselves much easier.

'I'll take him to a fish-and-chip saloon and see how he likes that,' said Dougal.

Alasdair was delighted, for this was a new and exciting experience for him, and to be with Dougal for so long was in itself a holiday for Alasdair. So Bobbie and I took the road south in our overloaded car. We left every road we could until we found ourselves in a glen of a few scattered small farms above Loch Nell. The road was rough, and a single track on which we did not expect much traffic, but it was difficult to get quite out of sight of any of the small farms. So, for the first time in my life, I went up to the door of one of them to ask if we might camp near the road a little way off. The little grey Highlandman was dour, rubbed his chin and hesitated, and then said yes, though he didn't go in for the camping sites whatever. I felt wretched and rather squashed. Later I told him we were from Lochbroom, where we were presently bound, and why we had come to ask him this night.

The dour little Highlandman disappeared entirely, and instead there was a laughing little man with the brightest of twinkling blue eyes. Bobbie went to talk with his wife and could not get away because she was made so welcome, and I learned from himself that he was from Ardnamurchan and that many were the good days and nights he had sailed round the Treshnish.

It rained a good deal in the night, but we slept happy and were ready to leave again by eight o'clock. Our little Mr McPhee waved us goodbye and called:

'Man, I'd like fine to be going with you the day.'

All that in less than twelve hours!

We continued along the narrow, winding road and drew alongside the harbour steps in Oban at precisely half past eight. An officer was on the steps above a grey launch full of men. He stepped forward and shook hands.

'Dr Fraser Darling? My name is C—, Second Officer of FC —. You are right on the dot for time.'

I heaved a sigh of relief; for weeks and weeks there had

been on my mind the responsibility of this zero hour. You start badly if you start late. I moved towards the car again to start unpacking.

'No no no,' said Mr C— in a shocked voice, 'just leave that to the boys.'

The half-dozen boys ranged from about twenty to sixty years of age, but they were all equally proficient in stripping my car of gear, and would have taken seats, tool pack and all if I had not watched them. A lorry came along with our stock of paraffin loaded into petrol tins, and almost at the same moment I saw Dougal and a porter coming from the little station lock-up shed, with our gear on a platform truck. Everything going like clockwork. I deposited the car in a garage for four months' rest and got back in time to go aboard the cruiser with the first load.

There I met Captain M—r and Mr O—, the First Officer, who gave me a cheerful reception, more cheerful than I had hoped for, because I had wondered for a long time if the cruiser folk would think we were just a party of silly asses out for a lark. They treated Alasdair with extraordinary kindness and not as a nuisance of a small boy. I had already given him a drilling about behaviour on board, not to go poking where he had not been asked and not to attempt to walk up to the bridge. In fact, he was generally to make himself scarce. And this he certainly did, for I hardly saw him again during the voyage. The little blighter was having a magnificent time in the fo'c'sle and in the galley with the cook. I remember once seeing him with a mouthful of green peas.

Captain M—r said he would like to wait for the post at 10.15 AM. So Bobbie and I went ashore again to do one or two oddments of shopping. Just as we were about to step aboard again a lady came running along the quayside clutching a handbag and umbrella, looking like many elderly women do when they are flurried and not quite sure of trains, boats and buses. There were we just stepping down into the smart launch when she called out breathlessly:

'Is this the six-shilling trip to Kilmorich?'

Mr C— shook his head, closed his eyes in shock and turned away; it was all too much for the poor man. I pulled myself together and pointed to a McBrayne steamer across the harbour, and the poor lady turned about and started running again, handbag, umbrella and all. The shattered Mr C— held the handrail as he walked down the steps into the launch.

There was a freshening north-westerly breeze as we crossed that choppy stretch of water at the south-west corner of Lismore and near the Lady Rock, but we felt nothing of it once we were into the Sound of Mull. At noon Captain M—r asked me on to the bridge, where we looked at charts of the Treshnish Isles and one of the Summer Isles which showed the anchorage of Tanera.

'I have always promised myself a night in there,' he said.

'Well,' I replied, 'perhaps if we are living there you will make more sure to keep your promise.'

'That's fine, I will.'

And in due time he did come.

As we had not emerged from the north-west end of the Sound of Mull by one o'clock, I thoroughly enjoyed my lunch. In fact, I enjoyed life for a while longer sitting in a deck-chair and watching the pleasant scene about the mouth of Loch Sunart and the south shore of Ardnamurchan. It was rather different when we got out beyond the north end of Mull and my beautiful lunch became a libation to Neptune. The swell was strikingly deep and a big surf was breaking on the west shore of Mull. I managed to stagger around in between times, pointing out the approach to Lunga and the landing place at the Captain's request. Nobody else felt the slightest bit squeamish, of course, and I cursed my misfortune in that direction. But it could not utterly take away the thrill I felt in the fine day and the sight of these plateaued islands which were now so near us. I remembered the first time I had ever seen them, long years ago on a May evening, from the top of Ben More Mull. How deeply I had longed to visit them then, and how near I was now!

We anchored off the eastern shoulder of Lunga after the

sailor who had been swinging the lead from the starboard bow
had called 'Mark thirteen, sir,' which, from looking at the
chart, I took to mean six and a half fathoms. The anchor
settled snug, the launch was lowered from the davits, and we
passengers went aboard her with Mr O— and six men and a
light load of gear.

The idea was that we should find the channel between
Creag a' Chaisteal and Lunga and nose about for the landing
which Ian Mackenzie had explained to me. Well, there was
no channel to be seen and we had to land ourselves and the
gear on a skerry by Creag a' Chaisteal. A very light-coloured
grey seal cow came alongside and looked at us calmly while
the sailors made remarks of various kinds, cajoling, complimentary and otherwise. Mr O— and I went to spy out the
ground, for we could not understand this dry crossing to
Lunga. According to information, the channel did not dry
out. What had really happened was that we had arrived at
the dead low of a new-moon spring tide, the only time when
the channel is dry. It was not pleasant going over those
weed-covered rounded boulders, but we thought we could
just carry over this small lot of gear before the tide came in.
We did not know that sound of water as we do now.

We picked up loads and started for the channel, but there
was water among the stones already and it could be seen
rising. Dougal waded through with a case and a young sailor
in sea-boots followed. They found it bad going; Dougal ran
back after dumping his case, and Sea-boots came over a
minute later and rather slower because of his rubbers. The
water was up to the top of those thigh-boots before he got
back on to the rock. All we could do was to wait for the tide,
so we lay on the skerry in the sun, enjoying our ease; the
work would come soon enough.

The cruiser's launch came back with the steward aboard,
who with professional slickness produced an immense teapot
full of tea, and a small mountain of tomato sandwiches. This
was truly a marvel, for my mouth was on fire and I was
famished after that round of sickness. It was one of the high
spots of this memorable day.

There was now more water and we left the skerry and Creag a' Chaisteal, ran slowly through the channel and landed on a small spit of shingle, the only bit of its kind on all that island. Then began that gruelling task with which we were now familiar – carrying the gear from the shore to the camp. Here we had to camp about ninety feet above the sea and a quarter of a mile from where the stuff was put ashore. Bobbie and I ran ahead as fast as we could and found a sheltered hollow near the old houses which we thought suitable for the tents. By the time we were in full swing carrying, there were eleven men crawling up and down the steep path from the shore, just like a lot of pirates or smugglers with contraband. Those men were great and remained entirely cheerful under a succession of loaded Tate sugar-boxes.

Captain M—r had told me earlier in the day that a patrol job tended to become monotonous and that a job like ours was a godsend. When we had finished, Mr O— said:

'Well, if your ears are burning this next day or two, you'll know it's the boys.'

From the shelf on which we were to camp we watched the launch return to the cruiser, being hoisted aboard and the ship's anchor drawn. We saw white handkerchiefs waving as she steamed away, and then, when well out of the skerries and going northwards, she gave us a few notes of farewell on her siren.

Lunga is a green island, full of rabbits, and rabbits mean that creeping thistles will grow well. Our feet were so hard that we could chase about the rough rock of Clerach at top-speed barefoot, but thistle thorns are quite a different proposition. If one gets into your foot, the flesh will fester until it comes out. We pitched our little brown portable tent for Alasdair and the small bell tent for ourselves, and Dougal pitched his new and specially made light tent. How thankful we were for this fine calm night!

We did not wake until eight o'clock the following morning, by which time the sun was lighting all the inside of the tent. Breakfast was soon out of the way, for we wanted to have the camp looking shipshape as soon as possible. There was the big bell tent to pitch and this smaller one to move a hundred yards to a place we thought better than where we were.

Lunga is a lump of an island and we could not get inside it to pitch our camp in a sheltered place as we could on Clerach, so we naturally pitched on the north-east corner near the water and near the remains of the old houses. A few yards east of us was the cliff edge, a ninety-foot sheer drop to the big boulders at the foot, and then the sea; a few yards the other way rose the steep, rocky slope of the hill of Lunga which reaches three hundred and thirty-seven feet and is known as the Cruachan, meaning haunch. Perforce, then, we had a magnificent view from the camp. Creag a' Chaisteal was out of sight of the tents, but we could see reefs to the north-east of it. Then to the north we could see Fladda and the tops of Cairn a' Burg beyond. Along the whole eastern horizon was Mull, a fine skyline indeed, topped by the shapely cone of Ben More. Between us and Mull were Gometra and Ulva and Little Colonsay, and as we gazed we were impressed once more with the characteristic features of this country of the west side of Mull. The cliffs are sheer, then there is a little flat; then another steep slope and cliff and another flat on top of that. Lunga itself is like that, and so is the Dutchman or Bac Mor, two or three miles south-west of Lunga. But the other Treshnish Isles have only the sheer cliffs rising from the sea, and flat tops on which you could play cricket. The formation is volcanic, and the Treshnish cliffs themselves are of grey amorphous rock lying on a platform of lava near the sea level. This laval erosion platform runs out into the sea at certain points and forms suitable breeding grounds for the seals.

If we go up the Cruachan of Lunga we see the white sands of Iona to the south and the little hill of that island, Dun-I. Westwards lies Tiree, the one-time 'Granary of the Isles' because of the good corn which could be grown there, and the island which, in the language of the Gael, 'lies below the waves'. It is indeed a low island for the most part, and many were the queer effects of the mirage; sometimes the island would seem to be cut in two and the houses would stand like skyscrapers with their feet in the sea. Beneath Iona and Tiree were the two isolated lighthouses of Dhu Artach and Skerryvore. A little north of Tiree begins the long, low, rocky coastline of Coll, over the top of which we could see the Outer Hebrides on a good day. North again was the spectacular outline of Rhum with its mountain cones rising over two thousand six hundred feet. Beyond Rhum we were able to see the Black Cuillin of Skye, and Blaven, and also the Red Hills of Skye. We could see Muck and the prominent Sgurr of the Island of Eigg. East again was the tall columnar lighthouse on the point of Ardnamurchan, the most westerly point of the mainland of Great Britain. We could see the high mountains of Ardgour over the top of the peninsula of Ardnamurchan.

That evening I thought I owed it to Alasdair as well as to myself to take a look round a bit of the island, and we set off westwards. We found that the Sanctuary Rock so-called, or more correctly Dun Cruit or the Harp Rock, was actually an island, cut off from Lunga by a narrow channel and sheer cliffs. The upper eastern face of the rock is riddled with puffin holes, and even now there were a few fulmars and young kittiwakes still at their nests. The buzzards were busy overhead engaged on their evening rabbiting. We also saw a flock of curlews and peewits and a couple of shelduck in a little inlet at the north-west of the island where the water collects an immense quantity of marine detritus. Later we came to call this place the Dirty Inlet, from the mess and stink which was set up as the weed and rubbish rotted. There were shags in hundreds, but few cormorants.

We found the west coast of Lunga an imposing place. The cliffs are rugged and sheer, and their foot is washed by the open Atlantic. The erosion platform, running out there just below tide level, caused the waves to break in a fine roll as they never did about the cliffs of Clerach where the water is deep close in to the face. Halfway down the length of Lunga the island nips in suddenly to a narrow, low neck only a few feet above the sea. This place is called the Dorlinn, and figured largely in our later life on the island, as it must have done years before to the earlier inhabitants. Beyond the Dorlinn is a long, low plateau with sheer cliffs almost all the way round, sixty to seventy feet high. Apart from the Cruachan itself, on which the soil is necessarily thin, the island is covered with rich grass, and in the frequent hollows the brown volcanic earth reaches a depth of two or three feet. If you could make shelter here you could grow anything on such soil.

We had already become acquainted with the nocturnal habits of the Manx shearwaters. These birds make an indescribable shrieking cry which is enough to frighten anyone not knowing the reason. It is a cracked, half-choked scream, and you do not hear the beat of wings as the birds come nearer and recede again. There is the story in the West that a mainland shepherd took service on the island of Eigg many years ago; the shearwaters were nesting in burrows near his house, he being unaware of their existence because they are not obvious about their breeding haunts during the day. He had not been in the house a week from the May Term when the shearwaters began shrieking, and then nothing would induce him to stay another night.

One of the young birds took to doing exercises of a sliding nature up and down the roof of Dougal's tent. It did not seem to have any animosity towards us when we picked it up and took its photograph; in fact, it came back for several nights and kicked up a fuss. Each night, also, we heard the storm petrels churring in the walls of the old houses and under boulders near the tents.

Two days after taking up our abode on Lunga we had a visit from the Robertsons, the family which has fished lobsters about these islands for three generations. They have a little hut on Fladda where they spend the summer fishing, and they return to Tobermory for the winter to make good their creel stock and equipment for the following year. Our visitors today were the old gentleman of eighty years and his son Donald. Donald was one of the biggest men I have ever

seen, with an immensely strong face and a voice as soft as
new milk. It was for me one of the greatest disappointments
of our expedition that we saw him only once more before he
went back to Mull. Our hope had been that we should have
made a deeper acquaintance and got about the islands with
them. But an extremely rough spell of weather and an illness
of the old gentleman prevented contact between us and
caused them to leave Fladda earlier than usual.

They brought us lobsters and crabs this day, told us the
news they had heard on the wireless, and then a lot of useful
stuff about the seals. The animals did not mind them and
would allow them quite near, but they were frightened of
strange boats and tended to go out westwards into deep water.
The Robertsons' work about the islands had made the seals
their friends, and I could tell how proud they were of the
seals and how anxious to take care of them. These men were
also good observers of bird life and had kept records for
several years of the spring arrivals of the nesting species on
the Treshnish Isles. In this intelligent interest in the wild life
of their territory the Robertsons reminded me of Shetland
folk, many of whom are first-rate observers and recorders of
facts, but our West Highland people as a whole have an
extraordinary ignorance of any animal life that does not directly concern them. It is a difference of outlook between the
two areas for which I cannot account. There is a lot of Norse
blood in the West after all, though the social traditions have
remained very distinct.

The good weather went out with August, for we woke to a
high wind and showers from the south-west on September
1st, the first day of what proved to be a trying fortnight. But
we had come to watch seals and were full of eagerness and
joy when the great beasts began to collect about the place in
increasing numbers. There was one bull of tremendous size,
probably nearly ten feet long and weighing, perhaps, nine
hundred pounds, who came to lie out at a particular place in
the sound between Lunga and Creag a' Chaisteal. His personality soon became evident to us, and I think it was

Dougal who christened him Old Tawny. What a magnificent head and proud bearing he had! Never since, either on the Treshnish or on North Rona, have I seen a bull seal to equal him in size or majesty.

His movements ashore were delightful to watch – the way he would make himself comfortable on the rock and then the expressive movements of his forelimbs, which I prefer to call hands because they can be used in ways so like the human hand, fingers and knuckles as well, rather than as some awkward mittened limb of whale or manatee. You would see Old Tawny scratch his belly delicately with his fingernails, waft a fly from his nose, and then, half closing the hand, draw it down over his face and nose just as men often do. Then he would smooth his whiskers with the back of his hand, this side and that. His hands would be at rest over the expanse of his chest for a while, and then you might see him scratch one palm with the fingers of the other hand, or close his fist and scratch the back of it. A seal's movements are often a most laughable travesty of humanity, but considered more carefully as seal movements they have great beauty.

The wind increased to a gale from the south-west and we saw waves breaking three-quarters of the way up the face of Dun Cruit or the Sanctuary Rock, which is one hundred and fifty feet high. Between there and Creag a' Chaisteal great rollers were coming in and breaking long before they reached the shore. The seals were out there obviously enjoying themselves. I saw Old Tawny letting the waves break on him and coming up again in the trough to wait for the next one. None of them was fishing; it was just the fun they were having.

The gale and rain seemed to reach a climax on the night of September 4th, and we had no sleep before 3 A.M. Then we went off oblivious of everything until six o'clock, when the wind had dropped and the rain stopped. Blessed peace. We turned over again, and the next thing we knew it was a quarter past nine. The seals were calling loudly in their high falsetto while we had breakfast, and I was thinking to myself that the tide should be low enough about noon to let us

across to Creag a' Chaisteal. I looked over the cliff to see
twelve cows lying out at Old Tawny's place. Soon there were
sixteen, and then Old Tawny himself came out of the water
and lay by them.

I had much to learn about the Atlantic grey seal at that
time. This was the first time I had spent any considerable
spell at one of their breeding grounds at the breeding season,
and I was much afraid of being too eager to stalk them and of
frightening them away. Money from scientific bodies and
much good-will from individual people had put me in this
favoured position in which I could do a self-chosen job of
work. Therefore, it was not for me to amuse myself with a
very close stalk, if by that act I imperilled later research. My
previous attempts at stalking seals at home and elsewhere
had shown me that they were extremely wary. But as I
looked at that mob of seals and at Old Tawny, then at every
inch of the ground between me and them, and felt the wind
coming from the west, I thought the job could be done.
Surely a photograph of Old Tawny would justify my
going.

Dougal and Alasdair wanted to explore part of Creag a'
Chaisteal, so we three started together on condition they left
the group of seals to me and kept well out of their sight and
wind. We crawled over the floor of the sound on our bellies
in full view of the seals two hundred and fifty yards away.
But the wind and sun were in our favour and we went extremely slowly over that expanse of tangle and wrack, myself
encumbered with camera, lenses and binoculars – nearly a
hundred pounds' worth of stuff about my neck. It was agon-
izing but exciting, and we got over and out of sight without
arousing the suspicion of the seals.

Now I went on alone, a big stalk ahead of me and all over
seaweed, or so I thought until I came to a place where I
realized it would be better tactics to be in the water than to
be in full view on top of a rock. I left my boots, stockings,
binoculars and some of my camera gear, and waded in slowly
until the water was nearly up to my middle. The bottom was
so slippy and my tackle so precious. Then a cow seal came

near to me in the water and was most interested in my slow and laboured progression. She was not frightened, just curious, and I changed the lens of my camera without mishap, took careful aim and got the photograph which later turned out to be a favourite. She was kind to me and went away quietly. Metaphorically, I raised my Sunday hat to the lady, for indeed it was the Sabbath, and then carried on.

I was over at last and crawling up a sunken skerry, along the top of it and in full view of the seals at less than fifty yards' range. By this time I was sweating and excited but had managed to keep my large red face to the ground. I took advantage of cover to shed more clothes and go forward with only the bare camera; then down the rock into some shallow water, moving so that it did not splash, crawling on again, and then a peep to see where I was. Only twenty yards, but a rotten position for a photograph. On again with my face to the rock; foot after foot.

And now I was lying alongside Old Tawny, near enough to tickle him, and he was still dozing. I looked at the great furred belly of the seal, at his powerful hand with its five black claws. He rumbled inside and the very rock seemed to shake; never have I felt more insignificant. There is six feet three of me, but I was a dwarf beside him and he was twice as high through the shoulder as I was, lying there beside him. I do not know how long I lay there in wonder at the beauty of the seal, but at last I brought myself to the serious and technical job of photography. The focusing, the exposure, the stops – and him. Was he in a good position? No, I was too near, his head was down and eyes closed. I edged backwards, using only my body muscles, then I whistled gently and he raised his head to look about him. My chance had come and I took it – and it was the last exposure in the film of thirty-six!

Old Tawny looked round, lay his head again for a moment and then up again. He looked calmly at the recumbent figure beside him. It was strange; he had better get away from it, but he moved leisurely and without fright. If a human being can get close enough to a large animal I find it will not take precipitate flight as it would if it saw him several yards away. I had got through the barrier of this beast's watchfulness and I should have had to make some positive movement to frighten him now. Luck was with me that day, the twelfth anniversary of my getting married, I noticed, and the portrait of Old Tawny* is in my house, while Old Tawny himself, I hope, is still swimming the seas of the Treshnish Isles with his usual joy and serenity of carriage.

I crawled back from the seals as carefully as I had come, collected my clothes and gear, and later my shoes and stockings, and then Dougal and Alasdair. Bobbie had been watching all this from the cliff edge on Lunga, but now she had hurried back to the camp and had a special anniversary lunch on the sugar-boxes. It was one of the great days of my life, and I was not much bothered when the wild south-west weather set in again at night for another long round.

A curious squall occurred on the evening of September 7th, a day when there had been incessant wind and rain from the south-west. Wind and rain stopped just after tea, then there was a sudden darkening as if a curtain had been drawn over the earth. Two minutes later the rain fell in torrents and there was a terrific squall from the north-east which made us fear for the tents. Then again, quite suddenly it abated, and within a few minutes the wind was back again to south-west and blowing hard. It veered in the night to north-west and reached us in gusts, and the following evening I wrote in my diary that it was the worst night we had ever had in a tent. Those thunderous and terrific gusts kept us awake, and as soon as sleep was about to overtake us again another blast would come. Then there were hard showers and I was out tightening and slackening the guys. We had had our bell tents fitted with long rope guys to the apex and extra short ones inserted between the normal guys from the eaves. Thus, each journey outside in the night meant handling fifty-four guys, and if things were very bad, giving them a tap all round with the mallet. Certainly these nights tired

*Reproduced in *Wild Country*: Cambridge, 1938.

us, but we expected them, and after all, we had no set hours of work to fulfil in the daytime. The work of observation of animal behaviour is in itself restful. We are talking enthusiastically at this time of the projected expedition to North Rona in the following year.

Before we had been a week on Lunga we made the acquaintance of some very old inhabitants of the island. The acquaintance ripened into much too close a contact and we were caused a lot of trouble during the first month or two of our stay. I allude to the house mice.

The people of Lunga left the island eighty years ago, but they did not take the house mice with them. When St Kilda was evacuated in 1931 there was some fear among zoologists whether the distinctive house mice of that island would become extinct. Our experience on Lunga dispels that fear.* The mice must have lived a truly rural existence for eighty years, for when we came to the island they greeted us with open mouths. They threw off their field habits immediately and became house – or rather tent – mice once more. They inspected everything and found it good, and the trodden floor of a bell tent made an excellent sports stadium for them at night-time. The bolder spirits would climb on to the sugar-box table and make it a sounding-board on which to slap their tails in bravado. Oh, it was great fun, but we had to curb their hospitality in self-defence and do something about them.

This was another emergency in which Dougal's ability as a handyman came to the fore. With immense patience he

* *Note.* The house mouse almost certainly is extinct on St Kilda; at least we could find none in 1948. The fallibility of arguing from Lunga to St Kilda lies in the fact that although there are no long-tailed field-mice (*Apodemus*) on Lunga, they are present on St Kilda. *Apodemus* is a dominant active species and country dwellers will know that if you have these mice in the house, you do not have the house mouse. The situation on St Kilda would seem to be that when the island was evacuated, the special environmental factor of human occupation was lost and in the presence of *Apodemus* the house mouse could not persist. In the absence of *Apodemus*, *Mus* could adapt himself to rural life without human beings on Lunga.

fashioned water traps which would lead the mice to suicide. He rounded the ends of a piece of wood so that it would rock when set across a bucket, and across this piece he set another, on the end of which he stuck oatmeal with the help of black treacle. The unsuspecting mouse climbed on to the mainstay, ran along to the cross-piece, turned at right angles to the oatmeal and – plomp, he was in the water at the bottom of the bucket; the devilish engine which had been his ruin came back into position again to entice the next victim to his doom. The mice never got wise to this device. For myself I am very fond of mice and I felt it hard to bring myself to catch them, for they are sprightly and diminutive, and tame ones have given me such pleasure all my life. But here on this island where we had no protection of bins and so on; and where, when there was a calm night, we were anxious to enjoy it, we were compelled to be drastic and put sentiment on one side. It was horrid letting the little things drown in a smooth-sided bucket, even more horrid and callous when we ourselves lived so often in some danger from the sea, and, lastly, we had butted in on their island, so to speak. Nevertheless, if we had not caught any of those seventy-five mice which we killed during our stay on Lunga, I fancy our stores would have been in an indescribable state. There are plenty of mice left there yet.

I have already mentioned that Lunga seethed with rabbits. About two-thirds of the population were wild-coloured, about a quarter black and the rest a pretty silver-grey. They were as wild as rabbits usually are, but round the tents they began to take us for granted and one little black one became quite tame. Dougal kept the pot going with about two rabbits a week, using his .22 Winchester. But he was always going back to nature and all that, and catching them by other means. One of his tricks was to look over a rock at a crowd of about fifty or a hundred rabbits feeding down below, and then with a leap and a flourish to be down among them. Perhaps one would be so taken by surprise that it would run to a hole which was only a make-believe, and Dougal's arm would fetch it out. Those he killed this way seemed to give him far more pleasure than those he shot with the rifle.

Normal people should never try to eat more than two rabbits in the family in a week, however plentiful they are. I should never eat them from choice at any time, because I once worked for a month on a farm where rabbit came on the men's table thirty days out of thirty-one. But here on Lunga they were a useful source of fresh food, and Bobbie was not like that wretched farmer's wife, who was not averse to stewing the gall-bladder as well sometimes. Bobbie would bake them one day, jug them another, and Dougal and I saw to it that only the best rabbits went into the pot.

There was also the stand-by of the fishing. John McInnes (Ian Mor) of Iona had lent us a funny little nine-foot dinghy which we called the Water Beetle, and which probably weighed more for its size than any boat in Northern Europe. She was also very leaky, and if you were out rowing it was very nice to have someone else in the boat to keep baling. Otherwise you rowed a little and baled a little and got a long way in a long time. Dougal and the Beetle became good friends, and he went about the enormous flat skerries east of Lunga which just showed through at low tides. There were big lythe in there, but it was remarkably easy to lose your tackle in those acres of tangle-covered rock. We used to beach the boat on the east side of the Dorlinn where there was a steep shingle beach. The swell was often very bad, but Dougal was never bothered. He would sit there just behind the breakers, laughing; then when he thought the moment right he would pull like mad and I would run in to help pull before the swell turned the crazy little boat broadside on and swamped her.

More cow seals came into the island during the first week of September and would spend most of the day lying out on the Creag a' Chaisteal side of the sound. The first seal calf was born on September 9th; I could see it flopping about the rocks several feet above the high-tide mark, and then I heard its little baby-like cry that is more human than that of any other animal. I crawled over to Creag a' Chaisteal at low tide after noticing that the mother was coming out of the sea to feed it about every two hours. There was a fair wind from the north that day, and when I found myself over on the rock there was a strong eddy coming towards me from the east. If I stalked the main body of seals under Old Tawny which was west of me I felt sure they would get my wind, and as the sun was in their favour and working against me I stalked a smaller bunch on the east end of Creag a' Chaisteal. I reached them in good order and got several photographs. Then I stalked away without disturbing them and worked my way along far behind Old Tawny's bunch until I was west of them. It was not necessary for me to work closer than twenty-five yards, because I now heard the cries of the baby near me, and for this I was thankful because the wind was snatchy and tending to come in from the west as well. These seals, like the deer I knew better at that time, have a habit of taking up a position which will bring them olfactory information from two points when that is possible.

I crawled along to the calf and my heart warmed to it immediately. Its long, silky hair was not white, but a kind of wind-swept grey and white like the wind passing over a field of green barley. The eyes were large and black and the head long. I was reminded of my companion of years ago, the great hound bitch Grainne, who we used to call the grey seal sometimes when we were plaguing her. This calf looked rather flat against the rock, because it was not as yet muscled up nor fat. And just as the legs of a lamb or foal look much too big for the body just after birth, so were the limbs of this baby seal out of proportion. I took a few photographs of this little thing which snuffled round me unafraid, and then stalked all the way back to the other side of the sound. I was delighted to see all the seals lying where they were when I set out, although I had been so near them. That is what a stalker with a rifle can never do; he cannot stalk *away* from his quarry and leave it undisturbed, as can the hunter with the camera.

Next day we found more calves born on the erosion platform at the south end of Lunga. They could be watched as a
group quite easily from the cliff edge seventy feet above
them. Bobbie, Alasdair, Dougal and I were all down there
that evening watching them with delight. How jealous of
their babies were these mothers, and how attentive! The
mother lies on her side to suckle the calf, and the two teats
come out beyond the level of the belly only while the calf is
sucking. Then they seem to be retracted and rest almost in a
little depression. The cow is able as a result to move over the
rocks on her belly without fear of chafing her teats. The seal
mother indulges in a lovely pattern of behaviour each time
after the calf is fed, by turning round a little and scratching
the baby on the back with her hand. She scratches all the
way up to the head, which she fondles with her hand exactly
as a human being might play with a dog. The baby obviously
likes this and later rolls on its back, waving all its limbs in the
air, in ease and well-fed playfulness.

We saw many scenes of idyllic maternal care from that
point of vantage on the cliff above the erosion platform.
Mothers and calves played in the quiet pools with charming
gentleness, and yet whenever another cow or calf came near,
the mother became all teeth and snarls. The bull seals were
usually innocent of any wish to hurt the calves, and if the
mothers were away would allow the calves to play round
with them and even tease them. But if the cow was there the
bull was treated with suspicion. Often have I seen a cow rush
open-mouthed at a bull and inflict a wound in his neck
though he, poor fellow, never retaliated. He just backed
away to safety.

Dougal and I were down there one day just in time to see
a terrific fight between two bulls. I have watched animals too
much to call every little sparring match between males a
great battle. Animal story-tellers would never sell their tales
unless the poor beasts were constantly engaging in these
rousing affairs, but in real life male animals do not fight any
more than they can help, but challenge each other and spar
around until honour is satisfied or one is scared. Only man

and such animals as he has bred expressly for the job are idiots enough to be continually fighting seriously; if the human species fails in the course of evolution it will be because of its warlike qualities. It is not content to spar, but is suicidal enough to subjugate the whole life of a nation in the practice of war until the society is left in an utterly exhausted state. In all my later watchings of the seals I never saw a fight like that one Dougal and I saw on the erosion platform of Lunga that mid-September day.

There was a bull seal on the tiny beach and he looked bad-tempered. He was running blood from new wounds in his neck and shoulders, and the cows were snarling at him as he edged his way down to the sea. He came near the calf of a mother we had found to be particularly attentive, and took hold of it in his teeth and began to worry it. The mother went for him, but he had given the calf nasty bites on the hind-flippers and on the back. The calf shuffled hurriedly to safety – a very frightened little man. Soon a great bull showed his head from the sea and looked intently at the one ashore. The latter saw him and showed he was afraid because he snarled. The great bull came up two or three yards more on the crest of a wave, and with the same undeviating look at his enemy. But the frightened bull did not run away. Suddenly the big fellow from the sea launched himself forward with surprising speed and his teeth closed in a great mouthful of the other's neck. He was so strong that he could actually shake the other bull and we could see the skin tearing in his jaws. They tore at each other and bellowed, and the blood ran freely. The frightened one saw a chance and made for the water, but an Atlantic seal is many feet long and the big bull was round in a moment with his teeth deep in the runaway's hindquarters. He was dragged into the water in this way, and now we saw the even more impressive spectacle of a fight not bounded by the two dimensions of dry land. The depth of the water and the fact that it is their natural medium enabled those two seals to fight at a much faster tempo. Over and over, rising and falling, grappling and biting until the sea was red about them. This continued for a full five minutes, until the big bull came victorious from the waves, his sides heaving and blood dripping from him.

Later in the morning Dougal and I were down on the erosion platform, stalking and photographing. We wormed up to the little fellow who had been bitten and found the wounds to be nasty gashes. We scratched him as his mother did, and he liked it, but Dougal was examining his hands and feet carefully while I scratched, and when I stopped for a moment he looked round and saw that we were strange. He lunged towards us as if to threaten, swelled out his nostrils wide and emitted a throaty snore of great violence. Dougal laughed so much that he fell over. We left the little one alone and he was soon asleep again.

I had some magnificent sport down there when wind and tide allowed me to get on to the platform. Some of my best photographs were taken there, including some of cows fighting, and others of mothers with babies suckling. But I was never lucky enough to be able to let fly at a bull fight such as we saw that day.

CHAPTER EIGHT

TROUBLES AND SUNSHINE

ON MONDAY, SEPTEMBER 13th, the time had come
for Alasdair to go to school, not to Achiltibuie but to Gor-
donstoun in Moray. This meant that one of us must go with
him, and after much discussion it was decided that Bobbie
should go. Had I gone myself I could have taken him in the
car and got back to Iona in quick time. But the question was
whether the weather would hold for me to get back to
Lunga. This was a highly important time in the work, and I
could not afford to be away more than a day or two. On the
other hand, if Bobbie went she would see about his clothes
and things better than I should. Ian Mackenzie happened to
come that afternoon, and with much sorrow I saw Bobbie
and Alasdair go away with him. What a journey it would be
for them! Back to Iona that night, to Oban the next day by
steamer, and then a God-forsaken journey of changes across
Scotland to Aberdeen and out to our friends at Williamston
where Alasdair was to stay until school began. Then the
nightmare journey back again to Oban and Iona – and back
to Lunga when the sea allowed.

Dougal and I were busy while she was away and managed
quite well for ourselves except that I put too much Hol-
brook's Sauce in a rabbit stew one day and nearly took the
skin off our throats.

We explored a cave on the south-west coast of the island
and found that the cave came in from the sea's edge to a
great hole in the middle of the southern half of Lunga. The
floor was thick with pigeon-droppings accumulated during
countless years, and even now there were two young rock

doves on a ledge, not quite fledged. We could not resist taking these home to see how they shaped as pets, but we paid dearly enough for succumbing to this temptation. They would not feed themselves yet, of course, nor did they much like pellets being thrust into their crops with a little stick we smoothed for the job. Eagerness to be fed made them no easier to feed, and we never gave up until their crops bulged with oatmeal and tinned milk. Nevertheless, the pigeons throve and fledged and ultimately flew, but they would not feed on the pellets we threw down for them; instead they would fly into the tent, sit on our knees and beg, and then be awkward when we put food into their mouths. They began to peck about outside in the grass as the days went by, studiously avoiding anything thrown there by us. Each night they came to a box we put for them near the store tent, but when we had drained a hollow a few yards away and moved the tents down there, the pigeons were quite upset and would not come to the new place though tents and box fulfilled the earlier conditions. It showed once more how significant in a bird's view of things is a particular point in space, and the irrelevance of previously relevant objects moved but a short distance from the former positions. This change seemed to snap the personal link between the pigeons and ourselves, for they came no more for food and were much wilder. Thus, our rock doves returned to their natural habitat good and strong on the wing and less likely to be snapped up by the peregrine falcon than if they had emerged naturally from their cave so late in the year.

We were surprised to hear a launch below us just after lunch on Friday, September 17th, and running to the edge of the cliff we saw Bobbie in Ian Mackenzie's big launch. By Jove, I was glad; fancy getting back here in four days; it was a grand performance. Dougal and I ran down to meet her and listened to a long story of an awkward journey. What struck me most was that she had received much kindness from *individuals* of the railway staff, usually when exceeding their duties, and extraordinary wooden-headedness and even discourtesy when in contact with the railway company as an

A young herring gull

One of the primitive crosses of native hornblende gneiss in the burial ground
on North Rona, now at the bottom of the sea after some Niseach thought
evidence of Popery should be removed from Rona

Guillemots and kittiwakes on North Rona

Kittiwakes nesting at Ailsa Craig

A fulmar petrel and her chick

'Did you say you had come all the way to North Rona to see us?'

Seals play in the Atlantic surf on the west side of North Rona

Cow and bull grey seals courting, North Rona

At the end of the breeding season, the bull seals are wrecks of their earlier magnificence, being now thin, scarred and bleary-eyed

A one-day-old Atlantic seal calf

The camp on Lunga of the Treshnish Isles

A wild day on North Rona

organization. It is a phenomenon not confined to railway companies. There are, for example, magnificent fellows in the Civil Service, really big minds, but as an organization they are often exasperating. Even learned societies suffer from the same disease, in that members as individuals have rangey, fluid, liberated minds, but when they act as a committee, their personalities freeze. My own technique for getting anything done nowadays is to short-circuit committees and take lunch instead. I am not alone in developing this technique; there is more done and decided over a lunch between two or three people these days than by large committees. But you cannot practise the idea so easily on a railway company.

Exactly two days after her return Bobbie felt ill – really ill, because she went to bed. Next day she was worse and very feverish. She had brought back scarlet fever. This ran a flaming course for nearly a week, during which time she grew very thin. We had no invalid diet for her, and on this expedition we were making soda bread because we had not yet learnt of the dried flaked yeast which we were later able to obtain from the Distillers' Company. We were also using tinned margarine, which keeps better than butter, but is not so appetizing. The poor girl could eat little or nothing.

All this time the wind was blowing hard from the southeast and south, directly on the tents. These two winds are always unpleasant ones in this part of the world, and at this time they were more nerve-wearing than ever. Oh how I wished it to be calm to give Bobbie a bit of peace, but no, it just kept on blowing hard. I was very troubled. Ought I to put up a flare and get help, supposing a launch would come in these high seas? What was the good anyway? Looked at from the social point of view, Bobbie was at least in a natural isolation hospital, and as for her as an individual she was better where she was than being carried away. What does the treatment for this kind of disease boil down to in the end? Waiting till the fever has run its course and keeping the patient open and warm. So Bobbie endured her adversity and said she felt much better a week later; then she began the characteristic peeling of the skin, but she got none of the pumice-stoning of the soles of her feet which is my chief remembrance of convalescence in childhood. I was much relieved when she stood on her feet once more.

The danger of scarlet fever is in its sequelae: no sooner had Bobbie begun to feel a little better than I came in one morning to find her in great pain in her ear. This troubled me far more than the scarlet fever, because this might mean a complication we could not relieve. That afternoon I put her to bed again with nearly a quarter of a pint of rum inside her. She has told me since of the blessed feeling of disassociation it brought her, and I crept about quieter than a mouse for the three hours she was asleep as a result of my dose. Then, of course, the pain came back when she awoke, but I did not wish to use more rum until last thing at night, because its effects would obviously lessen and a system full of alcohol is being handicapped in setting its house in order. But severe pain is also dangerous, so I immobilized poor Bobbie with rum for those dreadful hours of the early morning when pain is at its worst and hope is lowest. Dougal is a veterinary surgeon, and in advising against any interference with the ear in the way of pouring in olive oil or hydrogen peroxide, held out the hope that if it was an abscess of the external ear it should burst soon. We gave Bobbie hot bottles to put to her head and these helped a little.

Then suddenly at ten o'clock the next night she felt a quick relief from pain and pus began to flow from her ear. It was as if pressure had been lifted from the whole camp. Now at least we knew that the trouble was not in the inner ear, Bobbie was out of pain and time should put her right. And so it did. Gradually, very gradually, she grew strong again, and seemed completely herself by the end of October. Good air, fresh fish and rabbits and winkles must have helped her. I still think I did right to keep her on the island (and she herself refused to leave it), but there are some people who think me a callous devil.

Whenever the wind let us, Dougal and I would make little expeditions about the islands in search of information. There was Sgeir nan Erionnach and Sgeir nan Giusach, between which ran a shallow channel where the water showed green above the white sand. Dougal thought he could get flat fish there, but the current ran at about three knots and he was no sooner set for fishing than he was carried out at the south end.

This continual and rapid current must have been the reason why no seals bred on Sgeir nan Erionnach, a point which always puzzled me until I knew the rate of drift, for the shoreline was perfect for the young seals and the water appeared calm in every wind. It was while we were poking around those skerries one day that we saw a score or more of common seals lying out on a rock. This was their chosen territory, and we never saw them in the waters round Lunga. They looked very small now that we had become accustomed to the Atlantic grey seals.

There was another day when we thought Bobbie fit to leave for the time it would take us to get to Fladda and back. It was beautifully calm when we pulled into the southern anchorage of that queer little island. Apart from that low-lying neck between the north and south anchorages, Fladda is a plateau about forty feet above the sea, bounded by small sheer cliffs, and, unlike the rest of the Treshnish Isles, has a poor herbage containing more sedge and rinze heather than grass. We explored the island clockwise, and it was for that reason we did not come upon a little bay on the south side until last. There we found great quantities of brambles and Dougal and I stayed much longer than we ought to have done, picking them as hard as we could, filling handkerchiefs and scarves with the welcome fruit. We took back nearly half a stone for our trouble, but the sea was whipping up white with a north wind so that we had rather an anxious journey with the Water Beetle. Bobbie was also anxious, wondering why we did not come when the wind freshened. The sight of the fresh fruit happily eased our path towards a lunch kept waiting.

The year was changing, and that more obviously when we had a respite from the wind. October 4th was a lovely

autumn day of sunshine, marvellously peaceful to us who
were ridden by wind and rain. It was the high spring tide at
the new moon of the autumn equinox, and it drew me to the
south end that evening, to see how the young seals would be
faring on the erosion platform. The year was dying, and
comfortable as the sunshine had been, there had been that
golden quality in it which spoke of the failing light. As I
walked down that flat plateau the sun was setting behind the
southernmost point of Tiree, whereas it fell behind Coll
when we first came. Where there are trees, I thought, the
leaves will be browning, but still the year will have a
graciousness as of summer. Here there were no leaves to
brown and the signs of coming winter were of harder kind.
Already the grass was withering and the stems bleaching, so
that on a dry day the landscape was turning from green to
light buff and many shades of brown. There is a cold dignity
in the way the little islands accept the coming of winter. We
noticed it on Clerach and now here; this night it surged
through me going along in the half-light. A flock of peewits
rose, calling ahead of me, and here and there snipe flew from
the edge of little pools and zigzagged into the gloaming. The
grass was dark as I came back and those irregular pools of
rainwater threw back the fine light of evening, and I was
reminded of those lines in my favourite hymn of *Lead,
kindly light*; this scene was ever in my child's eye as I
sang:

> 'O'er moor and fen, o'er crag and torrent, till
>   The night is gone.'

Down there at the seal nursery on the south end of Lunga
the surf was tremendous, and because of the high spring tide
reached over the erosion platform to the foot of the cliff.
Two well-grown calves were washed off their ledges into the
surf and were dashed unmercifully among the boulders.
Then a great wave lifted them high to the foot of the cliff;
they held on desperately while the swirl receded, and as soon
as the pull of the water released, made their way out of reach
of the next wave as quickly as they could move. A cow was

lying below her young calf, taking the force of the waves and preventing the little one being taken down in the backwash. A bull came out near her; for a moment I could see indecision in her face before she chose the wrong thing to do! While she went to drive the bull away, a wave took the calf far out, but happily the next one brought it back to almost the same place and the mother came back to her patient task of sheltering the calf. The encroaching sea had driven the seals on to a much smaller space than was their usual nursery ground, and it was a wild troubled scene upon which I looked down that night. The mighty sea.

I remember that the day after was one of bright sunshine and strong south-east wind, a bad day for seal-watching here. If I went to the south end of the island I should have to approach from the west side and have the sun in my face all the time. The seals, on the other hand, would detect my slightest movement. If I stayed on the cliff and looked over, there would be a vertical blast of air which would soon make my eyes run and further watching would be most unpleasant. It was also impossible with this wind to watch the seals on the west side in the tiny bays; they were all very wary there and the slightest puff of my scent would drive them into the sea in a panic. And at the north end I could not go to the edge of the sound because my scent was carried over directly to the seals on Creag a' Chaisteal. In fact, I did go down there for a few moments and their noses were up in no time trying to get a line on me. So I took up a position on the cliffs between Dun Cruit and the Dirty Inlet, where I lay out of the wind, in the sun and in sight of many seals.

The study of animal behaviour, at least of wild animals in their natural habitat, is an amusement which has not been followed much by your high-class scientist. Here is no set of experiments you can devise or timetable to which you can work. In short, the animal cannot be hurried, and if you are not getting on fast enough there is not much you can do about it. That is why lazy fellows built on my pattern find it a pleasant sort of existence. One thing is certain: if you can be patient and watch long enough you will get your story, and perhaps there is such a thing as having a *flair* for being at the right place at the right time. This *flair* might bear analysis and turn out to be the reaction of the mind working with long familiarity of animals, but to all intents and purposes it is intuitive and you have it or you have not.

This day I was lucky in seeing one thing I had never seen before. The mother of a calf in the Dirty Inlet went into the sea about half past three and when she was but a few yards from the shore I saw a quick movement by her on the floor of the sea. She came to the surface with a good-sized flat fish in her mouth. She rolled over and over in the water, and by the way the fish's tail kept flapping it seemed she had not yet bitten it hard, but was playing with it as a cat does with a mouse. In a minute or two she took the fish from her mouth with her right hand and held it horizontally, fingers upwards and knuckles outwards. Then she took a good bite out of the fish just as you and I (or perhaps only I) might from a large jam tart. Two bites more, still standing upright in the water, and then she took the fish in both hands, pushed it into her mouth and held her muzzle high until the tail gradually disappeared.

We had made an arrangement with Ian Mackenzie that we would go in his big launch to the Dutchman one day if the weather was fit. But that day which opened so full of promise for me ended miserably. Ian Mackenzie did not come because, as we found later, he was asked to move some cattle; but I, looking through my glass over the calm sea, saw another boat come from Iona and anchor off the Dutchman. The distance was three and three-quarter miles from where the boat lay to where I was on the Cruachan, the sun was in my eyes and there was a slight haze. But my glass is a good one and I can use it; I saw a dinghy pulled up on the flat rocks of the erosion platform at the south end of the Little Dutchman and figures of men coming towards it and going away again. Then I knew it must be a raid on the seals there. I saw the dinghy rowed towards the launch, and then a heavy mass which caught the glint of the sun pulled aboard. A figure carrying a gun walked along the skyline and came down to the platform between the Little Dutchman and Dutchman's Cap. Later I saw two men bending low for a long time, and they held something up at last and threw it down again. It was a sealskin. They were there altogether for five hours, and here was I on Lunga, helpless to stop this shameful thing.

Ian Mackenzie came next day to take us to the Dutchman, and as he wished to take some sheep from Cairn a' Burg we went there with him also. Cairn a' Burg Mor is an island of high cliffs all round, and on top are the remains of an old fortress where a MacLean chieftain used to retire in troublous times. One of them held out for three years against the Hanoverians after the Rebellion of 1715. Cairn a' Burg was considered as impregnable as Dumbarton Rock, and I suppose it was until heavy artillery changed the whole notion of impregnability. There is some fine masonry built into the cliff to make it impossible to climb, and we were amused to see the several dykes and wall built to hinder attack. The island feels a romantic place and full of history. The remains of the living-quarters of the fortress are on the flat top of the island, and there is also left the form of the old chapel and its altar stone. What a place this must have been in a battle! Imagine bearded gentlemen rolling rocks and pouring boiling water on to the invaders!

The grass is short and good, and the seven grey-faced lambs we took from the Blackface ewes were bigger than their mothers and very heavy. We found seven seal calves round the shores of Cairn a' Burg, and on the way over we noticed two calves on Sgeir an Fheoir, east of Sgeir nan Erionnach. These small nurseries all contain very young calves, or in other words, the larger nurseries begin breeding earlier.

We ran with the wind behind us to the east side of the Dutchman and did not have very much trouble getting ashore on the apparently flat expanse of rock between the Little Dutchman and Dutchman's Cap. Actually the rock is very much cut up and the passage is by no means easy. When the tide is dead-low it is possible to jump the channels between the rocks, but the tide was now past the ebb. There is a shelf of lava a few feet above sea-level all round the Little Dutchman, and on this we found nineteen calves. Not an adult was to be seen except an old bull in the water. We found several pools red with blood, and at another place we saw the blood had evidently pumped out of the wound into a pool and clotted here. Now, when the seal calves are a fortnight old they change from their white coat to a short, beautiful blue one in which they can go to sea. We thought it significant that among all these calves there was not a blue one.

We joined the launch again and landed a little farther north on the Dutchman's Cap. There were no seal calves here, nor did we expect to find any, for the sea washes the base of the cliffs. There is one way up the cliffs at the south end of the island and another at the north – ways good enough up which to get cattle on a calm day, but there are more days when you cannot land on this island than when you can. There was a fine white-capped sea coming from the north as we came back to Lunga, and the spray flew merrily from the bows. Life seemed better altogether today.

The night north wind persisted for a few days, and that meant good, fine weather. We woke on the following Sunday morning after having felt it cold in the night, though the temperature had not been lower than 44° F. I felt brimful of energy in this northerly breeze and sunshine, so promised myself a morning's close stalking down the west side, where the wind was just perfect for the job. I went down the cave from the top of the south end of the island, came out on the west shore and worked up to my seals. A day-old calf was on a rock ten feet beyond and slightly below me, and the mother was idling in the water. I just lay there waiting, the wind in my face and bright sun behind – the stalker's idea of heaven. The mother came out of the water on to the rock and arranged herself to feed the calf. I got a lovely series of photos, but was waiting particularly for a photograph of that scratching and fondling behaviour which almost invariably follows suckling.

The wind was cold; being so near, I could not move and the rock seemed like a spike-harrow and I got more and more uncomfortable. That calf was really lazy, for he went on feeding in a desultory way for three-quarters of an hour, and at the end of that the cow just slid into the sea. When I rose I fell over again, and it took me some time to straighten my limbs. Then I ran back to camp as hard as I could go, arriving warm and ready for the big, steamed bramble-pudding and custard which Bobbie had made. This again was living.

There was never a week passed without a gale or succession of gales, so that when the single calm and sunny pet days came along there was always a great temptation to lie at peace in the sun. October 20th was a day like that. Dougal was out early fishing, and I, after some time watching at the north end, thought I would go down to the Dorlinn to help him up with the boat. He had done this already when I got there, and I whistled him, not having seen him go back to camp. An answer came from behind me, and I looked up to see him lying at the top of a fortress-like rock which is north of the Dorlinn. I joined him succumbing to the old urge of the sun, and we talked lazily of the affairs of the world. The seals went unwatched, except one which had a calf near the boat – a yellow-throated cow, blind in one eye and as nervous as a cat.

'It seems to me,' said Dougal, 'though it is one of those things you hesitate to say in a sophisticated society, that it is doubtful whether all that is meant by art and culture is the right thing by which to judge a civilization, nor should it be considered one of the major ends to which a civilization moves. Surely the true criterion of a civilization and its aim should be the right behaviour of people one to another. If a society exists in which behaviour has reached a state of justice, mercy and rightness, and the pitch of individual sensitiveness is high, can it achieve a much higher state of civilization by technics? I doubt it. The art and culture part of it is a symptom of civilization, a kind of creative froth coming out of the beer. If the beer is inert, you get no froth, in which case the people will lack the social and civic sense I am talking about.'

And so we went on till it was almost time to go home to lunch and Dougal asked:

'How high would you say that cliff was?'

'Seventy feet,' I said.

'I should say not more than fifty.'

'Well now, in the interests of truth,' I said (but actually to prove myself right), 'I will go down to the foot of that cliff and stand upright, and as I am six feet three inches, you can take your pencil and reckon the height of the cliff.'

'Och, the labour of going down,' said Dougal, 'and it is just on lunchtime.'

But I went and stood there, and when I came back he was smiling.

'Ten times,' he said.

'Sixty-two feet six inches, then; that's two feet six inches on my side.'

'Hm, yes; but the error of technique doesn't really allow you to credit yourself with that.'

We then discussed the place of the analytical and synthetical types of mind in science, his being markedly the former and mine just as much the latter. We were agreed that the extreme of his type believed too little or would accept nothing, and got nowhere, and mine was too credulous and apt to build on evidence not sufficiently sifted. One tends to be pessimistic, the other optimistic.

A week later we had one of the loveliest days of the year after an intervening bad spell. The wind fell in the early hours of the morning and I rose before the sun appeared from behind Ben More Mull. The last clouds dispersed and the sun shone its full round. We sat on the summit of the Cruachan and examined afresh and in detail that great view I have described which runs the whole 360° of the compass. Applecross showed beyond the Ardnamurchan peninsula, and Ben Resipol in Sunart was deeply capped with a glinting snow. The lighthouse on Bernera at the extreme south of the Outer Hebrides was visible with the naked eye. Think of the pale blue of the sky, the general blue tint of the ring of land, and the deep blue of the sea; all seems blue, with a touch of green, white or brown here and there. And that night the sky was a dome of stars. Each one of the seven Pleiades was distinct, the Eagle shone in the south-west, and in the light of the Milky Way was the beautiful cruciform constellation of the Wild Swan. The grass beneath our feet was a silver carpet; the air, being so still, brought the crying of the seals to us undistorted, a more pleasing sound since the anxious maternal jealousy went out of it. We lived in a beautiful world and were thankful for it.

The seal nurseries were almost empty now and very few new calves were being born. As soon as the calves change coat from the white fluffy one of the first fortnight to the blue, sea-going coat, the cows cease to take interest in them, and the babies, now extremely fat, remain about the nurseries for another week or two, sleeping much and playing by themselves in the pools. Hunger must eventually call them to the sea. That afternoon I had gone down to the Dorlinn and sat beside a baby cow seal just over a month old, pale-blue coated and ready for the sea. She was lying on her back fast asleep with her hands lying open; hard places were forming on her palms where she pulled herself over the rocks. I looked at her a long time, gently stroking her silvery-white belly; it was cool, being insulated by the thick layer of fat; then I stroked the back of her hand and found it warm, for no layer of blubber covers that. Soon all my children would be gone. This little cow who now looked so fat and happy would not have been alive today had I not run into the surf of a westerly gale here on the day she was born. She was getting a terrible battering and would have been carried far out on the ebbing tide. How she had wriggled in my arms as I lifted her and ran for a safe place above the high-tide mark; and yet she had made no attempt to bite my ear, because she was only a few hours old and had not acquired the power of discriminating between big living things.

There had been a great immigration of thrushes and blackbirds to the island about this time, not dozens but

hundreds of birds. Every patch of cow-dung was well spread
by them as soon as it was stale enough to have gathered below
it the insect fauna characteristic of such an environment. A
ring ouzel or mountain blackbird was among them one day
at the end of October, and I was caused to pick him out by
the loud 'chacking' which I recognized to be his note and not
his cousins'.

Dougal was counting the number of flowers in bloom on
November 1st. There were primroses, violets, buttercups,
daisies, ragwort, chickweed, sow-thistle, wild sage, mayweed,
stonecrop, sea-pink, storksbill, bell heather, prunella, scab-
ious, a geranium-like flower I did not know, another little
low, pink flower and the rich blue flower with dull, blue-
green leaves which grows in the volcanic gravel almost down
at sea-level – eighteen in all. Summer lingers into winter in
this West if you will but seek her in tiny, hidden places.

And yet by the next night there was a full gale blowing
from the south-east. It was a bad dry gale which gave us the
worst night we had had since we had moved camp into the
brackeny hollow which Dougal had drained. The rain fell in
torrents with no slackening of the gale all day November
3rd. It was a spring tide this evening and we had pulled the
boat high because of it, but the surf was tremendous and
caused me a little anxiety. There had been a new calf born
the day before on the east side of the spit of shingle at the
north end of the island, a place which was getting the full
force of this gale. I saw the mother patiently engaged keeping on the low side of the calf to prevent its being washed
away. This is the time when you see the cow seals at their
best – all care for the babies; and their eyes soft with concern.

If it was a gale when we went to bed, it was a hurricane
later. I slept for an hour as soon as I got into bed, for I was
dog-tired, but then no more at all. The rain stopped at three
o'clock in the morning and I was sorry, because I knew the
tent would soon dry and I should have trouble getting the
guys tight again in this inferno. Trouble began at four
o'clock when the eave ripped from part of the windward side

of the tent. In half an hour another stretch of canvas had
gone, and the increased wind resistance which the tent now
offered was causing us concern. I felt, also, that I ought to go
down to the boat, because a spring tide on her shore with
such a gale might reach her. It was then approaching high
tide, and I wished she were well up at the Dorlinn instead of
at the north-east point where we had made an alternative
slip. I went down the cliff path at the north end of the island,
finding sudden breathing space there after having difficulty
in keeping my feet on the top. A thrush came up from the
ground and hit my electric lantern. I picked it up and placed
it in a bield under a rock, but the poor little soul had not
wits enough to stay there. It flew into the night, the wind
caught it and carried it towards the sound where the sea
roared, and I wished then I had kept the thrush in my
pocket until morning. The boat was all right, though the
spray was splashing into her and I could see the tide was
higher than we had ever seen it before. Then I went back to
the tent as fast as I could move, there to find the eave had
ripped off completely on the windward side, which was now
against the centre pole and cracking about us like a cannon.
Dougal now appeared and helped us get essentials from
inside while Bobbie went to the store tent and tried to make
room in there. Then we loosened the pole and let the tent go
before she ripped to ribbons. Both Dougal and I felt it
keenly, because this tent had been a good friend these two
years. Even now the guying system had worked perfectly
and disaster had come through the canvas itself giving way
and not by the tent blowing down.

By this time it was after six o'clock, so we made breakfast
in the cramped space available in the store tent. Plenty of
good porridge and endless tea. The sunrise was the most
wonderful I have ever seen – and the most dangerous. The
gale was blowing as hard as ever, and when I looked at this
riot of green and gold and steel-grey, with patches of bright
cobalt blue – a colour I had never seen in the sky before – I
knew we could expect no cessation yet. And I was right. All
through that day the gale blew, while we built a shelter of

driftwood and tarpaulins for the stores in the ruins of one of
the old houses. It was killing work carrying the stuff up there
in that wind because of the initial labour of keeping upright.
Bobbie had arranged things in the little bell tent which
would henceforth be our home, and I was immediately
struck by the snugness and tidiness. Women have a great
value at a base camp, for they can create the atmosphere of
home much sooner and more realistically than men can. I
had no anxiety about this tent, because it was smaller than
the other, new for this trip and of specially heavy material.

When I wrote my diary that night I said I was so sleepy
that I was doubtful if even this wind could keep me awake
much longer, and the next day there was this entry:

'I fell asleep soon after eight o'clock last night and knew
no more till one o'clock, when it was still blowing. Asleep
again and woke at 7.30 (6.30 Greenwich) to a blessed calm. I
just lay and enjoyed it for some time before making some
tea. When I had woken in the night I had noticed lulls of one
or two seconds' duration, which experience has told us are
the first signs of the finish of a gale. Well, today has been
lovely, the sea calming rapidly; in fact, it was good enough
weather to have our lunch outside in the sun. Such are the
day-to-day changes in the West Highland climate. I went
down in the morning to see the little calf on the shingle spit;
it was lying above the tide fast asleep, and its mother
watched me anxiously from the water's edge. She has done
well. Yesterday afternoon again, just on dusk as the tide had
approached the high mark, I had seen her at her patient task
of holding her baby to the land. She has done this through
four tides of a terrific gale and has been successful in saving
her calf ... There are still one or two mushrooms to be
had.'

That calf was as good-natured as its mother: I used to
play with it without evoking those explosive snorts which
are the youngsters' first line of defence, and the mother lay
in the shallows looking on. The bull that was with her was
also an old friend of mine. He had been there much longer

than she had, and I had often gone down to talk to him; if I walked up and down that stretch of shore he would come with me, a few yards away in the water. He also used to watch me playing with his mate's calf, and never once did he make that characteristic sign of fright and warning – to throw himself backwards half out of the sea and bring his hand down with a great resounding smack on the surface of the water. When a seal does this, all the rest in the vicinity are on the look-out for the cause of disturbance.

Another snorter of a south-easterly gale came a fortnight after the one described above. It blew all the night of November 16th, getting worse until gusts of terrific force were hitting the tent at five o'clock in the morning. There was a slight abatement after breakfast, but it strengthened during the day until dusk when it backed to the east and became a hurricane. Spray was being blown up the face of the cliffs below us and was falling on the tents. I thought I had better have a look at the boat, and Bobbie insisted on coming to the Dorlinn with me. The Dorlinn was acting as a funnel for the wind, and the spray was being driven through this steep-sided gap in much greater quantities than if there had been heavy rain. I left Bobbie in the lee of a rock and then had to bend double and push hard to get to the boat. My double-thickness Grenfell suit became wet through almost immediately. As I was lifting big stones into the boat Dougal appeared out of the half-light, he also having been struck with the same idea. We yelled at each other but could hear nothing, but I saw his face and knew he was enjoying himself as much as I was. It was magnificent. As soon as we got out of the Dorlinn the wind bellied our clothes and we were dry again by the time we reached camp. We had had to hold Bobbie between us going home because of the sheer force of wind coming up that eastern slope. Once back, we had a grand tea with strawberry jam.

The gale continued all that night with these terrible gusts which were worse than a fortnight before; it blew all next day as well, though not quite so strong. I wrote in my diary on November 19th:

'I said the wind was slackening as we went to bed last night, and so it was, but hardly had we lain down to sleep than a series of great gusts came, and after an hour or more the rain began. Of course I had to get out to slacken the guys, but with these gusts I could do no more than half-slacken with safety. Then another wait in bed until the tent tightened once more, and out again to slacken fully. A drink of tea at one o'clock and attempts to sleep. End of rain at three o'clock, but continuance of south-east wind which dried up the canvas and guys. Bobbie, the rascal, went out at five o'clock to tighten, I then not being in a sufficiently conscious state to know she had gone. Out again a little later myself to tighten fully, and then some sleep until eight o'clock. Three nights of this sort of thing have made us look a trifle grey about the face, and yet we know how much we have to be thankful for. As I write, lying here in a warm, dry bed, the wind has gone round to north and fallen light, and the tent is in calm. All the cloud had blown away before I came in last thing and the moon had risen into a fine sky. The sea is a sheet of silver tonight, and the old grey rocks of the island are silver too in this light. How bright the lights of the lighthouses gleam! We were up the hill watching them tonight – Ardnamurchan, two flashes every twenty seconds; Dhu Artach, two every thirty seconds; and Skerryvore, one every twenty seconds. Such is the land of change in which we live: last night we could hear only the howl of the wind, its thunder on our tent, and the roar of the sea below. Tonight the sea but murmurs, the wild geese talk as they settle to graze on Creag a' Chaisteal and Sgeir nan Erionnach, and the cheerful note of the snipe reaches us as the birds come down near the tent. With the misery of last night so near, I say at this moment that life is good, whatever the morrow may bring.'

And then for those last days of November, and our last days on the island as it turned out, we had lovely winter weather which we enjoyed almost more than any other time. Bobbie was as fit as a fiddle once more and living every minute outside, our work for the season was about done and we had a better story than we had hoped to get. There was ample food and we had the appetites to eat plenty. Our main memory of this period is the leisurely way in which we were able to do things, such as washing and shaving – even going the length of a bath. And we remember the lovely sunsets which we used to watch from the Cruachan. At first the sky would be a blaze of gold, then the red came into it as the sun fell slightly to the west of the Dutchman. At the edge of the lighted sky and the blue there was a patch of mother-of-pearl cloud of the finest texture. The upper thousand-foot cone of Ben More Mull was white with snow and now made roseate by the reflection from the south-west. How can I describe adequately the multitudes of tints from violet, vermilion to red, rose and yellow which composed this great expanse of sea, land and sky?

I did not know when I wrote it that the ship was coming next day and that this would be the last entry in my Treshnish diary of those last November days:

'Tonight the starlight is wonderful and the air is very still. Long swells are booming rhythmically out east of us on Sgeiran Mor. One or two seals are crying full and clear, and I know what a nostalgic sound this will be for me now. It will go along with those of the barnacle and grey lag geese – noises that will stir me for the rest of my life and call me back to the islands. Indeed, this music of living things is becoming symphonic in the halls of my mind, and it moves me ever more deeply.'

I nipped out of the tent the following morning while the others were still sitting over breakfast, and I saw a speck in the sea off the Point of Ardnamurchan. It was a ship, of course, but the interesting thing to me was that we rarely saw a ship in that position and end on. I ran into the tent again and announced that the cruiser was coming for us.

Bobbie groaned, oh *no*! and Dougal just grinned, frankly incredulous, how did I know? Well, there was the ship off Ardnamurchan. But that doesn't mean to say it's the cruiser. No, but it is all the same – give me my telescope. With the aid of my glass I could see the ship was coming south and she was battleship-grey, though no other distinguishing marks were visible at that distance.

This was terrible, we expected to be here for another fortnight. We washed and shaved and packed and packed as hard as we could go. The ship was under Lunga two hours later and giving us a shout on her siren. I ran down to the launch which came off, and an officer I had not met before asked me how long we should be. Two hours, I said, and suggested he might drop a few men to save time carrying down. Several of our old friends now came ashore and were eager to know how we had fared these months.

Some of that final packing was not as neat as when we came to Lunga, and any inquisitive archaeologist of the future will find some weird junk rammed far down the rabbit-holes of that flat ground near the old houses. But we were aboard the cruiser in just over two hours and I did not let myself look back at the scene I had come to love.

When we climbed aboard it was not Captain M—r who greeted us but Captain P. We went down to lunch immediately, lots of fried haddock, and while we were eating Captain P. seemed most apologetic about not having come sooner. He said he looked in the log and saw when we had been landed in August and had come immediately.

'Don't worry,' we said; 'we had not expected to leave for at least another fortnight, and, in fact, we were a little disappointed to see you coming down the way today.'

But he still seemed to think it was an awful thing to have been left so long. It was calm going all the way, and once we were in the Sound of Mull we all had magnificent hot baths. What luxury!

We left the ship at Oban at about seven o'clock that evening. There was a drizzle of rain, and to our eyes and noses the town was a filthy place. Captain P. insisted on one sailor coming to carry our bag to the hotel where we were going to spend the night, and as he would not take no, we suffered having the little bag carried till we were into the darkness, then we relieved the sailor of it quickly, for we knew he had

designs on the cinema that evening. It galls me dreadfully to
have anyone carry my bag when I am well able to carry it
myself.

The hotel was almost empty, of course; it was centrally
heated, and the management evidently aimed at making
patrons *comfortable*. Dougal said 'phew' and went to the
flicks. Bobbie and I wandered about trying to find a cool
place, but for that we had to go out on the streets in the
drizzle and they were most depressing. We went to bed early,
pushed back all the curtains from the windows and folded
back the eiderdown. But the mattress seemed to rise all
round us until we were enveloped in a fulsome softness. I
finished the night on the floor in moderate comfort. The
bacon-and-egg breakfast seemed a heavy meal to us who
feed lightly in the morning, the walls and ceilings were
suffocating and the furnishings were ponderous after being
used to our lighter occasional table by Tate and Lyle. It was
good to get outside.

We unloaded our gear from the ship, put some on the rail
to be sent home, fetched the car from the garage and once
more grossly ill-treated it by overloading. It was just as full,
but not quite as heavy, as when we came, but now Dougal
was in front with Bobbie and me instead of Alasdair, and
there was not much room to spare. I felt we should never get
out of Oban, for there were many little odd jobs to do, and
on the hill going out of the town two plugs were misfiring. I
never lift the bonnet of a car if I can help it, but Dougal
patiently removed all the plugs, thoroughly cleaned them
and put them back. And, of course, they gave no more
trouble.

It is rather a narrow and bumpy road from Oban to the
foot of the Great Glen, and there was also a good deal of
rain, so that the first part of the journey seemed interminable, and to me tiring. Then the good new road made
driving much easier and it was a fine afternoon. When we
reached Invermoriston, Dougal said:

'Stop here and have tea on me.'

And a good tea it was. The hotel was empty at this time of

year, and the cases of salmon flies looked strangely like the decorations of some long-past festival.

We pushed on refreshed, and I decided to have a smack at the Kiltarlity road from Drumnadrochit. Bobbie swore I should never get up and that it would waste time, but when we got on to the hill I asked them to be ready to jump out as I said so. First Dougal went, then Bobbie, and at each lightening the car gathered herself for another effort, but I had to stop a hundred yards from the top and heave off two or three cases, which Dougal and Bobbie carried up behind me.

It was about dark when we reached Beauly, and it was after that we all began to feel tired. Would there ever be an end, I wondered, to the Dirie Mor and the home road over Feighan? On and on in the darkness, all of us singing Christmas carols until we were hoarse. Then down that last bit till we saw the lights of Corriehallie. Bobbie had wired the Morrisons from Oban, and these good folk had prepared an enormous meal for us. We seemed to go on eating and talking for hours.

How lovely seemed the trees of Brae next day, and the wood-smoke of the great fires we made to air the house and bedding! We had a fortnight more of Dougal's companionship, and because the Feighan road was blocked with snow we took him over the hill to Ullapool and there we said goodbye for the present. He was going to America.

CHAPTER NINE

NEARING THE GOAL

THE FIRST TIME I EVER set eyes on North Rona 'afar off in the lap of wild ocean' was from the summit cairn of An Teallach, from which place I was also looking down on the Brae House. And since those long years ago I have also seen An Teallach from North Rona, so you can understand how inextricably linked are all these places in my heart. As I lie here in my study on Tanera, the prisoner of a broken leg, I can see the summit of An Teallach also, and Suilven, whose peculiar lines were easily picked out from North Rona when a clear day allowed us to see as far as here.

But to return to my first glimpse of Rona: it was early morning of a June day, a time when Highland weather is often clear and dry, and at this hour the heat haze was not dancing to prevent my seeing through the telescope a small speck in the sea a hundred miles away. Just a speck with an apparently rounded top; there was no detail to be seen, but as it did not move from the absolute direction in which North Rona should be, I felt satisfied I had seen that island, which occupies less than half a square mile, attaining a height of three hundred and fifty-five feet and lying in the North Atlantic forty-seven miles north-west of Cape Wrath and forty-seven miles north-east of the Butt of Lewis.

I remember thinking that morning that the day would come when I should go ashore on North Rona, though at that time I had not thought overmuch of grey seals, nor even of going to live on Eilean a' Chleirich. I was busy observing the life and social affairs of the red deer in the wild country around An Teallach. But as that work developed I naturally began to think of the social life of other gregarious animals, that of the grey seal among them. How was their sociality ordered, and how did it compare with that of these deer?

Thus North Rona took more definite shape in my mind and I gleaned every bit of information I could find. *Ronay*, by Malcolm Stewart (Oxford, 1933), was immensely useful, and few of my books are more thumbed than that one, for, contrary to my usual finnicky care of books, I boldly used the wide margins of this for pencilled notes relating to the expedition. Stewart had spent two short periods of a week or more each on North Rona and had scoured the literature. This little book of his not only describes Rona but Sula Sgeir and the Flannan Isles as well, and gives bibliography for each. I also met and corresponded with John Ainslie, who, with Robert Atkinson, did a fine piece of research on Leach's fork-tailed petrel during a six weeks' spell on North Rona in the summer of 1936. Stewart and Ainslie, both hard lads, looked at us rather sadly over our projected stay of six months. 'A little fun, Josephine,' they seemed to say, 'but not that.'

It had certainly been rather a blow for both Dougal and us when he had to go to America, for he had been part of the scheme for so long. Several older groups of friends pointedly advised us that we ought to take another man for a trip of this order. But we knew enough of island life not to enter on such folly as taking another party we did not know well. There was also the question of the child. What madness! people said. If we did not take him with us, where else was he to go? And both Bobbie and I felt that we were not justified in depriving him of this experience. Alasdair had been on the other trips and had learned a sense of responsibility, so he could come on this and take his chance. It is a decision we have never regretted, and for him Rona is a treasured memory for life.

The boy's coming, and the fact that we were persuaded against our better judgement to take wireless transmitting and receiving gear, let us in for an awful lot of publicity in the newspaper Press. Even one or two of the London dailies printed a lot of nonsense about us. Their great aim, it seemed, was to create a scare about us. One of those so-called national daily newspapers with hotted-up circulations sent two men by car all the way to Dundonnell to 'get the story'. The weather had been consistently against us just then, otherwise those two professional 'snoopers', as I believe they are called, would have found us gone.

I curbed my initial impulse to refuse to see these fellows. Instead I gave them tea, briefly outlining why I was going to North Rona. One of them was a Yorkshireman, and straight-spoken to the effect that he said they wanted thrills.

'Yes, but I don't,' I said. 'Why not stick to the facts?'

'But the public wants a thrill. You're topical till Christmas, and while we don't wish you any harm, we'd like something or other to happen.'

So when we were well out of the way on Rona they and many other newspapers made up all sorts of cock-and-bull stories. I have endured this sort of thing more than most people, and academically a research worker suffers from this unwanted attention. How different were my good friends *The Glasgow Herald*, who printed a plain story and accepted my own articles and pictures. I would say outright that their courteous interest in the expedition helped me considerably with expenses, for I, like other expeditions, was short of money.

There was one delightful example of reporting, when we went to the Treshnish Isles.

'Are you taking a wireless?' asked the reporter.

'No, no wireless.'

'Not even a receiving set?'

'No, no wireless whatever.'

Imagine my feelings, therefore, when I was later sent a page from a newspaper announcing that 'scientist tries radio swing music on seals!'

But this takes me away from the preparations for Rona.

We had decided on two wooden huts, one ten feet by eight feet and the other seven feet by five feet, for our habitations and store space. They were made in very small sections and to a light specification by Messrs Cowiesons of Glasgow. Those huts stood up to terrific wind pressure, and though we saw the roof and front bend inwards in the gusts from time to time, they never gave us serious anxiety. They were intact when we returned to Rona in June, 1939, and if this wretched war ever ends, we still hope to live in them again in the continuance of our work.

We also bought a second-hand railway truck cover. These heavy tarpaulins are certainly not campers' gear, but they make an excellent buffer against the rain and spray on an expedition like ours. If it happens to be raining when the stuff is landed and before the huts are erected, the tarpaulin prevents rust, and we ourselves could use it as a shelter of a semi-permanent character if we found ourselves in difficulties. That cover has been consistently useful.

All our grocery stores were packed by Messrs William Dickson and Sons of Edinburgh in wooden boxes weighing not more than forty pounds each. This firm also tacked a label to each case giving a list of the contents, a course which saved us a lot of trouble when stowing the stores in the hut. The flour and meal had been purchased in half-boll (five-stone) sacks which were put inside proofed canvas bags made for us by Messrs Thomas Black and Sons of Greenock. The flour kept perfectly throughout the six months on Rona despite the saturated atmosphere during the last two months. As we went in July and did not expect any contact with the outside world, it may be realized that potatoes were rather a problem. Earlies would not keep long and no main-crop varieties were available at that time. So we got several cases of Chivers' tinned new potatoes and found them very good. We also had tinned vegetables of various kinds of this firm's packing. The vitamin content of these tinned vegetables is reckoned to be greater than that of the fresh greens cooked by ordinary household methods.

A Belfast ham gave us a series of magnificent dinners, cooked in North Country fashion, ie, a thick slice through the ham baked in the oven, with eggs. One experiment in the stores was highly successful – Walls' tinned sausages. We thought these better than fresh sausages, and always looked forward to the one day a fortnight when they appeared, removed from the tin and fried.

Messrs Maypole Dairy Company supplied butter, margarine and cooking fat in three-and-a-half-pound tins. The trouble they took over our order made us grateful to them, and everything kept perfectly.

From long experience we reckon our paraffin consumption at two gallons a week or rather less, certainly less in summer. We took seventy-five gallons to Rona, enough to have seen us right through the winter if we could not have been relieved. Messrs John Macrae and Sons of Dingwall washed out fifteen five-gallon oil drums and supplied the paraffin in them to Badantarbat pier. We had no trouble landing these on Rona, and had one or two fallen into the sea they should not have sunk, theoretically, but they were not put to the test anyway.

We had decided to make Tanera our base because of the excellent anchorage which would allow us to load up in calm water, and it is sixteen miles nearer Rona than Dundonnell. There were several points to check over on the mainland, so Bobbie and I came back from Tanera to Dundonnell by boat a fortnight before July 11th, the date set for going to Rona. We fetched Alasdair from school and all of us went to Edinburgh for a last tinkering at our teeth, for I am more afraid of toothache than anything else. I also got my photographic gear complete and bought an automatic flash-bulb outfit for my Leica, having in mind a few shots at the Leach's fork-tailed petrels flying at night-time.

We reached Dundonnell again with the car overloaded as usual, and with plenty of time to spare to let us get back to Tanera. But the weather had us beaten completely. Heavy rain and south-westerly gales were incessant all the early part of July, and the Little Loch Broom looked black with the peaty water from the hills when I went out each evening to pump out the launch which was lying on the mooring by the boathouse. One evening suddenly became fine and rather calmer, so I went down, or more correctly was going down, to the boathouse with a very heavy load of flour, cement and everything else, and I think we might even have chanced the run to Tanera that night. But that was not to be. Two miles from the Brae House, we pulled in to the side of the road to let pass a woman in an Opel car – she looked the sort that needs a lot of room on the road. We then felt a lurch to the left and our car was on its side in the ditch and Alasdair and I on top of Bobbie. The earth and stone road had become weakened by the rains and had given way under our over-loaded wheels on its edge.

What a job! Everything to be unloaded, help to get, and worst of all, my proud record gone of never having been ditched. Alec Maclean came along from the hotel with his car and gave me the *coup de grâce* by saying 'What are *you* doing in the ditch, Doc?' All because of bad weather and a little Opel car.

But the road in July is full of cars, and very soon a nice crowd of medical students from London came along and our combined strength put the old Ford on the road again. Nothing was damaged, for the car had just subsided into the ditch with no forward momentum.

July 11th was a Monday, but we were still at Dundonnell on the Sunday morning, with the weather unfit to take such precious gear as flour, meal and bedding round Cailleach Head in an open launch. I felt reduced at this late moment to the necessity of sending a reply-paid radiotelegram to the cruiser, asking the Captain to call in Little Loch Broom the following morning on his way to Tanera.

Gentle Reader, learn by my experience and never try to send a radiotelegram in Scotland on a Sunday. In the first place, the Dundonnell post office was completely floored by such an unprecedented request. That well-known and indispensable compendium the *Post Office Guide* was lying on the bench, and with the utmost difficulty the approximate method of procedure was decided. The *Guide* advised sending the radiotelegram by way of the wireless telegraph station nearest the ship. Good; but where was the ship? We also found there was no West Coast station other than Port-patrick, which is at the most south-westerly point of Scot-land. Wick was much nearer, but on the East Coast. Personally I fancied Wick, but Mistress C. was for backing Portpatrick; and then I caught sight of an instruction which said, if in doubt of a ship's whereabouts put 'Wireless'. So I said make it 'Wireless', but I think the euphony and Celtic glamour of the name Portpatrick was too much for Mistress C., for that wretched missive disturbed the air of Port-patrick, Malin Head and the whole West Highland Coast for another twenty-four hours.

I was not satisfied about the radiotelegram at all, so on Sunday evening I went down to the hotel to telephone for information about it. I was never more tired in my life than when I staggered out of there at eleven o'clock with no more news than when I began. First I rang the Inverness office; long wait; oh no, nothing could be verified there, it was Aberdeen I should try. Get Aberdeen; a nice little man replies and goes through a big pile of telegrams; yes, here it was, the message had been sent forth. Quite, but had it got there? Well, couldn't just say that. Was there anywhere I could find out? No, not on a Sunday night, but ring again in an hour. And so on, but no news came.

We were up early the following morning and I was at the post office by eight o'clock, to find no reply from the ship and she was not in the Loch and nothing could be done till nine o'clock. I rang up Inverness again then and asked if that radiotelegram had reached the ship. Had I been told it had not done so? No. Well then, it had, I was told pretty shortly. This may be post-office logic, but it did not satisfy me and I said so. The lady at the other end rang off.

There was one bright spot this morning; the weather was sunny and calm, so we brought our final lot of stuff down to the boathouse, loaded the launch and set out for Tanera as fast as we could. A ship appeared just beyond Clerach as we rounded Cailleach Head, and it was heading towards Little Loch Broom, which caused me some indecision. Ought I to go that way and make sure it was not the cruiser? —

because if it came into the Loch according to my radiotelegram and we had gone to Tanera there would be another
fuss. We went a mile or two towards Clerach and then saw
the ship turn northwards, obviously a trawler. Splendid; we
made for Tanera as fast as we could without shipping
spray.

The cruiser was there in Tanera Anchorage as we came in
just before one o'clock, and by George, I was thankful. Now
then, thought I, we will at least do the things well which are
within our control, even if the weather and radiotelegrams
are not. Alasdair went to the bows with the boathook and
stood smart and ready; I knelt at the engine and Bobbie took
the tiller. We came alongside the cruiser faultlessly under
the eyes of officers and men leaning over the side. We just
had to do this well for our own pride, even though those men
on board were the kindest on earth.

We shook hands with Cap'n M., as he came to be always
known to us, and with those of his officers present, and then
the Captain said he had just a minute or two before received
a radio message from us and was about to weigh anchor and
come to Little Loch Broom. That message, he said, had cost
him most of a night's sleep, for someone had been trying
to get him at all hours. Ultimately this message had come
from Malin Head and had been relayed from another
cruiser. Formalities over, the sailors came over the side to
strip our launch of its cargo. The Captain saw our three
hens, ancient and hardy heroines of our earlier island expeditions.

'Ah!' said Cap'n M. 'Hand those up to me.'

If an animal is in charge of a sailor you can forget about it,
for it will be well looked after henceforth. Those hens of
ours were soon living like fighting-cocks. They were installed
in a large, cylindrical lobster creel taken from a poaching
Brittany smack, and were surrounded with a quantity and
variety of food which would have kept those old harridans
for a month. Late that evening I found Cap'n M., leaning
over the side of the ship asking my one neighbour on Tanera,
James Macleod, to fetch half a bucket of gravel from the

shore. I think James was a little mystified and so was I, but when the stuff came alongside, the Captain took the bucket himself and leaned over confidentially.

'Hens must have grit, you know,' he said.

We worked hard all afternoon checking everything aboard, and were able to take things a little easier after tea. The Chief Engineer thought Alasdair and I needed a haircut, an opinion loudly endorsed by Bobbie, so there was nothing for it but to give in, sit on deck with the tablecloth round our necks and be clipped by the Chief. There was no doubt about it, he made a fine job of two unruly mops. Bobbie played deck-quoits and Alasdair shuffle-board, and I reeled off a last batch of letters. Last for six months I was telling myself joyfully, but in that I was too optimistic. Correspondence haunts me like a dark and persistent spectre.

I was deep in my first sleep that night when a sailor woke me to say Donnie Fraser was on deck asking to see me. I groaned and staggered out. There was Donnie supping a pint of hot tea and eating a sandwich given him by the crew; between the hearty gustatory sounds I gathered that I had forgotten to return the mail bags to Achiltibuie when we had collected two sacksful that afternoon, and he rowed over between midnight and one o'clock to fetch them for Mrs Macleod, the postmistress.

I could not get to sleep again, tired as I was, and just before two o'clock the engines started with a horrible rasping sound. Then the anchor was drawn, and with that characteristic jerk of a Diesel engine in a small ship we were away, steaming northwards at twelve and a half knots. This ship was built to look like a trawler, so the cabins below have no portholes or direct access to the open air. But beggars cannot be choosers, and I lay in moderate comfort until the ship was north of the Butt of Lewis, where the open Atlantic swell made her pitch and roll unpleasantly in a short, lively action. I choked back three bouts of sickness by lying absolutely still and exerting terrific will-power. Alasdair foolishly rose at six o'clock and went on deck, after which he was sick several times – the first bout of his life. It seems that this ship has turned up many a good man who has never been sick before. Bobbie was all right as usual and made up for my helplessness. I staggered on deck at the last possible moment when we were three or four miles from Rona. Will-power was no good now against anti-peristalsis.

All the same, cold and rainy as it was that early morning, and wretched as I felt, that first close glimpse of Rona thrilled me. Here was the speck in the sea at last. A noble shape she was, of rounded hill and sheer cliff on the east, sloping away to sea-level at the south-west; how green her mantle, and the band of white surf played along the black foot of her cliffs! I knew little more until I heard the engine bell ring for half-speed, dead slow and then stop. We were in the east bay of Rona and my spirit rose above seasickness, for it is the wonder of that first view that has remained. My heart was full of sheer joy. But immediately the great practical question leapt into my mind – should we be able to land on this island which is notoriously bad for landing? For the moment that was not my business, and wonder returned as I looked at the hundreds of thousands of sea birds which flew from the cliffs, startled by this most unusual advent of humanity and a ship.

It was tremendous and awe-inspiring. The swarms of puffins, guillemots and razorbills circled like bees from the hive of the cliff; kittiwakes flashed white from every coign of the rock-face which would hold a nest, and fulmar petrels glided silently on motionless wings like small monoplanes. Shags flew hither and thither, black and cumbrous compared with the grace of the smaller birds. The sound of it all was the most thrilling a bird-watcher knows – the composite skirl of a million throats proclaiming that it is summer. All I could think in that moment of wonder was – and we are going to live here and know every bit of this place as if it were home. After all, it was home.

Then I had to become more practical, for I alone knew just where the landing was. Cap'n M. said Alasdair and I were to go ashore first trip and take a certain amount of food with us as well as a little tent. This was an island with a sin-

ister history and he was taking no chances. The launch
was down now, and soon we were bobbing over to Geodha
Stoth on the eastern side of the northern peninsula of Fianuis.
There was certainly as much swell as we liked against those
low cliffs, but we saw one face where the swell did not break,
and being sheer it was almost like a dock. Many are the times
I have watched that curious place since then; you can land
there in quietness when as little as ten yards away the state
of the sea would make it impossible.

We sidled up to that rock carefully and I pushed Alasdair
ashore. It was a little gesture it pleased me to make, that the
child should be the first of the expedition to land on Rona.
I followed him and took the tent and stores thrown up by the
launch, which then cast off and went back to the ship.

Forty or fifty grey seals in an excited state came round
the boat and maintained a lively interest in us throughout
the day. I looked at them as beasts I now knew better than
most men. These individuals had never seen me before,
but fancy put it into my mind as I looked into their deep
eyes that they knew me for a friend and as one who knew
their language and civilization, though imperfectly. Those
sleek heads did not show fear.

Once ashore, it was for me to give up fancies and find the
right place for a permanent camp in the shortest possible time
before the launch came again. I chose the little sheep fank
at the narrowest part of the neck of Fianuis. If these dykes
have endured, I thought, it would not seem that the sea
comes right over, though at that moment the western ocean
was pounding the fifty-foot cliffs only forty yards away.
Also, these walls could be raised a little and would provide
shelter all round the base of the huts. My decision thus
rapidly made was one we never had cause to regret.

When people have looked at the map of Rona since our
return they have often said:

'But why did you not go into the middle of the island
where we see there are some ruins marked?'

The answer is this: Fianuis is only fifty feet high and the
journey from the fank to Geodha Stoth is one of a hundred

yards. Southwards from the sheep fank the ground rises very steeply to the three hundred foot ridge of the island. The ruins are a good way below the ridge on the south side. About once in a blue moon a man may jump ashore on the south coast of the island and then climb a hundred feet of bare rock to get on to the green. This was not one of those days, and even if it had been, we would not have got all our heavy gear up the southern cliffs. Ours was not a light camping on the island for a week, but a family expecting to stay six months and possibly longer. There was nowhere else for it but the fank on Fianuis, though we knew well we should long for the security of the middle of the island. Finally, the weather and possibilities of landing are so changeable that we could not afford to spend a long time transporting gear once it was ashore. The main job, not to be lost sight of, was to get it ashore and out of reach of the sea; and when the time eventually came for us to leave the island, we must be in the position to get the stuff down to the sea again in double-quick time.

The weather on this day became kinder and kinder. As the tide fell the little dock-like rock became better for landing and we were able to keep a continuous stream carrying up to the fank; all the stores were ashore and under the truck cover by one o'clock. How glad I was for a rest and a quart of tea! I lay on my back then for a quarter of an hour, all effects of the journey left me and I felt fit for anything.

The huts came ashore in sections after lunch, and a squad of men fell to erecting them. By seven in the evening both huts were ready for occupation, the larger one being lined with half-inch Cellotex for warmth and protection against draughts. The Chief Engineer passed wires over the top and tied them to large boulders. I was a bit fussy over this job, or at least I believe the Chief thought I was.

'But look at it this way,' I said. 'A ship at sea gives to the wind, and comparatively light structures hold together where the sea does not reach them, but here we are on solid ground where there is no give.'

'You're right enough,' said the Chief, 'but when this blows away the rest of North Scotland will go as well.'

There will be no trouble with that hut blowing away yet until the wire rusts through. Each evening during our first few weeks on the island we carried stone and built up the dyke to the level of the eave, so that when the winter gales came we had a very good shelter from the west and north.

With some difficulty we got these kindly men to stop working at nine o'clock that evening. They had helped us more than we could ever repay them, and later I was to learn the depth of their loyalty, after they had returned to ports of call and had been pestered for details of the landing and making camp on Rona by news reporters. They never let out one word. Grand fellows, every one of them.

We slept sound that night, feeling that things had gone better than we could possibly have expected. The job of landing gear, which had been the biggest problem of the whole expedition in my mind, and which had certainly taken up the largest part of my time in preparation, was now a thing of the past. Getting off an island is always easier than getting on, and we were content to let that matter wait.

The future did not bother me in the slightest because I felt in my own mind that our preparations were the best that we could do. When you have done your best there is no need to worry at all. Had any point in our earlier planning been passed over in slipshod fashion, that point would have stuck in my memory all the time and disturbed my well-being.

Though I do not consciously worry and felt no anxiety during our stay on Rona, there can be little doubt that the responsibility of the expedition, that long preparation and getting to the base, which is the worst part, did get at me in ways I did not know at the time, for during our first three months on Rona I often had anxiety dreams. It was curious how these came when the tension of preparation was over. I would dream of our flour whitening the waters of Little Loch Broom as great waves washed it out of the launch. They varied in their incidence and in terror, but always they woke me in the state I often used to wake from a nightmare as a child – wanting my mother. Sometimes the cruiser would be waiting for me to embark and I was miles away, unable to move hand or foot; and another time I dreamt I was to have my tonsils out a second time before going to Rona (safer, you know, someone had insisted), and the operation was to be done on a dray standing in a covered station goods yard. I knew the doctor to be old-fashioned and inefficient, and he was going to use chloroform, which would make me dreadfully sick, instead of one of the newer and less drastic anaesthetics. The dust and smoke of the station yard filled my eyes and nostrils as I climbed on to the dray to face the doctor in his shirt sleeves holding a swab of cotton wool soaked in the filthy fluid. I woke as he approached me, and thanked God when I discovered I was on Rona and that my tonsils had left me nearly thirty years ago.

The last of these dreams came when we had been on Rona for three months, and, as I will tell later, it came true all too soon. Enough to say here that we overcame the unpleasant circumstances when they befell and learned a little more patience.

CHAPTER TEN

NORTH RONA

We woke to south-west wind and rain on our first morning on Rona, weather which later became continuous driving mist through which we could see nothing of the island. That did not matter much on that first morning, for there was so much to do indoors, fitting shelves and unpacking boxes. The cruiser left by eight o'clock, as the wind was freshening and making that debatable anchorage unsafe. We learned a good deal about anchoring off Rona in the months which followed.

The sea floor of the east bay is of rock and does not give a good bite for an anchor. Very little wind is needed to make the anchor jump, and then it is time for a ship to be moving out. A thorough-going south-easterly gale can make the north-west bay a welcome shelter, for the cliffs are high there, but a ship will not lie quiet, for a big swell from the west is nearly always coming in. I have seen a trawler anchor for three days below the cliffs of the south side in a northerly gale, but watching her antics I have thanked my lucky stars I have not been aboard her. There are sunken skerries at about four and a half fathoms off Leac Mhor Fianuis and off the north end of Rona. These break spectacularly in heavy gales, and in such weather we have seen a break about two cables south-east of Leac Mhor. Below this place is a needle of rock at about two or three fathoms, not shown on the Admiralty Chart. It is probably the greatest hazard to shipping round Rona because it is so sudden, inconspicuous and unknown.

If you are on the hill ridge of Rona when the big gales

blow from the south-west, you can see the long lines of the immense swells cartwheeling round the north end of Rona and coming in white against the cliffs of the east side – a very fine sight as long as you are not wishing to leave in a hurry, for such seas take days to slacken.

I know of nothing more thrilling than the first day on an uninhabited island, when the exigencies of camp-making prevent me going forth immediately but whet the desire still more for the pleasure of exploration. No map can really show the thousand and one things that are awaiting my wondrous eye. It would be better now, I think, to depart from the narrative style for a while and describe North Rona as we saw it.

Man has such a little interest in North Rona that this island of less than half a square mile has disappeared from many maps of Scotland. Its true position is 59° 7′ 16″ North Latitude and 5° 49′ 44″ West Longitude. The island is completely rockbound, the cliffs varying from three hundred and fifty-five feet down to a great expanse of rock almost at sea-level on Loba Sgeir.

Rona is a northern outpost of the Hebridean hornblende gneiss, intersected here by several veins of pegmatite. These are more durable than the gneiss and thus influence the scenery of the cliffs, vividly so on the northern face of the west cliff where a sheer column stands three hundred feet above the sea. Crystals of quartz and felspar in the pegmatite make these seams a feature of great beauty. Curious foldings are evident in the western cliffs, and when Marcasgeo is reached the strata lie vertical and there are some curiously shaped upthrusts of rock. The idle collector of pretty pieces of rock will come away from Rona heavily laden; some are like coal, others salmon-pink, and the mica glints everywhere in the sunlight.

That peninsula of Sceapull and the island rock of Loba Sgeir must be one of the barest places in Scotland – a low, serrated expanse of rock ringed by a never-silent sea. We explored it well two days after getting to Rona; it gets at you in the same way as does the great face of quartzite which

slopes down into Gleann an Nid at the head of Strath na
Sheallag near home. For the first time I felt the remoteness
of Rona and the wild strength of the place. As I sat on this
bare rock I felt acutely what a frail hold a single human
family has, living alone on a small island. Times before, I
have realized the physical limitations of one family containing only one man – there are so many things you just
cannot do – but here I saw the elemental strength of wind
and water, and I was awed. Bobbie was wanting away from
the place, but I felt it good to sit round for a while and
dwell on my own insignificance. I have noticed it before
on the top of a mountain in mist, and I thought of it here,
a whole lot of stuffing goes out of you when the ground
beneath your feet becomes devoid of any vegetation. That
thin green carpet of more simple life is a thing of untold
comfort. Our place is above it, and when we are on a great
piece of bare rock we also are naked and of little consequence.

The main mass of North Rona is a hill ridge running
NW-SE, falling steep or sheer on the north-eastern side and
more gradually to sea-level on the south-west. This main
lump of the island holds much of interest, but it would not
be Rona, *Ron-y,* seal island, were it not for the northern
peninsula of Fianuis. Fianuis means witness or looking forth,
and from there an observer sees an unbroken ocean. The
peninsula is nowhere more than about sixty feet high, the
cliffs on the west side being sheer and jagged, and from there
the ground slopes eastwards to low cliffs and to the flat expanse of bedded rock, Leac Mhor – the big slab.

A storm beach of piled boulders set back from the western
cliff edge is a distinctive feature of Fianuis and it plays an
important part ecologically in the animal life of the island.
There is a layer of cemented sand below the storm beach,
which caused the geologist James Geikie to infer that Rona
was covered by the Quaternary Ice Sheet.

Although North Rona is geologically the northernmost
point of the Outer Hebrides, it differs much from them
botanically. The northern end of Lewis is one vast peat

bog which grows a characteristic herbage complex domi-
nated by heather. There is no peat at all on Rona. The rock
is covered a few inches deep with a sandy soil held together by
organic matter and the roots of a good turf of Yorkshire fog,
bents and fescue grasses. The sedges which are so commonly
found on the gneiss areas of the Hebrides and north-western
mainland are more rare on Rona, occurring mostly to the
west of the ancient village site where the turf has been cut
for fuel hundreds of years ago. Such scars never heal completely in our northern lands, where the soil is originally
very thin. The strength of the mat of turf is amazing, and
it needs to be strong indeed if it is to withstand those raking
gales from the Atlantic. I have seen the turf torn from the
rocks by the wind and rolled inland, and even stones as big
as a man's head pushed from their bed an inch or two in the
turf and rolled two or three yards uphill. The wind on Rona
has to be felt to be realized.

The drier rocky places are covered with a wealth of sea-
pink and a fair amount of buck's-horn plantain; the cliff
edges, heavily manured by the summer population of birds,
grow luxuriant sprays of scurvy grass, some sheep-sorrel,
Scotch lovage and mayweed. The village area with its large
numbers of lazy-beds grows wild white clover on the dry
banks of conserved soil, and in the immediate vicinity of the
houses silverweed almost crowds out everything else. There
is no bracken, no fern, no spleenwort, and few of those flowers
which make the northern lands gay in summer. The riot of
sea-pink makes up for the loss, many of the tufts being of a
very deep colour and others pure white. The botanist would
find Rona curiously even as a vegetative habitat, and Stewart
lists only thirty-five species for the island, but Robert Atkinson has since found forty-two.

Now once more the northern peninsula of Fianuis provides
something distinctive. The whole of Rona is washed by
salt spray in winter gales, but Fianuis is often impassable
under a continuous driven cloud of it. Only plants with high
tolerance of salt can grow there, annual poa-grass, sea-pink,
sea-milkwort and chickweed. Nowhere else have I seen

such a refulgent growth of chickweed as on the eastern side of Fianuis. There are about twenty acres of it growing to a foot in height.

There are no permanent pools of fresh water on Rona, and the human resident may find this to be one of the major problems of existence. The cruiser left us with about five gallons of water that first night, and in the afternoon of the next day, when we went for our first prowl in the heavy mist, almost our first thought was to look at the wells marked in such profusion on the map. They were disappointing, being very shallow, stagnant and full of ooze. There is a fair drain of water from the area west of the village down to Leac na Sgrob, but the birds use the temporary pools for bathing and make the water taste musky. We dug one or two of these pools deeper, but that was not a good thing to do because we had destroyed the waterproof surface of the pool and next time we went to them they had gone dry.

Bobbie objected strongly to this water, and I admit myself the tea was spoilt, and I did not look forward to six months of poor tea to drink. On the night of our arrival, the Chief and the Second Officer had dug a well about forty yards south of the huts, and the following morning the water looked clear and good. Unfortunately it was very brackish and soon dried out – or perhaps it was fortunate, because all that area in the wintertime is an indescribable mass of living and dead seals. Any water from north of the hill ridge is unfit to drink. Bobbie went hunting for a better well and found it at the head of Poll Heallair on the southern coast of the island. The true well is nearer the edge of the cliff than the one marked on the map. It has obviously been chiselled in the solid rock and then topped with stone. The water which drips constantly into this well, even in dry weather, makes a store of about ten gallons. It is only seepage from the slope above, but it is always sweet and cool. We used to make a journey over every day from the huts to fill a white-painted petrol can, marked with a brass label – WATER – which we found washed up on Lunga the year before. A journey of a mile to fetch a daily supply of drinking water – and yet I do not remember it as an irksome task at all.

Rainfall is fairly heavy on Rona, though we have known a whole fortnight without rain, and despite what I have said about there being no permanent pools of fresh water on the island and a lack of boggy places, it is surprising to find that the island is continually wet, wet in the sense that you could not sit on the grass in a pair of grey flannels without getting a wet seat. The steep northern face of the island runs a thin film of water all the time in winter, and passage up and down there without slipping a few yards now and again is almost impossible.

I have described caves on the other islands on which we have lived, and I wish I could say more of the underground world of Rona, which has never been explored. But this would be most difficult, because all the caves are sea caves running in from the west coast, and the sea is hardly ever calm enough to allow entry with a boat. We took our old kayak with us, but launching was always a difficulty because of the swell, even in Geodha Stoth, and I never felt justified in getting her down on the west side to go exploring. The responsibility of wife and child left above was too great.

The best-known cave on Rona is the Tunnel Cave running up from Sgeildige. From the head of the cave there runs a blow-hole over thirty yards long, coming out to the surface in the middle of the neck of Fianuis. The hole is about three feet high at the top, but broadens out farther down, and at the foot you can stand upright. The first few yards of the journey down are extraordinarily slippery because of a growth of algae, so it is best to go down the whole length on a rope. Once down, the play of light on water and rock make a scene of great beauty. But the days are few when you can get to the foot of the hole, and in a big gale I have seen a plume of spray coming from the top. The head of the cave must fill with water as the immense swells come in, and the pressure up that thirty-yard passage to the top of Fianuis is great.

Two more caves go under the island from Sgeildige Geo

and reach to just below the sheep fank. As we lay in bed with our ears near the floor of the hut we could hear the rustle of water in the caves below. That was a pleasant sound, but it became awe-inspiring when a deep swell caused great breakers at the head of the caves. These two caves were much haunted by an exceedingly vocal crowd of seals. They cried day and night in their rich falsetto voices, bulls and cows in different keys, and the sound was mixed by the acoustic qualities of the caves and given forth as a wonderful harmony, comparable in effect with that which reaches the listener at the foot of the nave of St Paul's Cathedral after the singing of the choir has been mixed under the dome.

The finest bit of scenery on Rona is Geodha Blatha Mor. It is possible to climb a little way down the cliff to the north of it and to look part way into the immense cave which runs inland from the geo. Three hundred feet of cliff face you, and the great mouth of the cave to the east and left. Every conceivable niche is occupied by kittiwakes and guillemots, even far into the cave. Thousands and thousands of birds, all crying; the sound is amplified in the yawning mouth of the cave and accompanied by the boom of the swell and the crying of seals within. I was so impressed with this place that I took Bobbie and Alasdair there the same evening when the sun shone into the cave. First they exclaimed, then were silent for a long time. It is one of those places that are wonderful as a whole but which repay examination in detail.

Such, then, is the face of Rona, a mere speck in the northern ocean; but such an island is much more than that biologically. Rather is it a metropolis for widely different animals through the seasons of the year, and a most important halting place for many others. The one occupation influences the other, and to the resident observer the island takes on a quality of wholeness in the mind which is denied the casual visitor.

Let us first consider man as a member of the island fauna, a singularly unlucky member on the whole, for he has not managed to persist. As far as we know, and this is not a

documented fact, St Ronan was the first human inhabitant
of Rona in the eighth century AD. He moved to Rona from
Eoropaidh at the north end of Lewis and adopted the name
of the island as his own. Thus we gather that Rona has been
the island of the seals for a very long period. Tradition has
it that St Ronan built the existing cell on Rona, and as this
building is in many ways typical of the cells built by ascetic
hermits of the early Celtic Church in other parts of Scotland,
there is no reason yet for disbelieving the traditional origin
of a building which is unlike any other on Rona.

Muir, a Scottish ecclesiological antiquary, who visited
Rona in 1857 and 1860, made careful measurements of the
cell and described the place as he found it. His sketches
indicate a very low entrance, and a paving to the cell is
implied. He also wrote of entering the cell on elbows and
knees; it was the unlikelihood of this being the original mode
of ingress that decided me to dig.

The east and west walls are almost perpendicular, but the
longer north and south walls slope inwards rapidly, and at a
height of over 11 feet are bridged by rectangular slabs of
gneiss to finish the roof. The length and breadth of the cell
at floor level are 11 feet 6 inches and 8 feet. This building
is in drystone, very beautifully done, and the technique is
the same as that of the black houses still inhabited in Lewis.
The inside edges of the flattish stones are set a little higher
than those reaching to the outside, so that all water draining
on to the top of such a wall must drain outwards and the
inside surface remains dry and free from condensation. The
beehive shielings are built on the same principle and the
courses reach inwards from near the foot of the wall. These
buildings are in direct descent from the culture of the Mega-
lithic Age. St Ronan's cell is the best example of this type of
construction I know, and into the south wall, near the east
end, he built a neat aumbry a foot square. There is a small
window 19 inches by 8 inches running through the thickness
of the west wall above the door. Whether there was a similar window in the east end is not known, because the upper
part of the wall there has fallen in. Earth and stones were

banked high round the north, east and south walls so that
the building was practically underground. The outside of
the west wall became the east inside wall of a chapel which
was built some time after Ronan's cell; Muir estimated about
two centuries later. This building, also in drystone but of
poorer workmanship, is 14 feet 8 inches long by 8 feet 3
inches, and forms in effect a nave to the cell as chancel. But
it is doubtful whether the two buildings were used conjointly
in this way.

The roof and much of the walls of the chapel have disappeared, and when I first went to Rona the south wall was
just a heap of stone fallen outwards. I had with me a copy of
Harvie-Brown's book aforementioned, in which there is
what is probably the first photograph of the chapel ever
taken. That was in 1885. The south wall was erect then, and
from the photograph I could see very well the height of the
doorway in the south wall and a curious bulge in the eastern
half of that wall. I began nervously to make a clearance of
the fallen stones and to find the foundations; I did not wish
to take down much in an effort to rebuild, for there was no
knowing where I should be able to stop. However, once the
foundation was clear, even showing that increased thickness east of the doorway, I went ahead with confidence.
The south wall is now back in the state it was in 1885, and I
do not think it will be easy to tell where I began work.

I now turned my attention to the inside of the chapel,
which had been occupied by fulmar petrels in the summer
and was half full of fallen stone and earth. This very low
doorway into the cell was intriguing, and it was there I
struck first with spade and pick. It was not long, as I cleared
my way north and south of the opening, before I struck two
blocks of masonry; they were piers 3 feet high and 2 feet
3 inches square, one each side of the entrance, and they had
at some time been faced with lime mortar. When I reached
the foot of these piers, which I take to be the altar supports
of the chapel, I found a rough paving running into the doorway of the cell. Here was no necessity for elbows and knees;
the doorway with its original paving and a tiny step was 4

feet and 4 inches high and 20 inches broad. The vertical section of soil and floor made by my digging revealed a thick bed of shell sand laid on the paving over the floor of the chapel. I found charred bones of sea birds and seals in this layer. A hard floor of rammed clay lay above the shell sand, and I was able to clear all the inside of the chapel to the level of the clay. As the east end and the entrance to the cell showed workings below the level of this floor, I built a course of drystone across the chapel, so that both the clay floor and the original cell front are now visible and should not easily become encumbered again.

There was now the cell itself to excavate, and I have not done this entirely, because at some time the sloping walls have been roughly buttressed on the north and south sides by large stones placed on end. But I have cleared to the paving inside the door, and at the east end I have gone right across the cell. I found an altar of well-built masonry 2 feet 6 inches high, 3 feet broad and 2 feet 3 inches deep. Muir said there was an altar *stone* 3 feet long at the east end of the cell, and he gave a sketch of it in position. Doubtless this was all he could see of the altar at that time, and I found this stone on a level with the top of the altar but at right angles to it. The altar being completely revealed, I have replaced the big slab. A visitor to Rona will now get the impression of a simple early church in a very fair state of preservation because it has been almost buried for so long. I am glad to say His Majesty's Office of Works is going to take the place in hand.

The only hint of a late age in the burial ground round the chapel is the hideous flat sandstone slab, complete with twirls and so on, brought here and raised to the memory of two penitent shepherds who, having had words with the minister in Ness, came to Rona in May, 1884, and died there in February, 1885. The weather of these parts is reducing the imported stone to decrepitude and the whole thing has taken a good lean eastwards. The legend on the stone is:

SACRED

TO

THE MEMORY OF

MALCOLM MCDONALD

NESS

WHO DIED AT RONA

FEB 18 1885 AGED 67

ALSO M MCKAY

WHO DIED AT RONA SAME TIME

Blessed are the dead

who die in the Lord

The composition of this legend is typical of West Highland English, primitive because it was a strange language to those whom the stone commemorates and those who piously erected it. But 1885 was a time when it was thought more genteel to have your gravestone inscribed in English, and this foreign stone would be thought to convey more respect than one of the rough crosses of Rona's own gneiss. These, indeed, were beautiful, and those which remain in the burial ground make the place a wholly pleasant one, far different from those places of stark, smooth monuments where civilized men bury their dead and attempt to immortalize them.

The first written mention of Rona and its people was made in 1549 by Sir Donald Monro, High Dean of the Isles. He mentions the ancient chapel and some of its magical qualities, and he speaks of the whiteness of the barley flour and of the method of its storage in sheepskins. Next comes Martin Martin, who made his famous tour of the Western Isles in 1695 and who took down an account of Rona and its inhabitants from Daniel Morison, the minister of Barvas, Lewis, in which parish Rona was and still is. The minister had been there about 1680 or before, and had received five sacks of the white barley meal, the sacks being the skins of sheep just as Sir Donald had described well over a century before. The minister's tale is of cattle and sheep and cultivation of barley and oats, but there is no word of potatoes.*

*Potatoes were first planted in Lewis in 1753.

He speaks of the altar in the chapel as being a 'big plank of wood about ten feet in length; every foot has a hole in it, and in every hole a stone, to which the natives ascribe several virtues'. The plank is gone, and how would we recognize the stones today? But I imagine that plank lay across the stone piers I have laid bare, and if so, it seems improbable that the cell would be used then for religious services. Presumably it was the clay floor now uncovered which the natives, according to the seventeenth-century minister, swept every day and kept 'neat and clean'.

From what we read of Martin Martin the life of these five families of remote people had a beautiful simplicity. He says 'they covet no wealth, being fully content and satisfied with food and raiment; though at the same time they are very precise in the matter of property among themselves . . . they take their surnames from the colour of the sky, rainbow and clouds'. It was very soon after this that a plague of rats came to Rona from a wrecked ship. These rodents ate up the whole sustenance of the people, who had no means of combating a new pest. A further calamity was the theft of the island bull by a passing ship wishing fresh meat. The people starved to death, and when the steward of St Kilda was some time later driven as far as Rona in a great storm, he 'found a woman with her child on her breast, both lying dead at the side of a rock'. The rats also starved, because Rona has no foreshore which would maintain them when they had eaten the people's harvests.

The ruins of the houses of this ancient people remain. They are half underground and each covers a considerable area, for devious low passages surrounded them and it seems probable that barn and byre were part of the house, just as they were in the black houses of Lewis, but the general plan of these Rona dwellings is round rather than rectangular, and the wind-baffling passages are distinctive. Nobody else has had my opportunities of digging and seeking among these ruins in winter when the silverweed has died. I have found one perfect quern stone twenty-two inches across which was buried in the floor of the largest dwelling. Two more well-preserved ones were lying visible on the wall of one of the houses, and I dug several fragments from the ground about the village. Bobbie made an important find of two fragments of stone vessels, one of which was evidently shallow and round and the other oval and deeper. I have gathered all these artefacts together in the west end of the chapel, and we have also made a plan of the cultivated area, showing the disposition and number of the lazy-beds, which appear to be in five main groups, possibly indicative of the five families which we are told made up the community.

I do not think thirty odd souls could have subsisted wholly on what they could grow on Rona. Their economy was helped out by the natural resources of birds and seals. The island is visited each year by an enormous number of sea fowl of several species. There are probably more now than there were in the days when the people took their toll. I estimate the guillemot population to be about 25,000 birds; the kittiwakes are in equal numbers and nest in nearest proximity to the guillemots. These two species do not come inland at all, and as they occupy the most sheer and the lowest positions of any of the cliff-breeding birds, their influence on the face of the island is negligible. There are about 1,500 razorbills on the island. The puffins are the most numerous of all the birds; they nest in burrows of their own making on the tops of cliffs and thus exercise a considerable effect on this area. They make for rapid drainage of the soil, so that sea-pink grows there refulgently, and they make for a certain amount of disintegration of the cliff edge, for sometimes the burrow-ridden soil sloughs off and falls to the sea after gales and heavy rain. They also manure this strip very heavily, and chickweed and scurvy grass become a luxuriant growth.

The puffins of the cliff edge are comparable with the rabbits of the mainland, in that both species become a food staple for other creatures. Man no longer salts thousands for winter use, but the great black-backed gulls feed on them throughout the summer, and there are more black-backs on Rona than I have seen anywhere else. I estimate there are at least 500 pairs nesting on the island, most of them on Fianuis. It is a magnificent spectacle to see from the hill ridge this great concourse of handsome black-and-white birds dotted about the peninsula. The black-backs of Rona are a migratory population, coming when the puffins do, breeding, and leaving with the puffins. Two or three hundred return a few weeks later in September when the seals begin to breed, because there are dead calves to be eaten. The departure of the black-backs is almost synchronous with that of the puffins, and though the few gulls remaining prey on young kittiwakes, which leave the cliff later and more gradually, it is obvious that puffins are the key to the numerousness of the predatory gulls. Let us suppose that each of the thousand black-backs takes a puffin once in four days – a very conservative estimate; that would mean 250 puffins a day for the whole ten weeks of the breeding season, a total of 15,000–20,000 birds. And yet there appear to be just as many at the end of the time as there were in the beginning. If there are 100,000 puffins on Rona, a depletion of 20 per cent would not be easily noticed even by a close observer, for there is always the number in the burrows, in the air and on the sea, as well as the large company on the cliff edge. Each pair of puffins rears only one chick a year; so, to maintain the population and serve as a food supply for other birds as well, it seems likely that the puffin's possible breeding life is a long one.

The cliffs of Rona are littered with the skins of puffins neatly pulled inside out from the carcass. Such is the technique of the black-back in eating any animal. The peregrine falcons also prey on the puffins, but there is only one pair of them on Rona and their influence on the population is small. The falcon takes the puffin to a little pool of water, wets the bird thoroughly and proceeds to pluck the feathers. A pair of untouched wings joined by the cleaned pectoral girdle marks the remains of a falcon's meal. They are not present in winter, though a food supply remains on the island in the shape of a resident flock of 300–400 starlings. We may assume that the arrival and departure of the puffins are responsible for a migratory movement on the part of the two predatory species mentioned.

North Rona was colonized by the fulmar petrel in the Eighties of last century, one of the first places to receive a surplus from St Kilda, where the human population was consuming fewer of these birds. It has been estimated that 600 pairs of fulmars breed on Rona, and my own census agrees very closely with this. But the three counts which have now been made were done in summer when the other birds were on the cliffs, and I am inclined to think 600 pairs is an under-estimate. It is possible that Rona receives an accretion of fulmars in the winter from places farther north; I am almost sure this does occur, for I saw among the winter birds a dark blue specimen characteristic of the northern type.

The storm beach of piled boulders on the top of Fianuis provides an environmental factor allowing the black guillemot and the Arctic tern to breed, the former deep among the stones and the terns in the open on the sandy, pebble-strewn places. Pebbles of hornblende gneiss are much like terns' eggs, and the nests and young are difficult to find on a terrain not duplicated elsewhere on Rona. Both of these species are migratory. As I have said before, the tysties do not stay on Rona throughout the winter as they do about Clerach. This is just one more example of the fact that different groups of birds of the same species will follow quite different rhythms, and an island such as Rona, with its peculiar set of circumstances, has its own story of animal life not closely comparable with its nearest neighbours. A casual visit does not reveal this story, only the watcher through the seasons can see the intricacy and beauty of the pattern.

There is no quiet on Rona in summer, day or night; the harsh rattle of the guillemots and shags, the cackle of fulmars, the high-pitched cries of kittiwakes, the coarse complaint of black-backs and the high, chittering scream of Arctic terns, all are blended into a splendid paean in our ears.

There are also the little storm petrels churring in the walls of the fank at night-time, and from midnight on the sound of the Leach's fork-tailed petrel may be heard on Fianuis and

about the chapel and village. Alasdair, Bobbie and I would
set out for the old houses about midnight on those calm July
nights, rather a subdued party, for we had tried to get a little
sleep in first. We would be wrapped up well and carrying
camera, lenses, electric flash-bulb gear and so on. Usually it
was good to get into the shelter of the main house and wait
until the first-comers arrived from the sea. Several were
flitting about by half past twelve, then more came in rapid
succession, and those already in their burrows in the drystone walls began to sing in an ascending trill most pleasant
to hear. It seemed to me that more petrels gathered near the
place immediately after these trillings. Soon the birds in the
air began to scream, but this was no unpleasant sound like
that of the Manx shearwaters. It was a succession of eight or
ten notes in a definite cadence and of varying pitch, rather
like a staccato, musical laugh. The swift-flying shapes increased in number and the volume of sound grew. We could
feel the excitement waxing in this community of little black
birds. Their flight is erratic and swift, and when two or
three hundred are flying in this way within a restricted
space, collisions are common. Our faces were brushed by the
soft wings smelling strongly of the characteristic petrel
musk. A pitch of excitement is reached after one o'clock in
the morning, and the laughter and erratic movements wane
before dawn.

How exciting it was for us the first night we went to hear
and see this aerial dance! We stood silent a long time, and I
was thinking how few people in Britain could have experienced this phenomenon of the northern summer night.
St Kilda, the Flannans, Sula Sgeir and North Rona; after
these you must go to Iceland or Greenland, the Labrador
coast or the Aleutian Islands in the Northern Pacific Ocean.
I shone a torch into one hole in a drystone dyke when I
heard that little trill coming forth, and there was the full
black eye of the petrel, its lovely grey face and the shining
black bill with its nostrils set in a tube above it.

I have wasted many flash bulbs in attempts to add a
Leach's petrel to my collection of flight photographs. This is

an almost impossible task, for you are working in darkness
with a dark-coloured bird dashing hither and thither at high
speed. But, as Nansen said, impossible things are only a little
more difficult of achievement, and during my visit to Rona
in 1939 I did manage to get a flying bird visible on the nega-
tive. The print shows a great span of wing, and the dark grey
face has shown white. It is a unique photograph which gives
me immense pleasure.

One of the birds of Rona which intrigued me more than a
little was the turnstone. Three days after our arrival, ie, July
15th, I saw two adults with three young birds which occasionally begged from the old ones. The youngsters were
well able to fly, but I thought it improbable they could have
migrated to the island by that date. There were plenty more
turnstones about also, and as autumn followed summer
many more came, and they remained in my memory as the
little companions of the great seals. You would see a seal
snap at a gull which might come near it, but the busy little
turnstones ran among the seals lying on the rocks or high in
the island, pecking morsels from the bodies of the great
beasts themselves. When winter came the turnstones and
purple sandpipers often joined forces on the seal grounds,
and they were as tame as a flock of poultry about our doors.
When I found them so common in July, including the young
birds, I wondered if the turnstone bred on this one island of
Britain after all. It was therefore with lively anticipation I
returned on June 18th, 1939. I hunted the island over immediately but never a turnstone did I find. They returned in
small numbers on June 24th. So it was not my luck to
definitely record the turnstone as a British breeding species.

Stewart gives a list of birds in *Ronay* which has the
authority of Tom Harrisson. Tom Harrisson's visits to Rona
have been short ones, and other authorities have given comparatively poor lists. I would much like to know when many
of the species cited were actually seen, such as the tree sparrow, crossbill, pied flycatcher, chiffchaff and lesser white-
throat. Several species mentioned by Harrisson I certainly
expected to see myself and was surprised not to do so in the

long period we were there. The hooded crow, for example, was absent, and I never saw a red-breasted merganser, a cormorant nor a pomatorhine skua. And though blackbirds were fairly common in November and December, I did not see a song thrush. Naturally I have many new records to add to the list for the island, and I will run through these with notes on their occurrences, for the information has not been given yet elsewhere.

Redwing: December 3rd, about the Tor, and later, December 11th, about the village.

Snow bunting: September 19th, common November and December on Fianuis and Sceapull.

Whooper swan: November 23rd, flying low over the island.

Blackbird: these birds were extraordinarily shy.

Mallard: common in winter Fianuis and Sceapull.

Merlin: September 12th and for several days.

Rock dove: three on September 19th, Fianuis, among the chickweed; occasionally in winter.

Buzzard: a single dark-plumaged bird, September-December, feeding on carcasses of seal calves.

Swift: over ruins July 27th, and flying across the northern slope for several days until August 4th; two more seen September 2nd.

Velvet scoter: August 3rd; a female on a pool on Fianuis.

Knot: August 14th, Leac Mhor Fianuis, common until end of September; one seen in breeding plumage.

Dotterel: August 30th, west side of island.

Pintail duck: September 8th, flight of nine on Fianuis.

Long-tailed duck: a pair frequented east bay November and December.

Great skua: August 17th, in a gale, on Fianuis.

Woodcock: September 5th, on Fianuis, again in December.

Spotted redshank: September 21st, Fianuis. Was doubtful of my own eyes, but saw the bird again next day.

Black-headed gull: one about pools on Fianuis most of September.

Raven: December 18th, after south-easterly gale.

Short-eared owl: December 9th, sitting on a rock on the ridge.

Barnacle goose: November 24th, four on Sceapull. Am surprised geese do not winter on Rona.

Great snipe: December 15th, Fianuis.

Jack snipe: December 16th, Fianuis.

Glaucous gull: many immature ones in December.

The autumn migratory season is a thrilling time on Rona. Flocks of young white wagtails came to Fianuis and were a joy to us for a month or more by their tameness about the huts. Then there was a surge of Greenland wheatears. I saw turtle-doves on two occasions, September 14th and 20th, and they seemed curiously out of place here. Ringed plovers paid us but a passing visit in August, but golden plovers stayed about for some weeks in very small numbers. And I remember the fine surprise of meeting a green sandpiper by a soft place on the ridge on September 24th. I stopped in my tracks, and the lovely little bird I had never seen in my life before walked about a few yards away in apparent unconcern. I saw a pair of little stints twice, in August and September, and one day in August my friend of deer-forest days, the greenshank, came through. I saw a sanderling twice in a flock of knots on Leac Mhor. Iceland redshanks were common in August, and dunlin were fairly common from August onwards. Two swallows came and flew round us in July, in the same confiding way they did on Clerach. A female hen harrier stayed about the island for most of September, and many were the fine views she gave me. I think I was never happier in my life than at this time.

Herring gulls were few on Rona. They nested on Sron na Chaorach and at the north of Fianuis along with a few lesser black-backed gulls; they had a poor chance against that immense flock of greater black-backs. That coarse complaint of the big black-backs was the one sound of which I tired, for you could not move without incurring their displeasure. One thing must be said in their favour: where they breed on an island as a colony they are largely responsible for a high state of fertility there. They bring a large amount of limey and phosphoric matter on to the ground, and their young add much nitrogenous fertilizer in the course of the summer.

Harvie-Brown mentions the commonness of the eider duck on Rona. Today there are very few resident, and I imagine their worst enemy, the greater black-back, is responsible for their decline. The pirates find the ducks' nests and swallow the eggs.

Some of my new records for Rona were made after big gales in December. I used to go out full of expectancy each day, and was seldom disappointed. But I felt some surprise, nevertheless, that some of these birds should be travelling the northern ocean at these inauspicious times. Where, pray, were the great snipe and jack snipe bound in December?

Another most noticeable fact was the importance of Fianuis and the north slope of the hill ridge as a resting place for migrant birds. I did not understand at first, but when I had seen the effect wrought on all that area by the passage to and fro of thousands of seals, I realized the extraordinary effect this must have in enriching the insect fauna of the island. No wonder the swifts hawked along the northern slope close to the grass, and the white wagtails were never found anywhere else but on Fianuis. I could do fine to become a modern Ronan and live there the seasons through for a few years more, watching the birds come and go and pass through, and the great seals populate the place in the wild autumns. Oh, Rona, Rona! and here am I on Tanera with a slowly mending leg, and a foolish outside world plunged into war. When will I be back again?

*Note. In company with other naturalists, I flew over and round about the Orkneys, the Shetlands, Foula, Sule Stac, North Rona, Sula Sgeir, the Flannan Isles, St Kilda, the Monachs and up the west coast of Lewis to the Butt, across to Cape Wrath and along the North Coast on September 29th, 1947. It was a bad day of north-west wind and snow showers. The sea was rough with a big surf against the island coasts, but what impressed me particularly was the degree of 'work' on the sea around Rona. It was as if it were alive, much more so than around the other islands.

I made an attempt to get ashore on Rona in October, 1949, but there was too much surf everywhere. Rona will never be easy game.

CHAPTER ELEVEN

GOOD DAYS AND BAD

THOSE FIRST DAYS ON RONA were a time of brilliant weather, especially early in the mornings when the sun would be shining on the northern faces of the cliffs on both the east and west sides of the island. Alasdair and I took advantage of the grand light by going out early with the camera for photographs of the sea birds. All of them were comparatively tame, and as we had to pass through a large puffin town to reach some convenient kittiwakes, the puffins would come down about us looking solemn and important with their bibulous noses, grey cheeks, black coats and white waistcoats. The birds stand upright in large companies like a lot of longshoremen on a harbour front; some toddle up and down and others take a short fly over the sea and back again; some come in with a catch of tiny, silvery fish in their beaks, all tails lying out. You would think when they came back the birds would make straight for the youngster in the burrow, but no, they often stand about for some minutes with the fish in their beaks. What are puffins thinking about all the time?

We tried colour photography for the first time on Rona, and though we wasted a good many exposures by our ignorance, there are some transparencies which could hardly be bettered. When thrown on to a screen they bring back the experience to us in a way no monochrome slide can do. Bobbie and I are agreed that one of the values of colour photography is the help it gives in the analysis and subsequent greater appreciation of natural scenery. You freeze a moment of time, as it were, and can study every detail at leisure. There are so many hidden beauties in the vast field of the eye's first glance.

The wind which drove the cruiser out on the early morning after we landed blew all day long and fell light on the following morning. Then the sun came out for a magnificent day and we spent a good deal of time on that grim west coast of Fianuis watching the surf and the seals. Enormous waves broke against these cliffs and the water was churned to white foam for seventy-five yards from their foot. The scene and the sound filled us with wonder. It was the sort of sea of which people sometimes say, 'Nothing could live in this terrible surf.' So you would think, but close in to the rocks and where the waves broke most fiercely were our friends the great seals. They were not battling against the seas but taking advantage of them for play. It was nothing but play and joy of life which was keeping them there, for they were not sounding as they do when fishing. They were keeping to the surface, nearly a hundred of them, enjoying the deep rise and fall of the sea and the spray of the shattered waves. They were living joyfully, and I in my own way rejoiced with them. The sky was a shining vault of blue, the sea was a deeper blue, and as we watched the surf grew even bigger. The whiteness of it shone in the sunlight and the movement and sound of it all were glorious. In those days I think we were lifted out of earthbound humanity for a space.

An engine rudely woke us one Sabbath morning in July. It was the cruiser returned to give us a hand with setting up the wireless gear. But the south-west wind was blowing up and the rain had already begun. A launch came away at breakfast-time to say it was not safe to stay and that they were going to continue their way to Orkney. I watched the cruiser draw off eastwards into the grey sea mist and felt a trifle grey myself. Now then, I must shelve my responsibilities no more but set to erecting a lot of apparatus about which I knew absolutely nothing.

The firm which supplied us with the wireless gear had made out a series of charts and instructions of the most careful kind and there was no good reason why I should not do the job myself. I began with the aerial masts, two of them, tubular steel, twenty-five feet high. Each mast was to carry twelve stranded wire guys, and we fastened these to the masts with a 'Post Office splice' explained to us by Cap'n M. earlier in the month. We got these up by tea-time and the aerial strung between them. The job looked quite professional and I became quite impressed with my own ability. I fixed another wire called the counterpoise after tea, took the leads through the walls of huts, earthed the petrol-engine generator, brought a lead-covered cable from the engine to the hut and set up the main switch. Then there were all the connexions and junctions to make inside the hut, but there was still a bit more to do when we stopped at half past eleven from sheer tiredness.

We were at it again first thing the following morning and had everything ready for the première at 10.45 AM. The engine started with a flourish, I drew down the switch, and lo, there came a little red light where a little red light should be. Marvellous! Then we turned on the receiver switch and the dial lit up also, and soon, as we turned the tuner, what do you think? There came the sugary tones of the BBC cinema organ – Bobbie's *bête noire*. What an anticlimax that this should be the first wireless sound heard on this remote isle! We kept on twisting and heard a trawler skipper talking to another one called George. He was a jolly man with a great laugh on him, and he was cursing the weather he had had round about the Faeroes.

And now, we thought, we will try the transmitter. How nice it would be to join in that merry talk with the trawler skippers now and again! I changed over the switch (*vide* working chart) and depressed another button. There was a splutter and the little red light disappeared and no pointers waggled as they should have done. Then a smell of heated fat greeted our nostrils and I opened a heavy metal box called a power pack, inside which some rolls of greasy paper were certainly melting. There was another thing in there also, a pretty lamp called a valve. Even as we watched, a lovely violet flame waxed within it, reached an ecstatic zenith, and quite suddenly went out. The smell of hot fat was getting worse, so we rightly assumed we were not transmitting; and that was the end of that. I put the wireless at the back of my mind altogether and went out to begin a count of the numbers of bridled guillemots. The wireless did not bother me at all, but back on the mainland the newspapers were screaming and making things unpleasant for relatives and friends. Had we not been badgered into buying these play-things I am convinced they would not have worried about us half as much as they did when they received 'no news from exiles'.

When we had been packing for Rona I had included a carton of insect powder – Keating's, you know.

'My dear,' said Bobbie in a shocked voice, 'we shan't need *that*.'

'You mean you *hope* we shall not need it,' I said in my superior, logical way, 'and I hope so too; but as we have it here, and the potentialities of this small cylinder are great, we will go prepared.'

The trouble was earwigs. Before we had been on Rona a week the huts simply swarmed with earwigs. I have quite a soft place in my heart for these orthopterans, and to begin with I carried them outside alive; but that had to stop, for earwigs were getting into every nook and corner – including the interior of the tubes of macaroni. They had a sweet tooth, these creatures, for they would easily nibble through the silver paper of chocolate and through the cellophane packing of blocks of dates. Bobbie cleaned out a box of dates one day and found over three hundred earwigs at the bottom. Another favourite place was in the niche made by the grooves of the matchboarding on the rafters of the hut, and at night-time they would emerge from these places and drop on to us – often on our faces as we slept. So we re-luctantly made war on the earwigs by spreading Keating's under the door each night and by clearing the rafters with a weapon of modern frightfulness which I made for the job and which was called the 'wigger'. This was a piece of wire which could be pushed through the grooves and which shot the unfortunate earwigs into a cup of boiling water which was waiting for them. We would get thirty or forty like this every night, but we certainly got top-side of them. Several of these remote islets off the North Coast of Scotland are similarly inhabited by swarms of earwigs. Silver-fish were also constant dwellers in the huts, but they were much less obtrusive than the earwigs and we did not bother them as they never attacked food supplies.

Every day we would see something new and wonderful. I remember a flock of about two thousand kittiwakes closely massed on the skerry of Lisgeir Mhor at the north end of Fianuis. They were a pretty enough sight like that, but when all of them suddenly took to the air and of necessity fanned out to give themselves flying room, it was a vision prodigal in its loveliness. It was a gigantic unfolding of resting life into brilliant animation. Perhaps two seconds after they took to the air they began calling; even a single kittiwake can make a lot of noise with the cry which gives the bird its name, but when two thousand throats cried out as one I stood in wonder listening to a paean of praise. Our bare northern islands often produce these moments of spontaneous exuberance and, in the right sense of the word, magnificence.

Malcolm Stewart asked me to do some ringing of young birds on Rona, and I agreed to do this because there was no good reason why I should not, and I am keen to have a lot of birds ringed because of the several scientific ends ringing serves. Ringing gull chicks is an easy job and causes the birds no inconvenience, but I am not happy ringing fulmar petrel chicks. It is a filthy job anyway because of the orange-coloured oil the chicks can project at you from their mouths. The first lot is pure oil, but the quality soon deteriorates till the final ejection is yesterday's lunch, so to speak, and your hands are in a dreadful state by the time each nestling is ringed. I did not like to see the little things upset, and after the first batch I waited some days to see if the loss of so much food matter had affected the birds. The puffins too – I like these folk and I felt absolutely ashamed, dragging decent parents and their children from the burrows. Their remonstrance was so quiet and dignified, and they are helpless in our hands.

It was not necessary to climb about the cliffs in order to ring a large number of fulmars, because on Rona, in common with a few more islands of the north, some of these birds nest on the top of the island. Over fifty were to be found on the storm beach and several more were among the ruins. Each corner of the chapel and cell was occupied by a fulmar chick. When Harvie-Brown visited Rona in the Eighties of last century the fulmars had only just colonized the island, and he remarked how the birds always flew on the seaward side of the cliff and appeared to have an active dislike of the land. How the old man would have stared to see these ones sitting nonchalantly in the chapel! Birds sometimes change their habits markedly in a few years.

Our three hens took to life on Rona like old campaigners. They came into a surge of egg-laying which surprised us, for within ten weeks the three of them laid one hundred and forty-four eggs, and then stopped suddenly. Bobbie always says cooking holds no fears for her if she has plenty of eggs. These twelve dozen eggs were a help to our store of pickled ones and they cost us nothing, for the hens lived on what they got from the island. The hens were very fond of the chickweed and were not alone in this. There were four grey lag geese which lived almost wholly on it; they would spend most of the day on the sea and come in to the chickweed in the evening. The few sheep on Rona lived like wild ones; they used to come down from the ridge during the night to feed on the chickweed, and then with considerable regularity would pass by the huts again on their way back to the main body of the island at about seven o'clock in the morning. It was two or three years since the Ness men had been to Rona, and there were two crops of lambs that had never been docked or castrated. The population of sheep seems to keep fairly constant, the heavy winter losses about balancing the annual increase of lambs. Had a fence prevented the daily

trek to the chickweed I am sure the sheep would have felt
the deprivation. We ourselves, also, were glad to be nibbling
this succulent weed and putting some into sandwiches. I
tried some scurvy grass one day, but found it most unpleasant to the taste; perhaps the thick green leaves of the
giant form of the plant are not so good as the tiny ones on
Clerach.

Although these were good summer days we thought it
wise to prepare for a possible winter's worst, by building up
and cleaning out a beehive shieling which stood two hundred yards away from the huts on Fianuis. We imagine this
place must have been used by the sealers in the eighteenth
and nineteenth centuries; it is about fourteen feet long and
seven feet broad, and oval inside. The door is approached by
a narrow and tortuous passage and you enter on hands and
knees. The stones of the walls have been laid in blackhouse
style, ie, they slope downwards and outwards to shed the
rain. I added two or three courses on the same principle, and
threw up more stone to the ramp of earth and stone all
round the outside. I had found a spar of timber some days
before on Leac Mhor Fianuis which just rested along the
top of the shieling lengthways. Thus, if our huts did blow
down in the winter we could bring the tarpaulin up here to
lay over the top of the wall and the ridge spar. Earth and
stone could have been banked all round and we should have
had an emergency lodging which would have kept out the
rain. 'Better a wee bush than nae bield,' said Burns. Happily,
we were not reduced to living in what would have been the
most primitive dwelling in Europe.

Bobbie and I went for a walk over the hill together on the
afternoon of the last day of July, thinking the end of the
month saw us a happier pair of people than did the beginning
when we were still in the stages of preparation. We
sat for a long time by the chapel saying nothing, for we were
enjoying the blue sky and the sea and the green of Rona's hill.
The warm breeze turned up the leaves of the silverweed and
dipped the heads of the bents, and dappled the hillside with
a shimmering pattern. Large white clouds stood out clear

against the blue, and the sheep were little less white, dotted about the green hill. This is Rona also, we thought, as well as Rona dark in the sea mist and windswept. Old Muir wrote well eighty years ago:

> O these endless little isles! and
> of all little isles this Ronay!
> Yet, much as hath been seen, not to
> see thee, lying clad with soft
> verdure, and in thine awful solitude,
> afar off in the lap of wild ocean, –
> not to see thee with the carnal
> eye, will be to have seen nothing!

That night the sun set at ten minutes past ten, going below the horizon with a green flash.

The first week of August was for us a giddy social whirl. Bobbie woke me rudely just after six o'clock in the morning on the first day of the month, shouting in my ear.

'There is a boat in the anchorage, what is it?'

In a semi-conscious state I leaned up and said it was the cruiser. Then I flopped back again, unable to feel as pleased as I really was when it really dawned upon me. Oh, how grey-faced you feel, being yanked out of bed like that! But a Primus does not take long to boil, and a cup of tea soon made me human again.

We sat down to letters immediately, for we knew there would not be much time for writing once the boys came ashore. They came soon after half past eight to Langa Beirie. We were met as old friends and they had a good laugh at my beard, which was neither one thing nor the other – I not being one of Esau's kind.

Cap'n M. began work on the wireless transmitter and found it was well and truly dead, but he brought us the news that as our wireless was not working, we might get a call from the cruiser now and again on her way to and from the Orkney station. This indeed was better than having the wireless, and I confess to being secretly pleased when the wireless did not work.

Alasdair was delighted to see his friends from the ship and a game of cricket was soon in progress – an empty oil drum for wicket and a batten of wood for a bat. Play continued hilariously until Bobbie made some coffee, when the team came into the pavilion to refresh themselves. It was one of those fine social occasions in summer when everybody enjoys themselves.

Next morning as I sat at breakfast I saw the smoke of a ship in the light of the sun a little north of east. I could see the hull of the ship after breakfast, and as it was a round speck rather than a long one it was obvious she must be end on to us and coming our way. We soon had no doubt that she was coming to Rona. We could see through my telescope that she was rather more fancy than a trawler, having a large bridge and boats in davits. She also had a cumbersome sort of boat hanging from a derrick forward.

'I don't think we'll wait for them to come ashore,' I said. 'We'll get the kayak down and I'll go out to them.'

I pushed off from the shore when their anchor grounded, and paddled over the quarter-mile to the ship. Several piratical gentlemen of the crew were leaning over the side and a civilian in a windjacket was firing a small cine camera at me. The very worst, I thought – reporters! But just then the Captain and First Officer looked over the side and introduced themselves, and I was completely reassured. The ship was the research ship *Explorer* on her way from Orkney to St Kilda.

The Captain pointed to the old flat-bottomed coble which was hanging from the derrick and which had puzzled me earlier as I had looked through my glass.

'We picked this from the sea twenty-five miles east of here. It is a danger to shipping, but rather than sink her we though it might be useful to you as firewood.'

I gazed with a new interest, for three days before I had seen this thing pass by the island from north-west to south-east, about a mile offshore. It had drifted at the surprising rate of a mile an hour and I had watched it carefully.

'She will do for more than firewood,' I said. 'What about using her as a roof for a store hut?'

This tickled the Captain's fancy, though he did not know just then the difficulties of getting such a hulk on to Rona. I felt that if there were enough of us it could be done. A dozen or more tumbled into the launch and we brought the coble and my kayak in tow. There was a bit of a swell running on the shore and the coble was leaky; when we got her nose on to the rock a wave pooped her and the rope painter broke. We were in danger of losing her, so I, being barefoot, leapt in and tied a long rope of tug-of-war to a ring in the floor of the coble. We got her up three or four feet on the rising swells and baled out the water from the stern. Then began the terrific job of getting this heavy old thing up rocks inclined at 30° to the sea. The Captain took charge and a big fellow called Jock did a lot of shouting by way of encouragement as well as doing a lot of work. This big East-Coaster, strong as an ox and kindhearted withal, gave me a private laugh. I asked him if he was from Aberdeen; his blue eyes looked at me blankly and shocked.

'Good gracious no,' he exclaimed. 'Stonehaven.'

I think I must be slow not to recognize immediately the difference between men from places fourteen miles apart.

The ship's company had been on a station all night and were ready to stretch their legs in a little relaxation ashore, otherwise I doubt whether my quiet rascality would have borne fruit. We gave many concerted pulls getting that coble up the rocks, and when she was on the chickweed at last we used the technique of a winning tug-of-war team, of spinning round and walking the boat up a long way. We were all a lot of lads together that day. The coble came to the sheep fank and we turned her over so that her gunwale rested on the lower part of the dyke; I knocked the stern and thwarts out of her later, and there we had a ready-made store for tinned things, tools and so on.

The poor old boat became quite famous because after our return I wrote to Alec MacFarquhar, Ness, Lewis, mentioning the coble. He wrote back saying it must be the one from Ness which had broken its moorings back in the summer. He said it was the one they used to take behind the big sailing-boat years ago when sheep were more regularly taken to and from Rona. Candidly I did not believe this could be the same boat, but Lewis evidently did, and the newspapers came out with a story of the boat with a homing instinct which floated home to Rona!

Some of the ship's company went over the hill to see the chapel, and the Captain asked us aboard for coffee. Big Jock took Alasdair in charge and showed him the tanks where live fish were – big pink sea-bream, young dogfish with yolksacs still attached to their bellies, and a few octopuses which changed colour as they swam across the tank. He also showed Alasdair the plankton net and the tiny life which comes out of it, under the miscroscope. It was Jock also who produced cream tarts from nowhere to eat with the coffee – and finally the visitors' book was placed before us for our signatures.

The kindness extended to us by the Captain and company of *Explorer* knew no bounds. Before we came ashore we were given a basket of fish – twenty big haddock, all split, cleaned and ready for salting, and a dozen fine soles. And just before we came off the ship one of the crew called Alasdair to the fo'c'sle and gave him a bag of sweets. I was very deeply touched by this. Big Jock also gave him some chocolate, explaining to me that he brought this stuff every voyage and never ate it. How typical it was of this big man that he should excuse his kindness! We had not yet stepped off the ladder before Jock said:

'What about giving 'em a real treat, Cap'n? Can I run and fetch 'em half a dozen salt herring?'

He was gone before the Captain could reply. Up came Jock again, all smiles, with a dozen wet and sticky herrings.

'Let 'em dry well in the sun and then grill 'em! Man, they're just beauties those!'

We had our lemon soles fried and served with chips before

Explorer finally left the anchorage, blowing her siren in fare-well. What a feed! What a morning!

We spent the rest of the day salting the fish in brine and hanging them out to dry. Our hut and the sheep fank looked like a Shetland croft by the time we had finished, what with the upturned boat and the haddies strung around. Perhaps this thought was in my mind that evening as I lay on the cliff edge in contemplative mood watching the puffins, my belly full of a second good meal of lemon sole.

The old people of the island salted puffins in thousands. I was glad I did not have to, even though I do curse at an advancing urban civilization which cuts across the self-sufficiency of island economy. It is difficult to know where to start and where to stop in this matter of taking life. If I lived here entirely I should eat puffins, but I would not take one puffin in the meantime, because I should not be taking toll of the race of puffindom so much as cutting short the free, and doubtless happy, life of one individual puffin when he was enjoying it most. Why should that individual suffer, of all his fellows, for a gastronomic experiment? I felt somewhat the same about the greater black-back gulls. There are too many of them here, I think, and I could at this date easily draw the necks of a dozen or more not yet in the air. But such a course would have no real effect on lessening the population, and the act of taking life would not be justified. I should have much less compunction about shooting three or four hun-dred of the adults.

Three days after this the weather was still brilliant, and after breakfast I went to a good place on the west side of Fianuis where I could watch seals, lie out of the light east wind and write in the slack intervals. But less than an hour afterwards I heard Bobbie's whistle blowing hard, and I ran back in an awful fright, thinking Bobbie must be in some dire trouble. There she was, running along the stony top of Fianuis, bursting her cheeks with the whistle whatever.

'A yacht going up the east side,' she called.

And when I got there it was to see a nice ten-ton, ketch-rigged yacht going north-about with her sails full of the

fresh south-easterly breeze, a pretty sight indeed. Bobbie said
she came round Sron na Chaorach into the east bay and
sounded her klaxon. Then, as there was too much breeze for
landing there, she continued northwards.

She lowered her sails at the north point, set her auxiliary
going and came into the west bay like a cat walking on eggs.
I did not smile at her extreme wariness, because the chart
shows no soundings there. We watched her drop anchor, saw
the dinghy, a Norwegian pram, come overboard, and then
we climbed down the cliffs on the south side of Sgeildige to
give him an idea where to make for. They did not venture
very close to the cliff-face, and when I called out that he
could land if he came in stern first, the man in the stern
said:

'Oh no, I'd rather not land unless you are in any trouble.
Can we do anything for you?'

'No, thanks,' I answered, 'as far as I know we're all right;
but you've come an awful long way not to be landing.'

'Not at all; we're sailing; we were in the Minch, and the
last we read about you was that no wireless message had
been received, so we thought we might come this length and
be able to report you all right.'

'Fine, thanks, but really, won't you come ashore and have
some lunch or a drink of tea?'

'No, no, I wouldn't climb up a dangerous cliff like that for
all the wealth in China. You oughtn't to have come down
yourselves.'

Bobbie and Alasdair were standing beside me, and none
of us had thought the cliff more than a walk; but there you
are, that was his outlook, and mine at that moment was to
admire his courage in coming fifty miles out of the shelter of
the Minch and then not to land. These sailing men are like
that. I would not wish to go a mile in a boat unless I were
going to land somewhere at the other end. We chatted a
little longer and learned that the yacht was SY *Judith*, Mr
W. A. Scott Brown, of Paisley and Glasgow. He was a
member of the Royal Clyde Yacht Club and told us he had
been talking to friends of ours in Lochbroom a couple of

nights before. So Mr Scott Brown drew back to *Judith* and I saw the little yacht disappear round the west point. This is just one of the short meetings we have had with strangers on islands, which have subsequently led to more solid acquaintanceship.

And Bobbie and I said to each other, 'What about the odd cup of tea?'

I did a little writing before lunch, but very little, because I was on the edge of the cliff above Sgeildige Geo, wearing polaroid glasses and watching the seals swimming in beautiful movement below water. I could see the shags going a good way down also, darting hither and thither among the swarms of tiny fish which I could just see. Arctic terns were dipping constantly and taking toll of these same swarms of seemingly indifferent little fish. The individual is nothing to them.

Down there in the mouth of the cave which runs under our huts is a rock which comes above water as the tide falls. Half a dozen seals play round it and lie out there sometimes, and among them was a big bull I called Big Willie. This seal came to know me well, just as that other one on the east side of the shingle spit on Lunga became intimate. At first Big Willie would let me talk to him only when he was in the water, for there a seal is master of his fate, as Big Willie well knew; but now he will let me talk to him as he lies lazily on the rock forty feet below me, and myself in full view. I can see his wise old face now in my mind's eye as I write these lines, and the present tense seems the right one in describing him.

The rest of the seals down there were immature bulls and two young cows. The bulls were playful lads, sometimes a bit rough with each other and even with the young cows. It is certain that some bulls prefer a sort of monastic existence outside the breeding season and young bulls will make up gangs. I do not think sociologists have realized the deep psycho-biological foundation of unisexual associations within societies. When young females come into these groups of young males the normal courteous relations of the bull seal to the cow are suspended. The young bulls might not be quite so rough with them as with their own sex, but the little cows are likely to get snarled off a rock, prevented from getting out of the water, or be snapped or scratched. Sometimes the young lady will lose her temper and flounce away, a sequence of behaviour very funny to watch, as it was on this morning. You get comparable conditions in human society; for example, there is a tacit understanding not to discriminate in a set of mixed tennis, and if a girl joins a climbing party (assuming she is worth her salt) she will not thank you for showing her preferential treatment or being shielded from hardship. But occasionally you do see a girl get cross when she cannot make equal headway and is still treated indifferently as an equal. Then she flounces away very much like my little cow seal who could not get out on the rock because these rough lads were teasing her and treating her as one of themselves.

They were just boisterous and full of fun. One of them had given me some fun five minutes before when he had mischievously given chase to a shag, not in a careful stalking fashion, but splashing heavily in a way that sent friend Shaggie flapping his wings over the water for fifty yards. The young bull dived and came up a few feet from the bird and snorted violently. The row sent Shaggie flapping in terror.

What chance had I, then, of doing much writing that morning? But I was not grumbling, for all these things were what I had come so far to see.

August 9th was a day specially worthy of notice, for the guillemots left their ledges on the cliffs. I went round the island and found the exodus had been a general one. Here and there was a solitary bird brooding over a very young chick, and these individuals merely heightened the forlornness. I imagine that the 'ledge' is the group unit in the social life of the guillemot, and that where I had seen the solitary birds the youngness of the chicks had made them more 'valent' for the parent than the larger loyalty of the 'ledge' which had now left the cliff and gone to sea. It is to

me a wonderful thing, and not easily explained, that thousands of guillemots spread about an island should suddenly
leave it in one night. What prompts this large group activity? All I can say about the birds prior to the event is that
they were extremely noisy in the darkness for two nights
before. Not until I saw those solitary birds that afternoon did
I realize that half the charm and beauty of sea birds is in
their busy life together.

The puffins were gone the next day, just as suddenly, and
now the cliffs had very much the appearance of 'the morning
after the night before'. Here, in a heightened form, was that
anticlimax of August which I have mentioned before in our
life on the islands. There is no doubt that the immense concourse of birds transmits some of its own excitement to the
human observer, and when the birds go the human being
feels lonely. I am not sentimentally fanciful in this, for I
have heard a hard-headed lighthouseman at an island
station make the same admission.

That night I removed the beard of a month's growth.
Bobbie said it was repulsive, and I had to admit it was a
failure as a beard. My razor had gone rusty in this oceanic
climate, and despite thorough stropping the removal of this
beard was in the nature of a major operation. The weather
had been so hot and calm on this day that I had been able to
enjoy a complete and leisurely bath in a pool on the south
side.

I sat up late that night carving for Alasdair a model boat
with mast and sails and working rudder, and when I had
finished at half past eleven I went outside to enjoy the
beauty of the night. The moon was at the full and the air
still, quieter than I ever thought it could be here. The petrels
were trilling among the stones and some were flying close
round my head. I picked up one which came to earth and
brought it into the hut for Bobbie to see. The little black
mite coughed up on my hand the food she was doubtless
bringing for her chick, and I was sorry.

Next day was so hot that we had both breakfast and lunch
outside. But the weather had no beauty in it, just oppressive

murky heat which promises thunder. These conditions, combined with the evening high spring tide, made me go out in
the kayak to fish though I had no wish to do so. I caught six
very large mackerel in a few minutes and came in again as a
low mist came down over Rona. We had not been in our bed
an hour when the heavy thunder rain began to fall, and
there was much thunder and lightning until three o'clock in
the morning. The closeness of the atmosphere and the noise
prevented our sleeping, but it was grand to see the island and
the sea lit up by the vivid flashes of sheet lightning. I called
out to Alasdair in his little hut early in the storm to ask him
if he was all right. He said he was and that he had not really
been to sleep yet. That could be readily understood, but
when a terrific clap woke me with a start from an unpleasant
sort of sleep I got out again and heard a cry from Alasdair.
The clap had woken him also and he did not know where he
was for a minute. So I called him into our hut, where he was
immediately very cheerful. I went through to his hut and
slept more or less well for the rest of the night.

It was still raining at breakfast-time, with a fresh wind
from the west. Then by ten o'clock the sun was out to make a
grand day of clear air, a white-flecked deep blue sea, and sky
with white cumulus clouds. Everything was fresh after what
had been nearly an inch of much-needed rain, and we felt
the better of it ourselves.

I went to the Tor and looked round with my glass. On
most days you can see no other land from there but Sula
Sgeir, the stark rock twelve and a half miles away WSW of
Rona, which just breaks through the ring of sea and sky. But
today the air was so clear I could see the gannets or solans
flying round Sula Sgeir and details of the rock were plain. An
immense panorama filled the southern horizon. Several of
the Orkney Islands were to be seen and the Hoy stood out as
a flat cone; then Duncansby Head at the north-east of the
mainland of Scotland. Next the fine line of the hills of the
North Coast, growing ever higher and more noble in shape
as the West was reached. Cape Wrath lighthouse was a
white speck forty-seven miles away, and then the mountains

began their southerly course until I could see shapes I knew well in Suilven and An Teallach. Now the circle of relationships seemed complete: I had seen Rona and the Brae House from An Teallach years before, and now, from that speck of Rona in the northern ocean, I was seeing the mountains of home which I see every day from Tanera. Rona is linked with our lives for ever.

Weather is the subject of constant interest to the island dweller, for practical as well as aesthetic reasons. Also, on a place like Rona, small, very remote and covered with an exceedingly short herbage, the sky and sea hold the interest still more. My diaries are full of descriptions of weather, and I admit to an experience of pleasure reading them over again. Here is an August morning which may please me more than you because when I read it I can remember the day itself:

'This morning was one of those calm days of soft colourings which are among the most beautiful for those who live on islands. The clouds did not wholly obscure the blue, and the clouds themselves were high and delicate. The sea answered the clouds with its diversity of colouring. The island was softened and its cliffs seemed not so sheer and terrible. I could see the mainland clearly, a distant skyline of isolated hills of fine lines; ships like toys seemed barely to move, thirty miles away. I lay for a while in the rich grass on the Tor enjoying the scents of earth and of the abundant white clover. It was a day for scents.'

The summer was reckoned a very bad one on the mainland, especially on the West Coast, but we called it a good one on Rona. There were gales, of course, but they did not last long and the number of sunny, brilliant days was remarkable. We agreed that we had rarely known such good weather anywhere.

When the three of us topped the ridge on such a day, September 1st, Alasdair pointed towards Sula Sgeir. There was a large brown sail on the sea just south of Gralisgeir, the skerry half a mile south of Sula Sgeir. We watched the boat tack in the northerly breeze until she came into the east side of the great rock, and there we could see no more of her, because the sun was going round out of our favour and Sula Sgeir was over twelve miles away from us. It was the men of Ness in their forty-foot open boat, come to take their annual harvest of the young solans or *gugas*. This boat is the last of its kind in existence, and it is this journey each year which keeps it in commission. The boat is a direct descendant of the ancient Viking type, skiff-ended and extremely buoyant. There are boats of similar type and lineage left in Shetland – the yollie, and in Caithness – the skaffa.

Since time immemorial the men of Ness, Lewis, have made the yearly journey to Sula Sgeir in late August or early September to take a toll of the young gannets, which are immensely fat at this time. The young birds are preserved for winter food. The present toll is about two thousand birds each year, more than the gannetry can stand, with the result that the stock is diminishing. There has been a considerable outcry from the preservationists pure and simple to put a stop to this practice; but the final result has been to harden opinion against any interference, and the boat went again in 1939.

The conservationist's point of view would be to consider man as a predatory animal and to include him in the ecological web. In an age when skilled physical effort tends to be dropped and ability lost, there can be little doubt that this open-boat journey has a social value in the small community of Ness. If these people did not eat the gannets, what else would they have? The answer is corned beef and margarine, a poor substitute which would bring in the money factor – always undesirable in a semi-primitive community – and allow the boat to rot. What I say in defence of this practice in no way excuses the appearance of roast gannet on the menu provided by the local steamship service!

A group of British workers headed by James Fisher, now Secretary of the British Trust for Ornithology, made a world census of gannets in 1939, but this was only the spectacular part of several years' work on the fluctuations of gannet colonies. There is now a good body of knowledge concerning the dynamics of population in this species, but in the heated correspondence and such official inquiry as has been made no reference seems to have been made to this research. If we had a Bureau of Biological Survey in this country, comparable with that excellent administrative body in the United States, the problem would have been referred to it as a matter of course, and the Bureau would have treated the gannets as a natural resource. The toll of gannets would neither be prohibited nor passively encouraged, but regulated. If a thousand instead of two thousand were taken for five years and the fluctuations of numbers noted on this remote islet, the safety of the gannetry would be ensured and the Ness men would continue their thousand-year-old custom.

The advent of September meant a new season in the life of the great seals. They began to come high on the face of Rona, the bulls first, to take up their territories for the breeding season, and then the cows a few days later. They came up not only on Leac Mhor but up the steep rocks from Geodha Stoth so that the huts were soon surrounded by the crying seals. Those in our immediate neighbourhood soon came to accept us as part of the island and did not go hurtling back to the sea when we passed to and fro. The wireless receiver was still working and we used to have the news each evening; the sound of the engine did not seem to worry the seals, for they would no more than raise their heads when I started and stopped it.

The first calf was born on September 14th, and after that they came in quick succession. The continuous falsetto crying of the seals was now augmented by these baby cries, a sound that pulls at your heart when you hear it in the night when the weather is wild and rainy. It was a magnificent experience to be living among these hundreds of seals, though there were times when Bobbie objected to the smell of them. It was an acrid, animal smell, smacking of the sea. Alasdair played with some of the calves but they would have none of him; even the mothers accepted him better than they did.

The breeding season of the seals was waxing, but autumn had come to Rona. A bleakness and hardness were there, and in the evenings we enjoyed more and more the institution of half an hour sitting on Alasdair's bed when we settled him for the night. This was the time when I played the mouth-organ and Bobbie and Alasdair sang. The conduct of Alasdair's *salon* as we called it was a matter for care because we found ourselves sensitive to the atmospheres evoked by music. If we wanted fun it had to be at the beginning with 'The De'il's Awa', 'McRory's Breeks' and other Scots and English songs. Then we would drift into the melodies of the like of 'Afton Water' and 'Drink to me only', and then into the still quieter and more primitive Gaelic songs such as 'Caol Muile', 'Grigal Chridhe', 'Caisteal na Gleann' and one of Alasdair's own compositions. Sometimes we had a round of hymns, and always we finished with two or three verses each of 'Lead, kindly light', 'Now the day is over' and 'The day thou gavest, Lord, is ended'. This nightly half-hour was an integral part of our lives on Rona, and had a great influence in making us feel bound together and strong in each other's love. It is one of the treasured memories we have brought away from Rona, and I know that Rona *salons* are in Alasdair's heart for evermore. If ever we made a right decision it was in taking him to the island; his spirit and life were enriched as well as ours.

The latter half of September, 1938, was clouded by the developments of the international crisis. From our remote corner of the earth's surface we seemed to see it impersonally as a tragic drama unfolding on another planet. And yet our perceptions were never clearer. On the Sunday, September 25th, I felt extremely unhappy and thought about the world which thoughtless men in Britain and the rest of Europe had created in recent years. I was still unhappy on the Monday morning when I went over to do a little more work at the chapel and cell. I sat a long while in that place where simple folk had worshipped in old time; I thought through recent events as far as I knew them, and then I stopped thinking and was conscious only of the island and the sound of the sea. Even these loved things became dim in a brighter light which filled my mind. Such moments are not ones to be dwelt on in print, but when they come I know them for truth. I came back to the huts that day with the unshakable conviction that war would not occur at that time, though knowledge was no cause for complacence.

Bobbie heard what I had to say; she hoped I was right, though the days brought still worse news. But to me those events were like reading a page of history, the result of which I knew already.

On the morning of September 29th I woke uneasily and began telling Bobbie of a most unpleasant dream I had had. The cruiser was coming for us and we had to leave Rona. And that was not the worst of the dream, for in it I had endured the misery of not being able to get back to the island because of the wild weather. How lovely it was, therefore, to wake and find that I really was on Rona all the time. I lay for a while in deep thankfulness at being where I was, for the dream had been so vivid.

My relief was short-lived, for we had not risen more than half an hour when the cruiser appeared off the east side of the island. I do not think I have ever felt my heart sink so completely as at that moment. We got the wireless receiver running and tuned in to our short wavelength. Cap'n M. was telling us to get ready to leave. All the same, there was a fresh south-easterly wind blowing and a deep swell coming in from the west, and I knew he could never get us off just then. He said so himself the next minute, and we saw the ship move away. Splendid. With a bit of luck this normally wretched wind would hold and we should remain until the international situation cleared.

This again was false optimism, for Cap'n M. is a tenacious man. He was back again in an hour because the Atlantic swell was dropping a little – enough to let him lower a boat. On this occasion we held conversation with him in an effective manner, but one which reflects no credit on me, because I ought to have learned to transmit and receive signalling in Morse code with flags. I went on to the steep hill-face with a pile of towels and my pyjamas. With these I spelt out letters and words on the green hillside, and the cruiser sounded a short blip on her siren after reading each letter. Bobbie was down at the hut receiving the spoken word from the cruiser on the wireless, and Alasdair was making liaison by running to and fro between us with the messages. No matter whether we wished to stay or not, we must go, and that quickly. Bobbie dropped a few necessities into two sleeping bags, while I tried to leave things shipshape about the camp. Our departure from Rona was that of destitute refugees. It was an almost hopeless task trying to catch our three hens in daylight on a bare island. One refused to be caught, and somebody dropped another going over to Langa Beirie where Cap'n M. had brought the launch. The seals were disturbed and I was thoroughly unhappy.

I endured misery all that voyage. We reached Stornoway about half past ten that night, and what a scene was there for such folk as we were! A large arc-light shone over the gangway of the mail boat, which on this night was packed with young fellows in naval uniform – Fleet reservists called up in the past two days. They all seemed glad, for there was much cheering and the sound of pipes was continual. Perhaps a few older men did not look so pleased, and my own heart ached to see the flower of the North gathered here like this. It but needed another war to finish the Highlands and Islands by draining their youth.

We reached Little Loch Broom next morning, and when we landed at Badluchrach I confess to the pleasure of seeing little stunted willows again, hearing a robin sing, and seeing and smelling corn stubbles and potato ground. We were at home to the Brae House soon after, drinking a few quarts of tea and enjoying the wood-smoke. What a mingled state I was in, of pleasure in loved things sensed afresh and of unhappiness at the calamitous break in my work towards which so much thought and money had gone. I felt some solace in going into the woods and on to the hill to watch the deer. It was rutting time in the forest and all was activity.

My dream proved all too true, for we lost the whole of

October and part of November, waiting from day to day for the seas to quieten and allow us to return to Rona. If ever I have learned patience it is in those days of waiting. Bobbie and I brought in great logs from the woods, sawed them and chopped them. We gathered wild apples and rowan berries and made jelly. Our bank passbook came and gave us a shock which sat me down to write articles for a few days. But we were living from day to day, and if you have ever lived ten miles from the nearest inadequate sort of a shop, with the car laid up, and without livestock, you will know how difficult catering was for us at that time. Happily, we had got Alasdair back to school the day after our return. I would go up the rock at the back of the house each morning to see the state of the sea and whether the cruiser was in the Loch and come down again disappointed. We shall never forget the goodness of our friends the Morrisons of Corriehallie then; they cheered us more than they knew with their good-fellowship.

And then one day came a telegram from Cap'n M. 'Purpose calling Little Loch Broom tomorrow Tuesday 9.30 A.M.' This set us doing our bit of packing and putting some of the things in the house in dry places. We went to bed saying 'Seven o'clock, seven o'clock' to ourselves, so that we should not be late up, but we need not have bothered, for both of us slept badly and were glad to get up soon after six o'clock in the morning.

CHAPTER TWELVE

RONA IN WINTER

Alex Maclean of the Dundonnell Hotel came to Brae for us in his car, and we got to the boathouse with our bit of baggage just as the cruiser was dropping anchor. Mac's last words as he said goodbye to us were to invite us to breakfast when we came back. We gave him a final wave from the deck of the cruiser.

It was good weather and calm going down the Loch, and I was able to enjoy myself for a little while. We passed between Eilean a' Chleirich and Ghlas Leac Bheag, where I saw a few grey lag geese flying about. Then the swell in the Minch proved too much for me, and my interests in anything were very slight thereafter. Black squalls came down from the north-west as we neared the Lewis coast, the wind so cold to me that it seemed to pierce my Grenfell suit and the piles of clothes I wore underneath it. That is one of the worst parts of seasickness, the dreadful, incurable coldness which just has to be borne. We anchored for the night north of Tolsta Head, where there was a trawler also lying. I felt an absolute mess and a milksop when I saw a couple of tough-looking fellows on the trawler leaning negligently over the gunwale stripped to the waist. They were not even working, just leaning around, arms folded over hairy chests. I was careful to do my walking up and down the other side of the ship so that the trawlermen should not see this specimen the cruiser had aboard.

The electric-light engine stopped about midnight, after which time I lay more or less at ease, listening to the west wind blowing through the rigging, and to the water lapping

against the side of the ship. The water showed phos-
phorescent, a beautiful moving pattern in the darkness of the
night. I slept off and on until four o'clock in the morning,
when the anchor was drawn and we got under way. I remained comfortable for a time, but I knew as soon as we
cleared the Butt of Lewis. Paddy the steward, who had been
a good friend to me these several journeys, came up to the
chartroom with tea and toast for me at seven o'clock and
said our home town was in sight. This was good news, which
I soon had the unwanted opportunity to confirm for myself.
Only a few miles more, and I lay listening for the bell of the
engine telegraph. I staggered out and looked to the landing
where the surf was hitting up white, but not so bad as it
might be. Once we were away from the rolling ship it was
my turn to guide the steersman to the landing and warn him
about a reef which is covered at high spring tide as it was
now; and as luck would have it, the swell got worse for a few
waves as we came up to the rocks. A wind from nor'-nor'-
east had sprung up since five o'clock time, and had made
things rather bad. We just had to wait a while for a few slack
waves, when we sidled in once more and made the most of
our opportunity by jumping for it. The arrangement was
that Bobbie and I should run up to the huts as fast as we
could, see that things were all right and come back to tell
them and let them away.

We had not time to realize this new Rona to which we had
come, but even as I was climbing up those slippery rocks I
noticed a pair of long-tailed duck and the fact that hundreds
of fulmar petrels were flying from the cliffs. We waded
through a sea of mud and grumly seals, saw a couple of seals
among our tinned stores under the upturned coble and
another one on the doorstep. The seals had brought down
the wireless masts and were romping through the wire en-
tanglements which had once been the stays. We looked very
hurriedly to see that the roofing felt was all right and inspected the flour and meal and other perishables. All seemed in
order, and we skated back to the launch to say that everything was all right as far as we could see. How thankful we

were then that we were ashore, for the swell had got much worse, even in those few minutes. That is the way of it on some of these small islands, the state of the swell changes in a very short time regardless of the weather. It was good to see the launch back at the ship and inboard again. We appreciated the kindness of Cap'n M. in keeping the ship in the east bay for a few minutes longer in case we found some trouble unnoticed in that first look round.

And now we came to consider the abomination of desolation. The place and mess were indescribable, but one thing pleased us – our two hens were alive and apparently well, uninterested in the food which we almost immediately offered them. No doubt this immense concourse of seals and the number of dead calves made a plentiful supply of food for birds.

Some rain had come through the roof of the big hut, and all the bedding we had left was very damp. The stove was soon going hard to dispel this atmosphere of chill. I ejected the seals from under the coble, where they had made a fine mess of the tinned jam, vegetables and fruit. Labels had come off and several cans were ground in the slime; happily, the outer environment has little to do with the contents of the tin, so, apart from having to guess at what was in them, we suffered no loss. The hens had also roosted there and found good shelter which must have enabled them to survive. Seals or wind or both had knocked down two five-gallon drums of paraffin and emptied them, and several tins of petrol had disappeared. We found some of these later nearly a quarter of a mile away where the great winds had blown them. The kayak had been broken to pieces by the seals, and bits of it were scattered half over Fianuis.

We turned away from the wreckage and ate a whole tin of fruit and cream for lunch. Lovely. Felt much better about everything after that. We had seemed to live on bread and tea, and venison and potatoes, those weeks of waiting at Dundonnell, but now we had returned to Rona where there was all manner of good victuals and many luxuries. Seasickness leaves me as soon as I get ashore, and now I was eager to be moving about the island again.

Those acres of Fianuis which had been lush fields of chickweed in the summer were now a sea of mud. The place was
black in the dull daylight of winter. The northern face of the
hill was a vast black slide down which we could see several
seals making their way at a great pace. We climbed up there
with difficulty to fetch water from the well on the south side
and had the surprise of seeing seals on the top of the ridge,
three hundred feet above the sea. It was altogether amazing.
There was another young seal at the extreme edge of the
sheer west cliff, one which a few days later I saw fall the
three hundred feet to its death. There were seals young and
old round the edge of Geodha Leis, a terribly dangerous
place, because if they take the hundred-foot jump into the
sea they are liable to fall on rocks which are just covered
down there. One day I saw a big bull seal go down when he
was chased by another, and he just burst when he hit those
rocks. I was thoroughly upset by this event, because I felt it
need not have happened.

I can see now that these Atlantic grey seals could be transplanted to new groups of islands when they are at the stage
of naturally starving at three weeks old, ie, before they have
any tradition of the sea. I can see that the population of
these seals could be much increased and drawn upon carefully as a natural resource of oil. If that ever came about
under the direction of a Bureau of Biological Survey, on
which I am so keen, it would also be possible on a place like
Rona to prevent a great deal of loss of stock, by fencing
these geos and sheer cliffs where the seals fall to certain
death.

Bobbie and I covered the island that first day, and by the
end of the second had counted 850 live seal calves and 150
dead ones. All the first lot which were calves when we left at
the end of September were away to sea now. My Treshnish
estimate of infant mortality was about 10 per cent, so I
reckoned there must have been 1,500 calves born on Rona.
That means a total population of seals about the place of
roughly 5,000, a figure I also estimated by actual counting.

This seems a lot of seals, but these big congregations of
breeding animals should never be taken at their face value as
representing vast numbers of the animals. This lot on Rona
probably represented half the total breeding stock on this
side of the Atlantic. Animals which breed in large congregations require our very special protection if they are to
remain in existence. The grey seals were nearly exterminated
in the last century, but fortunately for them a growing in-
dustrialism began to counteract the harm it was doing them,
by supplying the Hebridean population with rubber boots
which were more efficient than sealskin, and with paraffin oil
which gave a better light than seal oil.

It was good to get out of the muck that night and eat a
terrific dinner. Life was not too bad, I thought afterwards,
seeing our little world through the magic haze of a Havana
cigar. One of our Cheddar cheeses which had been in a flour
bin under the coble with the seals had ripened beautifully
into a blue-veined cheese which could only be described as
noble for its richness and fullness of flavour. It was one of the
cheeses of this generation. I was in a similar mood when I
wrote in my diary three nights later: 'The waves were going
green over Lisgeir Mhor this morning, and north of Rona
where the water is shallow the rollers are piling higher than
any waves I have ever seen. Now, after an immense tea and a
Larañaga (box getting distressingly low), I can hear the
steady roar of the sea outside and in the caves beneath us.
Now for a few tunes on the mouth-organ and then to bed.
This is a rest cure.'

Another night, November 27th it was, a southerly gale
was raging, and as I came in, just on dusk, I saw a seal cow
and her calf on the edge of the Sgeildige Geo, outlined
against the stormy sunset. It was too dark for me to see her
face plainly, but I could see her movements and the patient
carriage of her head. In that light, in that wind and in these
desolate surroundings there seemed to me to be the living
spirit of Rona in that silhouette.

The gale reached hurricane force in the night. The hut
shook and the roof went up and down as the great gusts

came down the hill. The pounding of the sea on the west side
of Rona was of itself rattling the crockery on the shelves.
The wind and rain being what they were, we stayed in bed
till ten o'clock that morning and got breakfast by the simple
means of reaching forth for various eatables, and the stove
was there with water ready for tea. The rain stopped and the
sun appeared, though the wind showed no signs of abating.
We went out to enjoy the spectacle of the island under these
conditions. The waves were breaking two or three times the
height of Fianuis and it was not possible to get along there
west of the storm beach. The waves breaking in Geodha Leis
and Geodha Blatha Mor were sending up clouds of spray to
over three hundred feet, which spray was then driven over
the whole face of the island, even over the Tor, which was
the farthest removed from the west and three hundred and
fifty-five feet high. From up there we could see that Loba
Sgeir and Sceapull were white with water going over them,
and waves were breaking over the north end of Fianuis as
well. The form of Sgeildige Geo saved the huts from the
worst of the spray, though we saw green water come to
within ten feet of the edge of the cliff there, just the rise and
fall of the swell.

Heavy rain set in again during the afternoon, herald of
another wild night. We could not sleep for the buffeting of
the wind and the roar of the sea, but we were snug and
warm, with plenty of books to read and tea to drink. Indeed,
Rona was a good place to get some reading done. I read
Robinson Crusoe again for the first time since schooldays,
and felt he was well off. When such nights as this frightened
us a little with the wind and sea I used to read Cherry-
Garrard's *The Worst Journey in the World*, and realized
that it was ourselves who were well off. I read Jane Austen's
novels, *A Sentimental Journey* and much of *The Bible
Designed to be Read as Literature*. The more I read of this,
the more I realized how wrong it is to make children read
the Bible and learn pieces of it by heart when at school. It
simply kills their appreciation of either the sentiment or the
English. The very mention of the phrase 'the twenty-third

psalm' would chill me and bring back those fruitless efforts
to learn it in school at the age of eight. The Lord was not my
shepherd in those days; my mother was enough for me, and
she was no shepherdess but a mother in every way she could
be to an eight-year-old child. Who was God, anyway? The
family Bible of 1830 showed Him as a stern, woolly-whis-
kered old gentleman who defied the laws of gravity by sitting
around on a cloud. He carried no conviction to the factual
mind of a child and meant nothing to me. But Jesus was my
mother's Friend, and acceptable in consequence. Now, on
Rona in the nights of storm, I could read 'The Lord is my
shepherd, I shall not want', and get the beauty out of it,
especially so in the form of blank verse given in Dr Sutherland Bates' edition of the Bible.

The wind suddenly slackened at ten o'clock the following
morning, and brilliant sunshine bathed the island. We were
out taking photographs for two or three hours before the
afternoon came grey and sullen once more and the wind
freshened from the south. There was a full gale blowing
from the south-east when we went to bed, accompanied by
incredibly sharp and intense showers. One of them was just as
if some mighty hand had hurled a fistful of rice on the roof –
then no more. I finished writing a book of essays on which I
had been working while we were on Rona, and a preface
which had escaped me entirely till now suddenly came into
my head and I was satisfied with it when I had put it to
paper. Broken sleep or little sleep at all in these nights of
storm seemed to have no effect on my mental brightness; in
fact, I do not think I was ever more keen in my perceptions.
I was happy, well fed, warm at nights, well supplied with
work and new things to see in surroundings I knew and
loved. The outside world did not exist for us now, the wireless being dismantled and ourselves not wishing for any contact until Christmas was near. The utter desolation of the
land and the might of the sea seemed to uplift us in some
strange way. Life was good. But as we look back on that time
of complete withdrawal from the world of men, it is the
weather which is the most vivid part of the experience. It

was not only wind and sea, but the sky as well. I wrote on
December 2nd:

'The wind has slackened a little, late this evening, though
it is still strong, the clouds have gone higher and the moon is
out for long periods. The northern lights are beautiful to the
north-east – a great curtain of greenish-yellow light and
glowing masses of this light rising and falling very rapidly. It
is interesting to look one way at the aurora and the other
way at the moonlight. How different they are! The one
seems unreal, intangible, almost mystic; the other is homely
and well known from childhood, and seems a light with
more body to it.'

We enjoyed a glorious calm night.

A southerly gale arose on December 4th of such intensity
that when I went for water I had to crawl over the ridge on
hands and knees. Fianuis was impassable for a short time.
The sunrise that morning had been a magnificent show of
blood-red and cerise, which always bodes ill. After the tan-
trums of the afternoon we had thunder and lightning at
night; the thunder came in single claps just like great explo-
sions and were rather frightening, because for the first two or
three I saw no lightning and could hardly believe they were
thunder, the sound being mixed with the great noise of wind.
We did a good deal of work about the chapel and village in
this time of storm, mapping the lazy-beds, gathering the
quern stones together and seeking for what we could find.

I excavated the altar in the cell at this time, and at its foot
on the right-hand side, buried under four feet of earth, I
found a round, polished stone of green marble rather less
than a cricket ball in size. My mind said immediately 'Iona',
for I know well the lovely green stone to be found in that
isle.

I brought the stone away for identification by an expert,
and it is serpentine marble of the same kind as that of Iona. I
have learned since that stones of foreign origin have been
found before in early Christian cells, and in one such cell
recently excavated in the Orkney Islands an Iona stone has
been found of the type one can pick up at Port na Churach

where Columba is supposed to have landed. There seems every reason for thinking the Rona stone is of Iona marble, and I have wondered if St Ronan was trained at Iona and brought this stone as a symbol of the earlier foundation. One newspaper critic pointed out that St Ronan was probably trained at Lindisfarne a century earlier than it has been assumed he lived on Rona. My answer to that is that there were about a hundred St Ronans in the history of the early Celtic Church. I put three little Iona stones of my own into Ronan's altar as a token of good faith until I brought back his own.

The seals of Rona were gathering at this time on the great skerry of Loba Sgeir to change their coats. The old hair came up white and gave the mass of two or three thousand seals a strange appearance. The animals lay quiet now, wrecks of their former selves, rarely crying or quarrelling. So they would lie until the old coat was rubbed out against the rock and then go forth once more to their habitual feeding grounds to regain condition.

I have complained many times in this book of the south-east wind and its devilish effects on the nerves. Here are excerpts from my diary of our last few days on Rona in 1938:

Tuesday, December 13th. Strong south-east wind all last night and all today, getting very strong since four o'clock. Bobbie and I went to the north end of Fianuis this morning, putting up two woodcock on the way. On the road home the wind was in our faces and I smelt the scent of burning wood. This troubled me a little, sufficient to make me quicken my pace, though I said nothing to Bobbie. Then she said:

'Can you smell burning wood, Frank?'

'Oh, so you're smelling it too, are you? Come on.'

I ran forward to a point where I could see the huts and was much relieved to see them still there and not smoking. Nevertheless, we wasted no time going back the other three hundred yards, but everything was all right. There were no ships anywhere to be seen, so I am wondering how both of us smelt that very distinct scent.

Did some packing and roping of boxes this afternoon, and
over the hill for water in the gloaming. It was clear enough
to see the alternate red and white flash from Cape Wrath
Lighthouse. How grand it was to come in just after dark, put
off heavy boots, peel off my Grenfell windproof trousers and
anorak, remove my stockings, let the knee-bands of my plus-
fours down about my ankles, put on two pairs of thick socks
and a pair of woolly slippers! Then peel off my heavy outer
jersey, have a good wash and comb my hair thoroughly –
and sit back and enjoy the smell and warmth of cooking
for a quarter of an hour until the meal is on the table. Cold
tongue, mixed vegetables and mayonnaise and new potatoes
tonight; finished up with I don't know how many beautifully browned raisin fritters with Demerara sugar. Then one
of the last half-dozen Larañagas and endless pints of tea.
Then to some writing and this diary, and soon to bed with a
good book until we are gloriously drowsy. Just enough
energy to reach out to turn the lamp out, and asleep in no
time. But not for unbroken slumber; I know we shall be
woken many times.

Wednesday, December 14th. Still the south-east wind,
slackening somewhat while it veered to south and freshened
to a gale. Glaucous gulls have come in today and are feeding
on carcasses of young seals. The young glaucous gulls are
more aggressive than the big black-backs and will drive
them away from a carcass. Sunset magnificent tonight, ex-
tending over the whole sky, east as well as west, but I
thought it indicative of a gale and I was right.

Thursday, December 15th. Last night when we came in
from our walk we noticed the gulls to be down on the ground
and comparatively tame, and the fulmars had not returned
to the cliffs. Bobbie asked me if I thought they were like this
because they were exhausted after the long period of high
winds, or was this portentous of something worse? I rather
imagined it meant worse to come but did not like to be
unduly pessimistic. But I have the devil of an eye for
weather; last night we suffered an absolute bombardment
from the wind in the south; then long before dawn it backed

to east-south-east. It increased after breakfast, and now at eight o'clock in the evening we are in one of the worst gales we have ever endured. We think it was at its worst between four and five o'clock, but it is still terrific. The hut was rocked and shaken before tea, and I had fears for the roof. We went out and piled more stones on to those which weight the wires running over the roof. The hens were in the fank all day sheltering from the gale, but when night fell they wanted to get under the old coble to roost. They could not go out of the hole in the wall because they would have been blown away into the sea, and they tried again and again to get over the dyke but were blown off. At one place the beam of the old boat projects above the dyke, and they eventually got on top of the stones there and slipped down between the dyke and the boat and crept round to the entrance.

Friday, December 16th. Last night was one to be got through somehow. The gale increased as we went to bed and kept us awake all night with the noise and shaking of the hut. I was anxious for the felting of the roof, and well I might be, for when we looked out this morning it was to find the felt had been ballooned up between the battens and had burst. I got it down again and nailed on several more boards to serve as battens; I also used a fair amount of putty, though my experience is that bitumen felt and putty do not agree together. When we got up this morning we felt as if we had been beaten all over – such is the effect of one of these terrible gales. And yet a blink of sunshine during the morning made us feel grand. Then in the afternoon it looked very threatening and there was a little rain; but within half an hour the wind veered to south, fell to moderate strength, the sky cleared and now it is a starlight evening. The seas are big in the east bay, though easterly gales, no matter how severe, never make the tremendous seas which come in from the west. Even with this great gale having blown for two days and the wind having been strong from the south-east for nearly a week, there is still a deep swell rolling in from the west, breaking high above the cliffs of Fianuis. The north point of Rona is in the position of having breakers on it from both sides. No one should ever get the idea that you can land on Rona in winter on the side away from the wind. Day after day goes by with landing utterly impossible. We had thought the number of seals about the island to be decreasing, but the gale seems to have brought them back to Loba Sgeir and Leac Mhor Fianuis, where they are lying in hundreds.

Saturday, December 17th. After a calm night the wind began to freshen again from the south-east about seven o'clock this morning. This is most disappointing, for we are sick of wind altogether. It blew fresh all morning, but the sun was out and we counted it pleasant weather; then the strength of wind increased after lunch, was blowing a gale by tea-time, and now in the evening it is blowing like the very deuce and the sea is as big as ever ... There has been an immense swell on the west side today, from which we infer there have been big disturbances in the Atlantic. Bobbie and I enjoyed a few minutes of absolute peace from wind in St Ronan's cell this afternoon.

Sunday, December 18th. It is no use going on using superlatives about these wretched gales. Last night was Inferno and we were very unhappy; we dozed now and again, but we read and made tea and listened for most of the night. How can I describe this dreadful south-easterly gale? The noise of wind and its physical effects on our hut were bad enough – roof lifting, all crockery rattling, creaks everywhere, and sometimes the upper half of the door bending in from the top. But as well as this there is the fact that we are not altogether ourselves in the night-time. We hear that dreadful sea a hundred yards in front to the east of us, and there is the pound of that immense swell forty yards behind to the west. All this tends to rattle you in the middle of the night, although in the daytime you see quite well that the water is unlikely to meet you green. The spray has driven across the neck of land all through the night and our windows are thickly encrusted with salt as with a heavy frost. When we rose this morning the sea was more white than green, and in a measure flattened by the force of the wind.

Bobbie and I battled forth to the south side this morning for water and had to crawl over the ridge. We were several times blown back some steps, and yet the queer thing is that but for this exceptional wind the weather is perfect; hardly a cloud in the sky, and the sun has shone the length of its short span. I was watching the swells come round the north end of Lisgeir Mhor to meet the full force of the gale from the east. One immense wave rolling forward to break was piled vertical by the wind, and its crest and half its body were just blown away as a great cloud of spray turned rainbow by the sun. The whole pillar must have been seventy or eighty feet ... Herring gulls and greater black-backed gulls are sitting close to the ground round the hut and inside the fank where there is a bit of shelter. They are regardless of our presence and allow us to pick them up and put them down again without trying to escape from our hands. Poor devils!

I have had to do some hammering with nails to keep the roof down today, and to put on extra wires as well. We have to yell to make ourselves heard even inside the hut; but Bobbie produced one of her usual treats for such a day as this – fried sausages, peas and new potatoes; strawberries-and-cream trifle and excellent coffee.

Monday, December 19th. The wind fell during the night but kept up a series of whistling gusts and dunts on the hut. We were so tired we slept through a good part. We were up and out as soon as it was light, for it is difficult to appreciate the sense of well-being in the blessed calm following one of these snorters unless you have experienced it under the conditions we have. Today Rona has been paradise, where for the last week it has been prison.

It was one of those days when we saw interesting new birds and ours seemed a good world.

The night was extraordinarily calm, and Bobbie and I found ourselves unable to sleep for excitement after four o'clock. We lay in our beds drinking tea until we could lie no longer. Breakfast was over long before it was light, and we took a walk up the Tor – to find an empty, flat-calm sea.

Considering the state of our excitement, we were not as disappointed as we expected to be. The scene of grey seas and skies and snow showers in the half-light of this winter morning was strangely beautiful; we put up ten woodcock from here and there – a sign of snow – and sure enough, before we were home again the snow began to fall. Then came a strong south wind and mist. I went over the hill for water later in the day, and on coming back saw a dim, white Fianuis washed by a green-edged sea, appearing from the mist. This glimpse of another Rona I would not have missed, a quiet, remote place indeed in this snow, despite the strong wind.

Bobbie and I put away our disappointment for another day, and then, when it seemed unlikely we should get away for Christmas, both of us suddenly and independently had the conviction that we should get home. Once that had come to us, all the little fears and doubts were gone and we were extraordinarily happy.

The snow settled the weather, and three days before Christmas we rose to a calm sea and a white, frozen Rona. It came light just after nine o'clock in the morning when we had climbed to the summit cairn on the Tor. Never had we seen the view so magnificent as on this which was to be our last morning. The sun was rising behind the far, clean line of the Sutherland hills and tinted the whole of our snowy world a rosy pink. The atmosphere was clear and still, and even as we watched I spied a dot thirty miles away between Cape Wrath and the Butt of Lewis. A ship undoubtedly, the first we had seen for a month. The dot was certainly coming nearer, and it must be the cruiser coming for *us*.

The two gale-battered folk of twenty-four hours ago became two carefree children. Was the snow truly rose-coloured by the sun, or had we donned the traditional spectacles with the sight of the ship? We slid down the snow slopes on the seats of our Grenfell suits; we rolled in the snow and turned somersaults. And rather more quietly we went over to Ronan's cell, the still vivid heart of the island. I know also that both of us silently paid our last tribute to Malcolm Macdonald and Murdoch Mackay who did not

live for such a joyful moment as this one in our lives. We
may never see Rona again as we saw it that morning early,
no one else alive has been there at such a time, but we felt in
those quiet moments by the chapel that our farewell was not
for ever. As I write these lines we are plunged into a war the
outcome of which for our society we do not know, and this
slowly mending leg and the depth of winter make me feel
that active and carefree days on Rona are far away. But I
would not like to think I had been there for the last time.
'Ane little ile callit Ronay,' wrote Dean Monro in 1549; 'afar
off in the lap of wild ocean,' wrote Thomas Muir in 1860,
'not to see thee with the carnal eye, will be to have seen
nothing!' Even beloved Eilean a' Chleirich has not affected
us so deeply as this little green island in the northern
ocean.

The cruiser dropped anchor in the east bay within three
hours, by which time we had carried some of our gear down
to the landing at Geodha Stoth. All this we got off eventually, but a lot of stores and heavier stuff had to wait till we
came back in June, 1939. We were rather glad to leave something so that we could come back for it.

Cap'n M.'s welcome to us seemed particularly warm that
day, and no one was more thankful than he was to get us
aboard. We heard later of Cap'n M.'s remarks when the ship
came in sight of the camp. Someone had said:

'Well, the huts are there all right.'

'I'm not thinking about the huts,' Cap'n M. had said. 'I
want to count the population first.'

The census of two souls was entirely satisfactory.

Our journey home was the most comfortable I had had.
Early next morning we came to Tanera Anchorage, and that
island, even in winter dress, looked sub-tropical to our eyes.
A hard frost was down but no snow. The high hills themselves were clear of it here, though Harris and Lewis were
white to the sea. We left some of our gear at Tanera and
made for the boathouse at the head of Little Loch Broom
which is for ever associated with our island expeditions. The
Chief gave me a farewell haircut as we came up the Loch,

but did we cut our hair by the weather I should have gone unshorn that day. We could feel the air getting colder and colder the farther up the Loch we went; the Ardessie falls were frozen solid; and the head of the Loch itself was frozen over.

I will not dwell on farewells to our good friends of the cruiser, for, after all, we were to meet and sail together again in the coming year. Rather let me say how kindly the Macleans at Dundonnell Hotel breakfasted us, and how delightful it was to meet the Morrisons again when we got the length of Brae. And once more the trees had their quality of wonder for me; I looked at the different branchings of oak and beech, and birch and ash, and enjoyed the quiet shelter of the pine trees.

Soon we had to be busy. There was the car to get and to travel across Scotland to Aberdeenshire for Christmas. We reached Williamston on Christmas Eve to find a white world again and frozen curling ponds. Our hosts and Alasdair came down the steps of the house to meet us and we were in a Christmas world of story-books.

Three nights before, I had peeled off those hard-worn Grenfell clothes, let down my knee-bands, put on dry woolly socks and slippers, and had a wash in preparation for one of Bobbie's Rona dinners. Now I had a real bath, climbed into my camphor-scented dinner-suit and boiled shirt, and could hardly believe it was myself. I looked across the polished table, through the light of candles and the glint of silver and glass, to where Bobbie sat in her black evening-dress and Spanish shawl. Our eyes met and there was nothing to be said.

Sir Frank Fraser Darling

WILDERNESS AND PLENTY 30p

A pioneer ecologist of worldwide reputation, Sir Frank Fraser Darling has spent a lifetime studying the relationship of man to his environment all over the globe. He views the wilderness as a shrinking natural resource, no longer an environment to be conquered by man. He looks toward the future with a plan for conservation and a plea for man's responsibility to nature.

His analysis of what man is doing to the world, of what it will lead to, and of what could be done to halt the rush of self-destruction, must be taken with the utmost seriousness.

David & Charles Series

These and other PAN Books are obtainable
from all booksellers and newsagents. If you
have any difficulty please send purchase price
plus 7p postage to PO Box 11, Falmouth,
Cornwall.
While every effort is made to keep prices low, it
is sometimes necessary to increase prices at
short notice. PAN Books reserve the right to
show new retail prices on covers which may
differ from those advertised in the text or
elsewhere.